Ready, Aim, Excel!
**The Expert Insights Weekly Guide to
Personal and Professional Leadership**

The Expert Insights
Weekly Guide to Personal
and Professional Leadership

Featuring
Drs. Marshall Goldsmith, Cathy Greenberg,
Relly Nadler, Ken Blanchard,
and 48 Top Leadership Experts

Ready, Aim, Excel!
The Expert Insights Weekly Guide to Personal and Professional Leadership
©2011 by Viki Winterton

Expert Insights Publishing
1001 East WT Harris Blvd #247
Charlotte, NC 28213

ISBN: 978-0-9837379-2-6

Printed Green in the United States of America by Greyden Press
Cover Design: Terry Z
Edited by: Chris Wallace, Brynn Burger
Interviews: Viki Winterton, Stacey Chadwell, Cathy Greenberg, and Relly Nadler

15 14 13 12 11   1 2 3 4 5

A portion of the proceeds from the sale of this book will be donated to world literacy, One Laptop Per Child.

•

Dedication

To my Dad, a great leader
whose silent strength
and unwavering support
fueled all he met with loving kindness
and powerful possibilities.
Namaste,
Viki

Table of Contents

Agnès van Rhijn

"Agnès has helped me access my personal leadership. I now have huge clarity on what I need to do next, and I am excited and inspired by these steps. I am now confident that I can do it!"
—Julia Velosa, Future Business Owner, Brussels, Belgium

Alison Forbes, Ph.D.

"Dr. Alison Forbes has redefined leadership and the new bottom line. In this book, she not only reveals the deep rooted challenges facing today's leaders, but connects us with information vital to fostering transformational change. You will be equipped with breakthrough concepts that will invigorate your passion and power with practical real-world application. Accelerate your leadership strength today."
—Elizabeth M. Lengyel, Radio Host, Career Juice Career Strategist and Advisor, Faculty, Conestoga College

Anastasia Montejano

"Anastasia Montejano is on my very short list for trusted partners in personal and professional growth. She possesses that rare blend of practical know-how with intuitive awareness. She listens beneath my words and weaves in real-world resources that support my next steps. She is a master at her craft!"
—Kathy Esper, MBA, PCC, CEFELI

Ann Farrell

"Ann has challenged my way of thinking, and has helped me identify and discover the kind of person, mother, and leader I want to be."
—Laura, Aurora, IL

Ann Van Eron, Ph.D.

"When I took Ann Van Eron's OASIS Moves™ program ten years ago, it had a profound effect on me like no other course previous or thereafter. It was the most useful and enlightening course I have ever taken. I am still using the process daily. I can see results at work and at home. I am a better leader."
—Senior Manager, Fortune 100 Company

Bernice Boyden

"Bernice quickly understands the issue you're dealing with and offers excellent solutions. She learns the people involved and offers excellent coaching guidance. Bernice is confident yet remains humble. She's about helping the people she supports and never about promoting herself—which I really respect."
—J. Peulso, Pittsburgh, PA

Bert Martinez

"You can't afford not to know what Bert Martinez is teaching!"
—Patrick Snow, *New York Times* Best-Selling Author of *Creating Your Own Destiny*

Candice Smithyman, D.D.

"Dr. Candice Smithyman is passionate about heart and skill leadership development. Leaders she has trained are known for being both authentic and professional with transformational influence. In times like these, we need the quality that she models and multiplies. Read and lead!"
—Dr. Joseph Umidi, President, Lifeforming Leadership Coaching

Cathy Greenberg, Ph.D.

"Recently I had the privilege and pleasure to work with Dr. Cathy Greenberg when she was a featured guest speaker at a webinar presentation for leaders of a large Fortune 100 company. Not only did I find the XCEL webinar to be extremely relevant, beneficial, and inspirational, but the comments I received from leaders who participated reflected sentiments such as "awesome," "fantastic," and "excellent," just to name a few of the unsolicited comments received. Webinars can be difficult when it comes to participants' engagement, but Dr. Greenberg's expertise, energy, use of exercises, and ability to connect with her audience keep the engagement level amazingly high. My only regret is that we could only spend an hour with her!"
—Executive, Global Fortune 100

Clara Noble

"Clara is a fantastic coach who has helped me grow tremendously personally and professionally and I am very grateful for her help. I feel that I have started a new chapter. I have more awareness of where I am and where I need to be, to be more successful."
—C.M. Corporate Trainer

David B. Savage

"Incisive, sensitive, and directive, Dave has a way of taking you where you wanted to go, even when you weren't sure that you wanted to get there. He is present for you, to you, and with you, and out of this powerful alliance, great changes occur."
—Daphne Kingma, Author

Diane Allen

"Diane Allen brings to her coaching an uncanny ability to meet a person where they currently are. By this, I mean that she is able to listen intently and then provide precisely the type and amount of support necessary to help him or her make whatever changes are required to achieve their goals."
—David Friedman, Author of *Fundamentally Different*

Duane Reed

"Through Duane's thought-provoking style, I have been able to tackle the hard issues of running a small business. His guidance has helped us establish best practices and his treasure chest of training and HR skills have really helped us grow when other firms are failing."
—Sandra C. Scanlon, P.E., SSG, Denver, CO

Eve Agee, Ph.D.

"Dr. Eve Agee is no doubt a scholar, but like the master storytellers of my childhood, she draws you in unexpectedly, holds you in suspense and disbelief, and then sends you off with a completely enhanced and altered way of understanding yourself and the world around you."
—Juliet M., Washington D.C.

Gilles Brouillette, Ph.D.

"Transformational leadership is an important part of our leadership program on creating a sustainable, continuous improvement culture. It is instrumental in helping leaders transform their existing mental models for working collaboratively while embracing change."
—Dave Legge, Senior VP, Air Canada

Gina Hiatt, Ph.D.

"Dr. Gina Hiatt is not only the embodiment of the courage, foresight and action it takes to be a leader in this field, her work—the Finish Agent software and system that revolutionizes how people get things done—will be recognized as a pivotal invention for personal development. I'm so grateful for Gina's contribution and invite everyone to pay close attention to what she's doing next."
—Andrea J. Lee, CEO, Wealthy Thought Leader, Author of *Multiple Streams of Coaching Income*

Joan C. King, Ph.D.

"Joan King is one of those rare jewels that a person is lucky to meet in a lifetime. She combines the wisdom of the ages, the purity of heart of a child, and a wicked thirst for adventure. She brings an extraordinary, courageous and undaunted approach to the journey called life."
—Paula E Chauncey, Managing Partner, Étre, LLC

JoAnne Ward

"I loved her enthusiasm and motivation. We quickly gained a wonderful relationship and the changes in my life were positive and permanent."
—T. J. Vancouver, BC

Joyce Odidison

"Joyce's coaching sessions are refreshing, enthusiastic, passionate, and absolutely positive! My team is very pleased with the work she does for our organization."
—Petra C. Rapmund, C.H.R.P., Senior Manager, Pension & Benefits, StandardAero

Juracy Johnson

"I want to thank you with all my heart for being part of my life's sunrise. Your coaching, to me, was the best gift I have ever given myself. Now my heart is healed through forgiveness. Thanks, Juracy, for being that instrument that allowed me to heal forty years of beating myself down."
—M. E., Costa Rica

Karen Wright, MCC
"Sure, there are some leaders who step effortlessly into their role and thrive both at work and at home, being deeply nourished by both. But that's not most of us. Karen Wright's The Complete Executive gives anyone in a leadership role the ability not just to "fill in the gaps" where things might be fraying a little, but to also to gather the resources to step up a level, connect to the Great Work that's there to be done, and increase not only a sense of purpose but the impact they're having in their role."
—Michael Bungay Stanier, Author of *Do More Great Work* and *End Malaria*

Kathryn McKinnon
"Kathryn is terrific, extremely perceptive, and intuitive. She guides you through a learning process that allows you to gain insight into what's going on in your life."
—Jordan Rich, Show Host, WBZ Radio, Boston, Massachusetts

Katinka Nicou
"Rarely have I experienced an Executive Coach with Katinka's level of compassion, empowerment, and breadth of wisdom. She has an uncanny ability to shine light on the heart of a difficult problem, and with dedication, creativity, and inspiration, helps her clients navigate toward the greatest possibilities awaiting them."
—Judith Glaser, CEO, Benchmark Communications, Inc.

Kim Zilliox, MA, MBA, CPCC
"Kim Zilliox has been an incredible and invaluable resource for our organization. She has significantly contributed to the company's growth through her uncanny ability to develop leaders to the next level, regardless of their title or experience."
—Senior VP of HR, Well-Known Internet Technology Company, Silicon Valley, CA

Laura Pedro
"Laura Pedro's coaching helped me grow exponentially in confidence and commitment to professional success. With her guidance, I established goals in alignment with my beliefs and took action to transform my vision into reality. She gave me a forum and a format that empowered me to step boldly into leadership."
—Marykay Morelli

Lee Strauss
"Lee is an inspiration. His intelligence, generosity, and warmth were widely acknowledged by his colleagues. Lee is always focused on how he can help others succeed and, with his wealth of knowledge and emotional intelligence, he enhanced the experience for all of us. I recommend Lee to anyone seeking a natural coach with depth of experience, integrity, and compassion."
—Rochelle Bright, Owner, Vita Activa

Linda Cobb

"Even the greatest athletes have coaches who help them improve their performance. Executives should be no different. Fortunately I found Coach Cobb. She helped me solve difficult people problems, become more effective as a leader, and re-create our organizational culture."
—Peter Weiss, M.D., CEO, Health First Health Plans

Lisa Hein

"This book is an honest portrayal of a mother's experiences raising her child in both the good and difficult times of teenagerdom."
—Richard Paul Evans, #1 *New York Times* Best-Selling Author and Emmy-Award Winning CBS Movie, *The Christmas Box*

Mary O'Loughlin

"To see Mary on stage as a motivational speaker is awesome. The attention in the room is incredible. Her message is simple and from the heart. Whether she has a dozen people in the audience or three hundred corporate personnel, the response and atmosphere is second to none. As a person, this lady is a delight! As a mother, she exemplifies the role. She is the ultimate in fun, caring, and positivity."
—Hilary Wood, RN, Bach Nursing, National Marketing Director

Michael Simpson

"The Northeast Region went from fifth place to first place in number of SSF units sold in less than four months. We have tried to get this type of focus from our teams in the past and have failed several times. The 4 Disciplines has allowed us to get the focus we need in just three months down to the front line."
—Frito Lay Regional Vice President

M.J. Jiaras, Ph.D.

"M.J. blends his remarkable gift of insight into human possibilities with consummate professional skills to provide great value for the continuous improvement of leadership. His talent is to deftly weave together the flow of executive experience to co-construct clarity of intention and strategies for powerful action. The result for the executive is new insight into the opportunities for effective leadership and deeper understanding of ways of being in this role."
—Terry Mazany, CEO, The Chicago Community Trust

Raymond Perras, CIF, CPC

"Ray has been a Master in delivering his Life Mastery program to both me and my organization. He has used a balance of process and human touch in helping me direct the orchestra of noise. It has become a symphony."
—Bruno Lindia, Principal and Owner, DMA Canada Limited

Rose Mattran, Ed.D.

"Rose Mattran has clearly demonstrated a natural ability for development of workable planning solutions with deep creativity aspects and attention to details. Rose is a master at seeing the big picture and not just the snapshot,

and her self-starter energy is always present. Instilled with a deep "do-the-right-thing" philosophy, Rose leads by example and is clearly capable of building and inspiring confidence among her peers and subordinates."
—Joe Curley, APR, CPRC, Senior Corporate Communications Counsel, Universal Studios Parks & Resorts

Ruth Littler
"Ruth has a deep connection with herself and an innate ability to tap into the needs of others."
—Veronika Honner, Colleague and Counselor, Perth, Australia

Sharon McGloin
"Sharon has helped me discover a new mental avenue to life. She has introduced me to techniques that help solve life's little and big issues. Personally, I have started to understand the boundaries related to my personal development as it relates to leadership development."
—Will Shields, Owner, 68's Inside Sports, Former NFL Great Kansas City Chief

Sharon Melnick, Ph.D.
"Sharon's portfolio of techniques is powerful. I was skeptical when she said I could make changes quickly after I had tried for so long to make improvements based on others' techniques. What we discussed were things I had heard about and known intellectually, but Sharon was able to break through to me emotionally and help me find and identify the internal 'glass wall' that had been holding me back. Now I am confident and act with clarity and purpose. It's been unbelievable and worth every penny—even much more!"
—Mark M., NYSERDA

Sherry Buffington, Ph.D.
Dr. Sherry Buffington is deeply beloved and respected for her graciousness, brilliance, creativity, generosity, and the nonstop, sustainable results people experience from the cutting-edge tools she has created. She makes a mammoth difference in others' lives. Thousands of people have recovered their authentic selves, gotten back their healthy lives, restored their relationships, grabbed back their sanity, found their self-confidence, or recovered their physical health as a result of her work."
—Jill Pickett, Executive and Personal Performance Coach

Susan Guiher
"Thank you so much for all you have done. Your coaching, your presentation, and your inspiration supported me in having a breakdown and then a breakthrough. You helped me and my company move forward. Thank you from the bottom of my heart. You are amazing!"
—Jennifer Jolicoeur, Founder, The Athena's Cup

Sylvia Lafair
"The concepts and strategies learned from Sylvia and Total Leadership Connections are invaluable. Working in a newsroom is competitive and stressful, and with new understanding of how relationships trigger tension, I

resolve pressure situations faster and with minimal dissention. Moreover, I can bring the techniques and tools home—a double win."
—Tyler Mathisen, Co-Anchor, CNBC's "Power Lunch," Vice President, Strategic Editorial Initiatives

Teresa Ray

"Teresa Ray is the only person I trust to work with our most precious assets, our people. I cannot afford to have anything but the best in executive coaching; without a doubt, Teresa is the best."
—Ramon Lugo, Center Director, NASA's John Glenn Research Center, OH

Theresa Garwood

"Theresa takes a thoughtful, meaningful approach to the human aspect of leadership. Whether in her personal quest for continuous learning or throughout professional experience, she lives by a commitment to helping others."
—M.F., Executive, Industrial Supplies

Tina Rasmussen, Ph.D.

"I have used the consulting services of Dr. Tina Rasmussen for many years with wonderful results. We were recently recognized for our progress in changing the climate of our organization, largely as a result of following Tina's process."
—Dave Thornton, Chair, National Steering Committee, YMCA of the USA

Tony DiRico

"My company has used Winslow reports and assessments extensively for the past two years. We have utilized the tools to aid us in staffing our newest store with much success. In addition, we have used the reports with our existing staff to aid in communications and professional development. Tony DiRico has been very helpful and responsive to our needs. I heartily recommend both Tony and Winslow reports."
—Mike Palmer, Owner, Hometown Health Mart Pharmacy

Yogesh Sood

"As a coach, Yogesh has a distinct ability to listen and patiently ask the right questions—questions that would develop greater insights and challenge the paradigms. During coaching sessions, he is very specific, factual, simple, and objective."
—Priti Pawha, Sr. Consultant/Trainer, DOOR Training & Consulting, India

Zeina Ghossoub

"Together we can make a difference; with this philosophy, you are welcomed in her office, you see it, you feel it, and most of all, you live it. Coach Zeina, this very professional, caring person makes you feel secure and understood. She made me see that it is never too late. Thank you for giving me back my self-esteem."
—Nancy Barakat, Financial Manager, Volver SAL, Beirut, Lebanon

We all have leadership roles. You don't have to have a title to be a leader. If friends come to you for answers, if a child holds your hand as you are grocery shopping, if a youngster is on the receiving end of a game of catch, if you are involved in an organizational activity and members ask what you think, if people look to you for direction, you are a leader.

We encourage you to explore leadership in new ways. Take a look around you and you will find lessons in leadership everywhere.

We live in the most confusing climate of our era when leadership theories and methods are just not as effective as they used to be. These days many are finding it challenging to be effective in their varied and demanding leadership roles. New slants on old models aren't cutting it anymore. Along with these challenges comes increased difficulty as we strive to form meaningful connections and communication in the midst of a technology-driven society.

We must face the reality that yesterday's solutions won't solve today's problems. To be successful in reaching out, maintaining relationships, generating new business, and remaining competitive, we must identify a new approach.

In this indispensable resource, top visionaries and experts share their leadership secrets, proven formulas, and the defining moments that have shaped their lives and careers. A wealth of information is delivered within these exclusive interviews for the purpose of guiding you on your own journey to the best you can be.

You have a vision for what you hope your life, your business, and your contribution to the world will be. But the road to get there often seems winding, uneven, and filled with pitfalls. Sit back, take a deep breath, and allow each of these experts to share with you about their own personal journey. Explore the dedication it required, which processes proved successful, where it led them, and what they learned along the way. Each conversation contained in these pages is empowering, inspiring, and priceless, and you will find yourself in the pages of these interviews and in these accounts of occupational achievement and personal triumph.

Let go of your fears, try something new, and step into a promising future, allowing these leadership experts and stories to guide you along the way.

Bill Cumming: Motivating the Unmotivatable

In 1979, one of my children was raped. I want to fast forward to today—that young woman is now the CFO of an organization called The Transformation Center in Boston that helps returning troops from Afghanistan and Iraq readjust to society using peer coaching. She's fine, but on that day, our world as we knew it stopped. My child was standing in my kitchen bleeding, and I knew that she had just been through one of the most traumatic experiences in the world. If I had caught the person responsible in that instant, I literally would have killed him. I've spent my life doing things that are nonviolent and completely antithetical to that emotion that arose, but there was no missing the emotion.

Obviously, we took care of my daughter, Joy. We immediately went to the hospital where there were police and social workers available. But for a period of a few days, I couldn't shake that desire. It didn't take me long to figure out that it was completely antithetical to everything I'd spent my life being about, but it gave me a little bit of an indication as to where some of the violence in the world comes from.

I realized that one of the reasons people engage in violent behavior is because they think they have no control over their circumstances. Riots break out—not the kind that have to do with looting and things like that—when people become overwhelmed by their circumstances and feel like they have no control; they will resort to almost anything, especially when it comes to protecting their children. It's been said numerous times that unless we end the issue of world hunger, we're never going to have a world of peace, and I believe that to be true.

What I discovered about my daughter was that she was a lot more together than I was. She would tell me later that it was simply because she was a better actress than I am. She really was stoic in relationship to what had happened, and those days are a blur to me. All I remember is my white rage and wanting to do everything I could to protect my daughter, which I clearly couldn't do. What I discovered, therefore, was this incredible courage and fortitude in my daughter that I was astounded by. I always knew she was a neat kid, but the fact of the matter was she was tough as nails.

That same year, I met a man in a maximum security prison in Somers, Connecticut. There weren't any video cameras around at that time and there were no guards who could hear our conversation. What I didn't expect that day was to hear this man say to me, "Bill, I am sorry that your daughter was raped." I knew he meant it. I didn't know what to do with it, but I knew he meant it.

It began to dawn on me at a very deep level that I had spent my life trying to do things that I considered useful and worthwhile, and I just acknowledged to you that I have the capacity to kill (and you'll notice I didn't put that in the past tense), and here was a man who had committed violent crimes and admitted it—he was not only convicted, but he had also admitted to me that he had done those things—who was capable of loving kindness.

What really became clear to me in a relatively short period of time was that the capacity for everything is inside of us; the question is what do we nurture? What do we water?

I began building programs that allowed people who had never experienced their value and worth in the world an opportunity to experience that. But they could also experience the reality that inside of them is the ability to make choices that allow them to take charge of their own lives. That's what happened, and that's what I've spent the last thirty-three years doing.

In "Motivating the Unmotivatable" we wanted to address the fact that there is no such word as "unmotivatable," and you and I can't actually motivate other people; all we can do is create an environment in which they're more likely to choose to be motivated themselves.

Nelson Mandela went through twenty-seven years in a prison, and in the year following his release, he desegregated the country. That capacity resides inside of all people. Viktor Frankl said, "The last of the freedoms is to choose one's attitude in any given set of circumstances." He wrote those words while in a concentration camp, and the depth of our ability to do that is that deep.

It's not as if Viktor Frankl is the only one who has that capacity. Most of the doing-ness to solve the world's problems already exists. The issue is we don't treat each other well. We actually treat each other very poorly, and we need to be mindful of finding ways to nurture all that is good in people, and to be mindful of operating with one another with dignity, grace, and loving kindness. That sounds simple, but it applies in every situation.

I used to believe there was right and wrong, and now I realize there's only wellness and unwellness. People who are well don't damage other people in any way, shape, or form. If you're in a place of loving kindness, it's impossible for you to intentionally do damage. That doesn't mean that I don't do damage from time to time; I do, but that's because of moments of unconsciousness.

We are trained to believe that some people are good and some people are evil. I've read the source documents of about fifteen different major religions, and all of the spiritual traditions point to two things: love all people with no exception, and grow in wisdom. That's the message, which means it isn't ours to judge. That's not to say that I expect people to be running around the street who have not had an opportunity to do some work. What changed in me was the way I saw the world.

In my experience, we keep looking to the wrong things to make the changes. At the moment, we're looking to change public schools by doing more testing. The testing is getting better; at least now we're testing the same student to see whether they learned anything in a particular year. In the old days, they used to test a particular grade level every few years. That's not significant because it's like comparing apples and oranges; there's no correlation between test results for an eighth grade class three years from now and what's going on in eighth grade now.

However, the core issue is, if youngsters don't feel well about themselves—and this has nothing to do with being happy, it's about seeing themselves as valued and valuable—if they don't see themselves as able to be responsible for their own lives and well-being, they're not going to produce the kind of results we want to see produced.

In all of our struggle for freedom of every single kind you can imagine, we've forgotten the fact that raising children is more important than any other leadership role on the planet, and until that gets reinforced by realizing that it's got to be the primary responsibility of people in relationship to these young people, very little is going to change. The way we're operating with one another needs to shift; it's not about the doing-ness.

Youngsters need to know they're loved, period. What I mean by that is the same thing I mean in relationship to my own children: I want you to have a meaningful, productive, contributory, joyous life. I don't want food or shelter to be an issue. I care about you as a human being.

There is no scarcity of love. As a matter of fact, the more you do it, the more you're able to do it, and the clearer you become in communicating to a person their value and worth in the world.

People need to know that, and we need to stop being concerned about words and focus on intentions. Loving kindness is exactly what's wanted and needed.

Loving kindness is a problem solver. The problem is that we don't hold it that way because we've heard about it for a long time, and we think it's something we can't get a handle on. That's not true.

Consider any person who has ever moved from, "I don't matter, I don't value myself," to "I do matter, and I'm starting to produce results." I've asked thousands of people like that this question: "What was present at the moment you were able to make that transition?" The answer in every case but one was that first, there was an adult who absolutely cared about them, and second, they began to make changes that allowed them to take charge of their own life. When those two things happen simultaneously, all kinds of things become possible in people's lives.

Discover the love and wisdom from the leaders in this wonderful book, and you'll find that anything is possible for you and for our world.

Namaste,
Bill

Bill Cumming is a thirty-year coaching veteran to CEOs and executive teams of healthcare delivery organizations, businesses, school systems, and nonprofit organizations ranging in size from startup to three-quarters of a billion dollar corporations. Bill's work focuses on creating inspired environments where individuals can take responsibility for their lives and the organizations for which they work. Bill is also the founder of The Boothby Institute (www.theboothbyinstitute.org).

Ready,

Aim,

Excel!

Bert Martinez
Houston, Texas, USA

Bert's acumen as a marketing and business expert is grounded in more than twenty years of advising individuals and large enterprises on sales and business development in both routine situations and those charged with risks and high stakes.

He arrived in America at age six from Cuba, and retired at age twenty-eight. Bert is also a sought-after speaker and thought leader, speaking to thousands of people each year about business and success principles.

He is CEO of Bert Martinez Communications. His practice specializes in teaching organizations about consumer buying philosophy, latest trends, and how they're applied to marketing, publicity, and business development.

I: You are a great leader in the fields of publicity, business development, and helping people become successful. What do you tell clients about this rapidly changing economy we're all facing?

BM: That's a great question. I think people have to really inform themselves as to what is really happening right now. We are going through some significant changes, and I think that when you look back through history, every generation has faced some pretty tough changes at some stage. Some do it at a very early age; some do it later in life.

A few years ago, we talked about the Great Generation, and those who were part of the Great Generation were born in 1910. By the time those individuals were twelve years old, they were going through the Great Depression, and by the time they were twenty-two or twenty-three, their world was involved in World War II. I think our generation has had it fairly easy. We've experienced some pain and some uncertainty, which is what I think is causing a lot of what's happening in the world.

I'm sure that you've experienced some pain in your family; I definitely have in mine. But I think this is the first time we're experiencing it on this level—on almost a global level.

I tell our clients and our audiences that it's time to become resourceful, and I think the difference between someone succeeding and someone failing is their ability to be resourceful. Everyone thinks money solves everything. When the stock market is crashing and you have a possible recession, when your real estate isn't worth what it used to be, or when you've lost 40% or 50% of your retirement, those are drastic changes, but it's not the worst thing.

There are people who have suffered all of those different losses and in addition to that have now found themselves unemployed. The difference is in becoming resourceful—in knowing how to use whatever is available to you.

Most of that is internal; it's not out there. The real estate market isn't out there. The stock market isn't really out there. It's all inside, and I think what we see in the soft stock market, in the soft real estate market, and where you have this high unemployment is the manifestation of how people are feeling inside. When people are scared, this is what happens. When you have a government that is feeding that fear, this is what happens.

I tell my clients that they need to take stock of their resources. You need to learn how to manage your emotions, because ultimately, how you feel determines what you achieve, and if you're focused on fear, worry, and doubt, you're going to achieve those things. You're going to achieve a scarcity mind-set. You're going to achieve losing more, because that's what fear does.

If you manage your emotions correctly, you build up your beliefs, and you work on the things you know to be true. You do have certain controls over your own personal economy. Even if you get laid off, there are certain things you can do. This might be the perfect time for you to launch your own business, to change careers, or to go back to school.

There are always choices, and by being resourceful, you allow yourself to have more choices, and that's really what it comes down to. I guarantee that there are some people right now who are going through some massive changes; they're losing what they call "everything," and within a short amount of time, they will rebound and will come back stronger.

I: So the creativity that springs from being resourceful really is a powerful leadership quality, and we all have access to tap into it, but let's talk about the fear. How do you help people deal with the emotion of fear?

"How you feel is more important than what you know."

BM: That's another great question, and what you really want to do is train yourself emotionally and mentally. To me, emotion and mentality are two elements that go hand in hand. I'm a big believer— and I say this all time—that how you feel is more important than what you know. Call it emotional fitness, if you will.

This also goes back to what you believe, and so if you believe and you feel that you have no control over a situation and that it's all up to the government, you're pretty helpless, because you're giving your power to "out there," you're giving your power to the government, you're giving your power to uncertainty, and you're going to be full of fear and doubt.

At the same time, we've seen people who have been born in poverty, who have been born in a recession, who have been born with unbelievable disabilities, and they overcome everything because of their emotional fitness, their mental toughness. These people dig in deep and make changes.

For some people, it may not necessarily be a change. They may have this deep core belief in themselves that no matter what, they're going to reach a specific goal. They will do whatever it takes and are so focused on reaching that goal and achieving that dream—they're so focused on their belief—that it drives them. That's really what drives all of us; that really makes the difference.

Fear is really nothing more than focusing on uncertainty and a belief that you have no control. Zig Zigler said this, and I've always remembered it, "Fear is false evidence that appears real." Sometimes fear is useful. The example that I like to use is that if you're lost and you're going down a dark alley and you're a little fearful, that might be a good time to be fearful; that fear is giving you a signal to be alert and to be aware. But if you're sitting in the comfort of your home and you're afraid, then that is an internal belief system, and you have to look closer at what you're scared of.

If you're scared you can't find another job, that's an action signal, and you have to get out there and you have to look for a job. Maybe it won't be the perfect job. Again, you may have to make some changes. Maybe you'll have to move. Back in the 1980s and late 1990s people lost their jobs in the east coast markets and had to move to the southern states or to the west coast to get jobs. Sometimes you have to make changes to get things going.

I always tell people, "If you do what you fear, the fear will disappear." Again, I learned that from someone else. It's a great quote.

Think about it. If you're afraid of losing your job, chances are you probably will lose your job, but so what? It's not the end of the world. You will find another job. If you're afraid of losing a home, so what? It's not the end of the world. Is it going to be a challenge? Absolutely. Is it going to be heart wrenching? Absolutely. But it's not the end of the world.

Going back to what I said earlier about being resourceful, if you think you have no choices, then you just let things happen. There's an old saying, "Desperation is the mother of invention." When things are tough, make a list of all the things you have available to you. Some of those things may not be what you deem valuable at first, but being able to negotiate might be a strength for you. Not being afraid to ask for what you want or to do some research are some things you can list, because by doing research, maybe you can find the answer that solves your dilemma.

The bottom line is, I want to have people do an exercise of simply just writing down everything that is available to them—the public library, the Internet, friends, and associates—that they can tap into to get some advice, to get some help, and to make some connections.

When it comes to fear or uncertainty, I believe that people really can overcome anything. We see people do it all of time. Get on the Internet and you can find literally thousands of people who are overcoming great obstacles—much bigger obstacles then we have to deal with. There are tons of books written about people who have lived through concentration camps, through abuse, and through being incarcerated. Just recently in the news there was a young girl who was kidnapped at the age of twelve, and she was finally rescued at the age of thirty.

Some people overcome huge obstacles. Look to those people for inspiration. Use them as models. See what they did and how they overcame their situation. Then realize that you can do the same thing. Again, fear is an internal thing for the most part, and by taking control of your emotions and becoming emotionally fit, you'll overcome everything.

I: This shift in focus is really powerful. What do you do for yourself to ensure your personal and professional leadership growth?

BM: I do what I advise everyone else to do and that is to read books. You need to go to seminars. You need to stay sharp. The only way to do that is to get around other people inspire you and who will then inspire you to take action.

"Most people reach plateaus for two reasons: either they don't know what to do, or they're afraid to take action."

There's nothing more rewarding and more exciting than going to a seminar or an event with people just like you who are experiencing some of the same struggles you are. You attend the event and you walk away with two or three ideas that change your world, that help you hold on, and that encourage you to take that next step. When you go to those gatherings, there are also other people that you're going to be able to help, inspire, and encourage to take action as well.

I turn to books, CDs, DVDs, and seminars, because I believe they're absolutely crucial to staying sharp. You cannot be a leader without also continuing to grow mentally, emotionally, and physically. You have to stretch yourself. You have to go to these places and find out what the new trends are and what is happening that you can use in your world.

The next step then is to apply what you learn. To me, there's nothing worse than taking all this knowledge and never doing anything with it. Go and expand your resources, and then apply some of them. Maybe you can start a mastermind group or get involved in a mastermind group that will help you take more action.

We talked about fear earlier, and most people reach plateaus for two reasons: either they don't know what to do, or they're afraid to take action.

LEADERSHIP OPPORTUNITY:

There is an exercise that I have people go through that involves simply pretending that they are a superhero. If you pretend that you're a superhero, that you're wearing a cape and you're invincible, you become unstoppable. You will notice instantly when people put on this fake cape, because everyone can immediately see how their physiology changes. Their shoulders go back. Their chest goes up. Their tummy is tight. People know how to be confident.

The exercise then is simply this: if you felt confident and unstoppable, how would you approach this thing that's holding you back? People come up with their own answers. That's because now that they're feeling unstoppable—now that they know they're unbeatable—they can quickly come up with an answer, and the answer may be that they're just going to do it.

LEADERSHIP SUCCESS:

A client of mine lost his home and his fortune. He also lost his confidence and his belief in himself. However, he quickly got out of that, and rebuilt his confidence by doing some exercises. His daily morning exercise was the superhero exercise mentioned in the *Leadership Opportunity* above.

After he lost everything, he went and got a job. Every morning as he headed out to work, he would put on his fake cape and did the superhero exercise. In a period of thirty days, he was the number one salesperson at the organization he was working for, and at the end of that thirty days, his confidence was restored enough that he went back to working for himself. He has now rebuilt his business, and, like all of us when we do something for a second or third time, he has done it better. It is all because he changed the way he felt. How you feel is more important than what you know.

Change how you feel and you will have peace in your life, you'll have love in your life, and you'll overcome obstacles with ease.

My belief is this: We were created to succeed. People were not put on this planet to fail.

Marshall Goldsmith, Ph.D.
Rancho Santa Fe, California, USA

Dr. Marshall Goldsmith is a world authority in helping successful leaders get even better by achieving positive, lasting change in behavior for themselves, their people, and their teams. Marshall's book, *What Got You Here Won't Get You There*, is a *New York Times* best seller, a *Wall Street Journal* number one business book, and the winner of the Harold Longman Award as the Best Business Book of 2007.

***MOJO* was released in February 2010. It is a *New York Times* and *Wall Street Journal* top ten best seller and the *Shanghai Daily* number one business book in China. It is already scheduled to be translated into fourteen languages.**

I: Can you tell us a little bit about yourself and how you came to work in the field of talent management and leadership?

MG: Sure. I basically do three things. I teach classes for business leaders—either executives or high-potential leaders—either inside corporations or business schools. Then I do executive coaching, and there my clients are CEOs of big companies. I also write and edit books and articles.

I: Who are the key people that have influenced you as a leader?

MG: I've been very fortunate. I had the privilege of spending over fifty days with Peter Drucker before he died. I was on the board of the Peter Drucker Foundation. Richard Beckhard was a great mentor of mine. I got to spend a lot of time with him. Frances Hesselbein is a good friend of mine, a CEO today in a Leader Institute, and a woman who has greatly helped me. So, if I had to name the people who have influenced me, those would be the ones.

Again it's just very fortunate. The first book I did was called *The Leader of the Future*. It was many years ago and was with Frances Hesselbein, Richard Beckhard, and Peter Drucker. I certainly say I was a junior member of that crew. That would be a generous estimate. I was sort of the "nobody" member of that crew, and they were kind enough to help me. It really gave me a boost in my career and my life. So I've been very fortunate to be around some very influential people.

I: There's a lot of coaching going on out there. How does your coaching differ from other practitioners in the field?

MG: My coaching is very specific. I help very successful leaders achieve positive long-term change in behavior. That's all I do. So my work is very narrowly focused. I don't do strategic coaching or life planning or other types of coaching. Mine is focused strictly on behavior, and again it's not a good or bad issue, it's just what I do. I have a very unique approach to coaching. I work with my clients for a year to eighteen months and I don't get paid if they don't get better. And "better" is not judged by me, nor is it judged by clients. It's judged by everyone around my clients. So in that sense it's kind of different.

What I try to do in terms of teaching is that I teach people how to build in follow up so they actually achieve positive long-term change. In many ways I see what I do as a kind of trade school for executives. It's not really like graduate school. It's more like trade school. I'm not trying to help people learn. I'm trying to help people do. As I've grown older, I've come to believe that if you sit in a class and you learn things but you don't do anything different, the world does not become a better place.

> _"I'm not trying to help people learn. I'm trying to help people do."_

One of the great misconceptions of leadership development is that if someone understands, they will do. That's not true at all. When my book was a number one ranked business book in the whole United States, the number one ranked diet book sold ten times as many copies. Americans get fatter and fatter and fatter and buy more and more diet books. If reading diet books could make people thin, Americans would be the thinnest people in the world. The problem isn't that people aren't reading diet books. The problem is that they're not dieting.

The problem with what I do is not getting people to understand what to do, it's getting them to do it. If you read my book, _What Got You Here Won't Get You There_, you will read the story and laugh and think, _What a bunch of goofy people!_ Well, the goofy people in the book have IQs of 150. They're CEOs at multibillion dollar corporations, and they're the ones who are trying to get better. It's easy to understand. It's hard to do.

Leaders today manage knowledgeable workers. Peter Drucker said, "The leaders of the past know how to tell. A leader in the future knows how to ask." If you're managing knowledgeable workers, you have to be very good about including them, involving them, and making them feel valued. If you don't, they're going to leave. And by the way, this is true not only in the for-profit sector, it's also true in the not-for-profit sector, and it's true in the military.

> *"Leadership is not about what you say. Leadership is about what others hear. We'd all like to believe that if we say something, the world changes. Well, there's a big gap between* we say *and* they hear.*"*

For example, I teach in the New Admirals program for the United States Navy. These people are managing; in essence, they're high-technology leaders. The people I manage have multiple graduate degrees. They speak multiple languages. They are not idiots. There's an image in the military of an admiral or general yelling and screaming at people. That's history. They don't do that. If they did, the people they manage would simply leave. These people can get more money somewhere else. They don't have to be there.

The concept of what a leader is, is changing. The leader's role is much more about working with people as a facilitator. It's not about telling people what to do and how to do it, because the problem for the coach is that the subordinates know more than the leader in most cases. When you're managing knowledge workers, oftentimes they know more about what they're doing than their boss does. You can't just tell them what to do and how to do it.

I've come to the conclusion that 40% of my job is helping my client change behavior, while 60% of my job is creating an environment where people around them give them a chance, because we're all stereotypical people.

Leadership is not about what you say. Leadership is about what others hear. We'd all like to believe that if we say something, the world changes. Well, there's a big gap between *we say* and *they hear*. Especially *we say* and *they believe*.

There is one thing I encourage women to do more, and that is to promote themselves. I think a lot of women have a great deal of hesitancy when it comes to self-promotion. They have a sort of naïve belief. They think, *Well, if I do a good job, that's all I should have to do. My work should speak for itself, and I shouldn't have to promote myself.* If that were true, no company would need a marketing function. All the company would have to do is do good work and people would stand in line to buy their stuff. And we all know that's not the case.

I: What are some examples of how you would promote yourself? A lot of people say, "Well, that's just bragging." How do you do it effectively while keeping your integrity?

MG: Well, it's not just bragging. One woman I was teaching this to worked in a large bank, and she said, "So, this means I'm supposed to show off or brag?"

I asked her a question. I said, "If you get promoted, do you think that is bad or good for this company?" You know what she said? "It would be good if it would help the company."

I: That's an outstanding point. We're talking about some of the key behaviors that leaders may need to stop, one of which is speaking when angry. Could you talk a little bit about that?

MG: Frances Hesselbein said, "Why should we be expected to control anything else if we can't control ourselves?" The first person we need to learn how to control is ourselves. It's very important to avoid speaking or sending e-mails when you're angry or feeling out of control. Control is important.

I'd like to offer an example from my book that involves my daughter, Kelly. I'm very proud of my daughter. She earned a Ph.D. at Yale. She was prom queen and president of her class. She's a wonderful daughter. But when she was fifteen, she did something that daddy was not so thrilled about. She was a pioneer in the world of navel rings. She got a navel ring and a lacy little outfit to highlight the navel ring so we could see it.

I came home and there she was wearing the lacy outfit and the navel ring. I reacted with something less than wild enthusiasm — yelling, screaming, ranting, and raving.

Years later I was meditating in a little Buddhist monastery. We meditated on anger, and he said, "Think of a time in your life when you became angry and lost control of your behavior." I came out with this case study, and then he said, "Who is responsible for what happened?" I realized what was going on in my mind. My first thought was of my daughter walking down the street and someone saying, "What a cheap-looking kid. I wonder who her father is." Even worse, my second thought was of my own friends saying, "I'm amazed Marshall lets his daughter look that way." What was I concerned about? Her or me? Which was the biggest problem? Her navel ring or my own ego? Clearly it was my own ego.

And you know, if I had to do it over, I still might have said, "Get rid of the navel ring." But I didn't have to yell and scream and rant or act like an idiot. It's very hard when we get angry to take a breath, look in the mirror, and say, "How much of this problem is *out there*, and how much of this problem is *in here*?" Eighty percent of the time the biggest problem when we get angry is not *out there*. The biggest problem is *in here*. We can't necessarily change *out there,* but we can change *in here*.

I: This brings up some different questions. Could you talk a little bit about meditation or relaxation techniques that you have found to be successful with executives or leaders? I think that could probably be one of the most valuable things for those individuals, and I wonder if you've found any success in that area.

MG: I don't do that specifically in my coaching. One thing I do, however, is utilize a Buddhist technique called Feed Forward. Buddha said, "Only do what I teach you. If it works, make it part of your own life. If it doesn't work in the context of your life, don't do it."

In the Feed Forward process, I have everyone ask not for feedback about the past, but for ideas for the future. When you get the ideas, you're supposed to shut up, listen, take notes, and just say thank you. No matter what the idea is, you don't judge, you don't critique, and you look at the idea like a gift. If you want to do it, you should do it. And if you don't want to do it, don't. Just shut up, listen, take notes, and say thank you. Never judge the other person.

I: It would be beautiful if we could all focus on doing that.

MG: Yes, and most of our friends and family members would be more than happy if we helped more and judged less.

LEADERSHIP OPPORTUNITY:

I've done this exercise with tens of thousands of people around the world. Begin by selecting one behavior you want to improve. Ask as many people as you can, get ideas, and always say thank you. In return, share your own ideas, and the other person should also say thank you. At the end of the exercise, I ask people to give me a word to describe this activity. People describe it as positive, useful, helpful, and even fun. Then I ask, "What's the last word that you think of to describe any feedback activity?" I say, "Fun." A lot of people say this *is* fun.

It's about focusing on a future you can change, not on a past you can't change. It's about looking positively at what you *can* do, not at what you *can't* do. There's no judging involved.

For example, you would come to me and say, "Marshall, I want to get better. Please help me." It's about everyone trying to help each other as opposed to judging each other. It takes out that superiority/inferiority aspect to the point where we are just regular folks trying to help everyone get better. So the four words I think that tie into better coaching that I think Buddha would agree with are *help more, judge less.*

LEADERSHIP SUCCESS:

I was teaching at the Kaiser Permanente health company, and a woman in my class said, "There's one thing you've left out. You should teach people to do this with their parents."

So she went out and asked her mother, "How can I be a better daughter?" Her mother said, "Well, you know Dad is dead and I live alone. Every day I take a long walk up the driveway to the mailbox. Almost every day there's nothing in the mailbox, and every day that makes me lonely." She said, "It would mean so much to me, as your mother, if you would send me little pictures or cards or something, so when I go to the mailbox there might be something in it."

So she started sending her mother little pictures and cards. What does that mean to her mother? Everything! What does it cost her? Almost nothing. She sent me an e-mail about a month ago. Her mother just died. The last thing her mother said was, "Thank you for the cards, pictures, and letters you sent to me." What's that worth? I think you've got to be speechless here. It's very powerful.

Katinka Nicou

London, United Kingdom

An Organization and Leadership Development Consultant, Katinka Nicou serves client organizations by aligning their talent and performance with strategic goals. Her services include talent management strategic planning and implementation, competency and performance management, as well as leadership development and executive coaching. Katinka has carried out consulting and facilitation assignments for clients across the United States and Europe and is a frequent speaker and author on organizational and personal transformation.

Katinka holds a Master of Education in Leadership from Columbia University and a Bachelor of Arts in Organizational Behavior and Communications from New York University. She has several Executive Coaching certifications and is qualified in a variety of personal transformation approaches, including Neuro-Linguistic Programming and Hypnotherapy.

I: How does leadership impact your specific niche or area of specialization?

KN: Whether in an organizational or individual context, transformational coaching involves breaking away from unconscious beliefs that limit us from seeing our own abilities and the possibilities in front of us, so that we are more equipped to realize our highest potential. I believe every person has a sense of purpose which, when unveiled, unleashes a tremendous power in the individual. From this point, the unique individual's creative capacity becomes an active force in painting the vision of their future.

As a Coach, I have witnessed a profound longing for self-discovery and a sense of purpose among my clients, from senior Lawyers to corporate executives to social entrepreneurs. Professionals increasingly seek personal and spiritual development as a way of finding the sustainable inner balance necessary to tackle an increasingly stressful workload and environment, but few organizational cultures have fostered this kind of development.

Fortunately, more and more businesses have recognized the benefits of personal leadership development and Executive Coaching to successful business decision making and execution. Nevertheless, what is often taught in general leadership programs is research or models that were developed prior to the age of the Internet, globalization, and the intercultural communication that takes place at every level of organizational hierarchy and societal stratus. There is a significant lack of guidance on how to be a successful leader in today's sophisticated global context of world citizens and intricate webs of business and political relationships.

Hence, I think what is needed among today's leaders is not more templates for how to do business in a particular culture or how to communicate with general personality styles, but a facilitated path to a clear sense of identity and personal way of leadership—one that balances rational judgment and tact with internal wisdom and objectivity in the midst of the intensity and complexity of today's business and political landscapes—supported by such deeper transformation. More and more leaders in today's world recognize the need for transformational learning for effective leadership and wish to have an honest dialogue with themselves about their values, beliefs, needs and innermost aspirations to bring them closer to their highest capacity and deepest sense of self.

The role of the Coach is to question assumptions, address uncertainties, establish understanding, and carry light on the highest intention and constructive action. I feel blessed through my work to be able to facilitate these transformations and calls to action for my clients in the most respectful, expanding, and motivating dynamics. I have seen what power can emerge from individuals who make a conscious choice to make the most of their resources and sense of purpose—a charisma that can drive masses to accept challenges and accomplish goals.

I: How do you know what goals are right for you and what you need to work on to achieve them?

KN: A personal goal is a desired outcome of an activity, what you wish to create in your life in the best of all realities, how you wish to be, think, and feel once it is achieved. In other words, it is the result you wish to experience from having achieved the activities you engage in, not the activity itself. When you take this approach to setting milestones for your own life or career, you are sure to know intuitively what is right for you, and your coach will help you assess your goals against the wider implications for your values and your context. A lot of people think that coaching is mainly about setting goals and supporting the actions needed to achieve them. What is often overlooked, and what is often the most powerful process in enabling those goals, is identifying and addressing what holds you back from achieving them. Some of the most common blocks to the realization of our full potential are conflicting values, limiting beliefs, and fear.

"If you continue on a path guided by values you no longer hold, you will likely feel unfulfilled."

Our values change as we experience life; for example, when we leave home to support ourselves, when we have families, and when we begin to care for our elderly. Ask yourself regularly, "What is important to me at this point in my life? How can I let that guide my next life choice or career move?" If you continue on a path guided by values you no longer hold, you will likely feel unfulfilled.

Our beliefs about ourselves also determine success. Most of our beliefs are completely unconscious, and thus we just assume them to be true. Check in with yourself as to whether your belief system supports what you want to achieve. Ask yourself, "Do I believe that I can have this outcome, that I deserve it, and that it will be in the highest intention of others around me that I have it?" Sometimes we hold unconscious beliefs that are completely irrational but a powerful saboteur. By investigating and addressing unconscious beliefs, we clear the way to our own success.

Fear is another obstacle. We might think that the obvious response to one's own success is to embrace it and keep it going. But a lot of people are held back by fear of the consequences, responsibilities, or perceived expectations of their possible success. Making sure not to let ourselves off the hook, we should ask ourselves "If I am successful in achieving this outcome that I want, what additional responsibilities will I then have? What will be expected of me? What will I expect of myself? What will I have to give up? Who might be opposed to my achieving this goal?" So where the coach can be most helpful is in throwing light on what may prevent you from achieving what you want and addressing it.

I: How do you ensure personal and professional leadership growth?

KN: One of my most respected personal development teachers once said, "A great teacher is only learning ahead." Continuous learning is a term most people claim to live by in today's world, but to continuously learn means more than acquiring professional development credits. Owning up to our own experiences and challenges and turning them into insights that can be openly shared with others is a gift that keeps enlightening the people whose lives you help transform through coaching.

I try to proactively recognize what needs to happen for me to get to the next level and remind myself that all obstacles are subject to our interpretations. A lot of personal obstacles can be overcome, and I am a walking example of that statement. And I have countless stories of clients overcoming limiting beliefs or performance anxiety, dramatically improving their relationships with their managers or subordinates, or drastically increasing their compensation. But they put great effort and courage into their personal development to clear their own way to success.

I: In tough times, what has kept you going?

KN: Learning from them. My simple story has—to my great joy and sometimes surprise—inspired more friends, colleagues, and clients than I could have ever imagined to also embark on a journey of personal transformation. I have enjoyed a remarkable decade of transformational experiences and continuous evolution toward an integrated sense of self. I have confronted some of my innermost attachments, fears, and insecurities, and the emotional freedom and the space within which to creatively develop my strengths that opened up as a result has evoked in me a tremendous gratitude and a sustained sense of inner peace and joy.

Most of us would define a tough time as a reactive time, a time when we have had to react to an unforeseen event or unfavorable action by others. An important thing to remember is that we cannot be creative when we are reactive. We often don't realize that a situation has been traumatic for us until we have gained some perspective from it. The more self-aware we become, the better we are able to catch ourselves in the moment we feel thrown off and

LEADERSHIP OPPORTUNITY:

I am driven by a long-term "life vision" and a short-term "living vision." I wrote the long-term vision almost ten years ago, and it still serves as my guidepost in every aspect of life. Every New Year's Eve, I take a couple of hours by myself and reflect on what I am most grateful for of the events of the year that has passed, what I have learned, how that has shaped me, and how I wish to apply that wisdom to move forward in the year to come. I then review my long-term vision for my life and ask myself how I am progressing toward it. I may discover that I have progressed in certain areas of my life and not others, or that my values have changed and as a result, my priorities have shifted. I can then revise the guideposts I have set for the various aspects of my life or add newly acquired aspirations or values as motivating forces toward my vision. This is a beautiful internal dialogue that I look forward to every holiday season. That said, it is not something that should happen only once a year or at that particular time; it is just how I have structured it. Many of my clients do this for the first time with me, and I encourage them to do it on a regular basis— perhaps once per quarter or every six months in the beginning—to remind themselves of how far they have come and how they have expanded their capacity to create their own lives.

On one sheet of paper, write down your ideal personal life vision, imagining your life at least ten years from now. Describe what your life would look like and feel like, your career path, the people with whom you live and work, your activities, where you live and travel, and anything you wish to add in creating a life that is in perfect harmony with your greatest sense of self.

On another sheet of paper, write down what comes to mind as you consider the following questions:

1. What am I grateful for in the year that has been? Include events and people that have come into your life.

2. How have those things or people shaped me? As a result, how am I different? What positive qualities or skills have I developed? What wisdom have I gained?

3. How do I wish to apply those qualities and skills in the next year toward fulfilling my life vision?

4. What else do I need to learn and what people do I need to meet? How can I actively seek out those experiences?

Every time you do this exercise, remember to look back at your previous notes and recognize your progress. You will be stunned at how much you can achieve in a short time by having priorities and by focusing your efforts and aspirations.

LEADERSHIP SUCCESS:

I was working with the chairman and main investor of a growing real estate company and his executive team. Despite being in the midst of a recession, the company had been very successful, but the team was struggling with interpersonal conflict and loss of motivation. Occasionally, the chairman would fly in and find that the progress of the company was not where he expected it to be. He would explicitly and loudly share his dismay, but the team would not know what to do, as they were at a loss for goals and direction. It was necessary to get everyone on the same page, which required a process of asking, "What are we all about? What do we want to achieve? What do we need in order to achieve it? And how are we going to get there?" It was clear that the team needed leadership, but what that would look like had to be defined by the chairman *and* the team so that everyone would get the guidance and support they needed. I focused my facilitation on identifying alternative approaches for the chairman to share his feedback constructively.

He needed to be mindful of is his level of empowerment of the team. He came to realize that he needed to elicit as much thought and as many suggestions as he could before making decisions, and delegate all follow through so that team members would not lose trust in their own judgment. He also had to be consistent. While he was comfortable with change, several members of the team were not, and to grow a strong platform for business operations, his messages should not be disruptive. He had to be clear about his position and ask himself what he needed to do to maintain it. I asked him what he needed in order to feel in control without having to take charge or change direction. He also needed to find ways to mitigate silo behaviour so that team members were not pulling their own efforts in different directions.

The chairman set milestones for each team head and the level below. I also encouraged him to leverage the varying skill sets on the team to devise solutions for the company's growth. He tapped into employees at lower levels which offered them an opportunity to shine their strengths. He realized that he had extremely capable people on his team, and within a year, the company doubled its assets and expanded to three continents.

Tony DiRico
Keller, Texas, USA

Tony DiRico is the founder of Profit Hunters International, a company that provides talent management consulting services and features employee personality assessment tools to recruit, hire, train, develop, and retain the company's most valuable asset—their people.

Prior to founding Profit Hunters International, Tony was a hospitality industry executive with over thirty-five years of experience at senior management level positions including President, COO, and CEO in both private and public companies for up to five thousand international hotels. He's an expert in finding talent, determining what makes that talent possess great leadership skills, and being able to enhance those leadership skills.

I: You've spent over thirty years in senior leadership roles in the hotel business. How have your leadership skills and style changed over that period of time?

TD: The major changes were made when I first started. My leadership style was more autocratic. I was a hard worker and very good at my trade, which was the hospitality business. I thought everyone had to be like myself. You have to put in the hours and work really hard.

Another major change occurred when my first child was born in 1987. I was nervous to be a new father and wished the new baby came home with a manual. At that time I bought a book by Dr. Glenn Doman who founded the Institute for the Achievement of Human Potential. The book was *How to Multiply Your Baby's Intelligence.*

What I found interesting about Dr. Doman's work was that he was actually working with brain-damaged children. While working with these special needs children, they developed a system and method to help these children enhance their abilities. What they discovered was that these children were found to function significantly better than children who were at normal development. The basis of change was that the parents and people involved with the children that were challenged were always positive and excited any time the child attempted to accomplish something. The children that didn't progress quite as well had parents who were more disconnected and cold in their responses.

I related to that when my children were learning to walk. I still remember my wife placing our child standing against the couch, taking a step back, holding our arms out to catch them, and encouraging them to take a step. I think everyone does the same thing; you let your child take the first step and then they fall in your arms and you hug them. You twirl them around. You celebrate. You are excited that they tried.

Historically, my management style up to that point was autocratic. In regards to an employee, I would have approached them and said, "I don't understand why you are having a problem with this! I told you how to do it! I showed you how to do it! How come you can't do the job?"

Encouraging my children to take those first steps made me realize that my type of management was very limiting. A major turning point came when I realized it was the same thing in the workplace. When people attempt to do something—whether they succeed or fail—we need to make sure we provide positive reinforcement and celebrate the fact that they took the risk and attempted it. Then we can continue to encourage them to move forward and learn in regards to whatever activity they are working on.

With that experience, I went from a hard work, autocratic, get-it-done attitude to one geared more toward that of a mentor, coach, and enthusiastic cheerleader for the people I led.

I: It's really something that this amazing event of the birth of your children completely transformed your leadership skills and your methods of maximizing employee and team performance.

TD: Absolutely. It was a major event and a great turning point in my leadership style.

I: Was there anything else that drew you to that conclusion? It must have been quite an adjustment to shift your style.

"I went from a hard work, autocratic, get-it-done attitude to one geared more toward that of a mentor, coach, and enthusiastic cheerleader for the people I led."

TD: It wasn't as dramatic a change as it may seem. I was not that ogre supervisor that most people might have expected. I was fairly humanistic, but it was an evolution.

Another thing that had a major affect on my ongoing development as a leader also took place early on. Hard work had gotten me to where I was. A lot of times people would say to me, "Tony, you've been fairly successful. What made you so successful?"

I would say, "The first thing was that I showed up for work every day. That eliminated 80% of the people." When I started, most people took off work on a sunny day; they called in sick or made up an excuse, but I was a dedicated, ambitious, and very conscientious hard worker.

However, that attitude only got me so far. To rise to the next level, I started to read books and attend seminars. In the hotel business, one of our major jobs was to sell our services. And I forget who spoke about it—it may have been Jim Rohn or even Denis Waitley—but someone said that highly successful salespeople spent thirty hours a week in personal development, whether they were reading books, attending seminars, or attending training classes. Conversely, they also said that the average American spends thirty hours a week in front of the television. I decided if it worked for them then it might work for me.

I started to expand my reading and started to read a book a month. One of the first books that I gravitated to was *Think and Grow Rich* by Napoleon Hill. I attended seminars, whether they were sponsored by the company or if it was a Tony Robbins event. It has been a real evolution from where I was to where I am today.

I: Can you give us some additional tips that you might want to share with those just getting started?

TD: When I hired hotel managers, I gave them each a copy of the book *Think and Grow Rich*. Then I gave them an assignment to read the book, come back, and tell me what they learned.

Buying a rich man lunch is one of the principles taught in the book. I was with a public company at the time called Manor Care. They own Choice Hotels. To apply that principle, Stuart, the founder of Manor Care, was thought to have a very autocratic style of leadership. When he walked the halls, most people would walk the other way even though he wasn't overly involved in the day-to-day activities. I thought, *What better practice than to offer to buy Stuart lunch.*

I called his office and spoke to his secretary. I told her I would like to buy Stuart lunch. She told me she would ask him what he would like to do. One of my associates and long-time employee asked me if I was crazy. "You want to buy Stuart lunch? He's going to eat *you* for lunch!" he said.

I replied calmly, "You know what, that may be true, but let me see."

His secretary called me back and said, "Tony, Stuart would love to have lunch with you, but he'd like to have lunch in his conference room, and he wants to do it on Thursday. If you don't mind, he'd like to schedule it from one o'clock to two o'clock."

I joined him and he had lunch brought to the conference room, so I obviously didn't pay for it, but we did have the chance to talk. I simply asked him, "Stuart, you've been really successful in your life and you've been so impactful in the lives of other people. How did you do it? What were some of the things you did when you were starting your business?"

It's amazing the amount of insight he provided simply because I asked him. I suspect very few people would have asked him because of his stature and his wealth.

That illustrates a piece of advice that I'd give someone starting out. If you see someone who's been highly successful, don't ask them to buy you lunch; offer to take *them* out to lunch. Let them know you'd like to know more about how they've been successful. A lot of highly successful people are sometimes the loneliest people in the world. It's kind of like the most beautiful girl in the room: everyone thinks she has hundreds of people asking her out, but she is sometimes lonely too.

I: How do you balance the demands of your leadership role and family life? You seem to do a beautiful job; we don't all do that well.

TD: I'm like a swan; I look calm on the surface, but I'm paddling like crazy under the water. Part of it is about visualization. One of the ways I process information is to use visualization techniques. I visualize a stool and the top of the stool, and I say, "This is life balance." That stool has four legs and each of those legs stand for something: my personal life including fitness and how I maintain myself, my professional life, my life at home with my family, and my spirituality.

To maintain balance, you want to make sure that all four of those legs maintain a certain length. If I stop exercising and gain twenty pounds and become less fit, that will create an imbalance. If I don't spend quality time with my family, that also creates imbalance. So I make a plan. For example, if I get four weeks of vacation each year, I make sure to spend them with my family.

The first of the year my wife—and also my children when they were old enough to participate—would say, "Let's plan our vacations. Let's get the calendar. Where and when do you want to have these times together?" I would put them on the calendar and they would be hard-coded, meaning that if someone called me up and said, "Tony, we want you to do this in this period of time," I could look at my calendar first and if it said "family vacation," I would decline the work opportunity. Those are the kinds of activities that balance family life.

I: What do you find are greatest challenges for leaders today?

TD: What I find to be the greatest challenge is leading a diverse group of people and getting them to perform to their optimal level. You can label the groups Generation X or Baby Boomers and further identify them based on whether they work on the front lines, in the warehouse, or as the Senior Vice President of sales and marketing. As a leader, you have to ask yourself, "How do I get this person to be number one—to be highly effective in their role and also extremely effective as a team member?"

I typically assist them in understanding the unique characteristics of the employee as an individual and then collectively as a member of the team. Offering guidance as to how they can better coach their team is the number one best piece of advice I can give them.

LEADERSHIP OPPORTUNITY:

I would suggest that anyone look at their own personality style or traits to determine their personality makeup. It kind of goes back to the idea of the general practitioner; if I have a patient, one of the first things I would order would be a blood test. This helps the doctor pinpoint areas of weakness and strength. Similarly, a personality assessment pinpoints areas of strength and weakness which allows the opportunity to suggest solutions for performance improvement.

I would suggest that even family units today should have a behavioral characteristic assessment to determine compatibility. Some of these things can be found for free on the Internet. My whole family has taken personality assessments.

LEADERSHIP SUCCESS:

We were working with a manufacturing company out of Cleveland, Ohio, and one of the challenges they were having one was in the area of sales area. They were looking to hire a regional director, and they came to me through a consultant in the manufacturing distribution industry.

The consultant had met with an individual, who happened to be from Texas, and both the company and the psychologist thought he was an inappropriate fit. When we assessed him using our tools and my intervention with him, we predicted that the gentleman would be a highly successful salesperson in the company. The challenge they found was that he was from Texas, he had a southern drawl, and they weren't sure he would fit with their customers. That was their bias because they were—for lack of a better term—Yankees from Cleveland, and they thought this good old boy from Texas just wasn't going to be able to sell.

They took a chance. They said, "You know what, we're going to contradict what our local programs have told us, and we'll go with yours." They hired the gentleman. That was three years ago, and he has been one of their top performers since the day he started.

We always advise people, "If you hire only the people who look and act just like you, you're going to end up with a lot of duplication of thought, and you're going to have a lot of waste."

Sherry Buffington, Ph.D.
Dallas, Texas, USA

Dr. Sherry Buffington has been immersed in the study of human nature, motivation, and success principles since 1978. She is a leading authority on behaviors and motivations that lead to success.

She is the founder of NaviCore International, Inc., a research and development firm focused on human potential as well as the owner of Quantum Leap which provides leading-edge advancements for personal and professional prosperity. Her programs consistently receive rave reviews for the rapid, measurable, and powerful results they provide.

Sherry is a psychologist, coach, consultant, trainer, presenter, and author of a number of books. She is also the creator of The Accelerated Mind Patterning Process (AAMP), which immediately and permanently removes internal blocks and barriers to success.

I: You are a leading expert in the area of human behavior. You've been training and leading coaches and leaders for more than twenty years. What do you consider to be the top skills leaders absolutely need to be highly successful?

SB: There are actually ten competencies that are important to effective leadership, but if I had to choose just one, I'd say it's the ability to get the intended result. To get intended results requires good communication skills. Without the kinds of skills we need to genuinely connect with people, the likelihood of having a misunderstanding becomes very large, and poor outcomes become a factor.

Most of us have a similar communicational style, and that style—unless a leader recognizes that they have that style and purposely modifies it—tends to get substandard results when we give directives. Leaders have no idea that they are inadvertently creating the very things they most want to eliminate, which include errors as well as wasted time and resources.

A few years ago, in trying to explain to leaders what that style was that I see so frequently, I coined the term, *Swiss Cheese Communication.* I use Swiss Cheese Communication as a descriptor because the style is full of holes and yet most leaders like the holes; they are communicational generalists.

Most leaders fall into the generalist category of communication. They get to the point and are bottom-line oriented. They want someone to give them just enough information to make a decision and then get out of their way. They dislike too many details, and that's true whether they're giving instructions or giving or receiving information, so they get impatient when people ask for more details. As you might imagine, general instructions with a lot of holes in them will not usually result in the outcome that the leader set out to attain.

I: I could see where that could create some significant problems. Is that type of communication highly prevalent?

SB: Yes. The interesting thing is that leaders who communicate this way actually like the holes. To them, the holes allow room for creativity and innovation, but not everyone approaches projects that way; not everyone is looking for innovation or creativity.

The problem occurs when leaders are looking at the "cheese," so to speak, and embracing the holes because of the room for creativity and innovation while their employees are looking at the holes and wondering what goes into those holes. So you have a leader thinking that he or she is communicating clearly, and employees who are looking at those holes in the communication and saying, "I need to understand this." They're being left far behind while the leader continues to move ahead to explain what they want; often they're not even hearing it.

If an employee who is looking at the holes starts asking questions, the typical leader who has a generalist communication style will get impatient with that. When the impatience shows, employees then sense that impatience and stop asking questions, so the holes don't get filled. Then the employee goes away, forced to assume what goes in the holes. And we know where assumptions lead, don't we?

I: I had never quite thought of it that way.

SB: It is a huge problem that rarely gets addressed because the typical assumption on the part of the leader is that poor results are the fault of the employees. You frequently hear leaders say that they can't delegate because employees can't follow instructions.

The reality is, when I talk to leaders about their communication style and point out to them where they're getting less than stellar results—especially if that's applies to more than one team member—I try to help them see that they need to look at the common denominator. The common denominator is always the communicator—the leader.

I: In working with leaders in major corporations, what would you say are their greatest challenges?

SB: Clearly, it is being blind to their communicational style and to the communicational style of their employees. There are eight distinct styles of communication.

For example, extroverted communicators—people who are bold communicators—tend to think out loud. Introverts tend not to; they process internally. Most leaders tend to possess a bold leadership style. What happens—and you've probably seen this happen yourself in a meeting—is that you'll have a lot of bold leadership types along with more reserved leaders or employees in a meeting together, but you don't hear anything from the reserved leaders. The reason for that is because often the bold types think out loud and throw ideas on the table while the reserved individuals take it all in as though it's real. If the reserved type of communicator doesn't understand communicational styles, then they don't realize that the extroverted communicator is just tossing out ideas, so they're taking them seriously. That is one common problem.

The other problem occurs when a bold type of leader asks a reserved individual a question. The reserved person—because they process information internally—will hesitate and pause as they process the information. The bold type assumes they didn't understand because there's that silence and bold types don't like silence. So they fill in the silence by re-asking the question another way or assuming the person didn't understand; they try to explain further, which only irritates the silent type. The more reserved individual, who is trying to process internally, becomes irritated, and that is when communications break down. You can see where that would be a big problem.

Under those circumstances—with miscommunications occurring—costly mistakes are inevitable, and they happen daily.

I: What's the solution for this? How is a leader to know that his or her communication has really been heard?

SB: I'm not sure who stated it first, but the observation is that, "The greatest barrier to good communication is the illusion that it has occurred." To prevent that illusion, leaders need to take it upon themselves to give and receive feedback consistently. When they are giving instructions, feedback is essential to excellent outcomes in what they are striving to attain.

Leaders are often surprised when I point this out to them. They can't believe that they're leaving holes in their instructions and not being patient with filling in those holes. This leaves their employees to make assumptions, and those assumptions are often wrong. Leaders are often shocked and surprised at how frequently employees are unable to feed back to them what they thought they had clearly conveyed. We need to communicate frequently and clearly.

"Leaders are often shocked and surprised at how frequently employees are unable to feed back to them what they thought they had clearly conveyed."

When asking for feedback, it's best to say something like, "Would you feed back to me what you understand the instruction to be so that I know I communicated it to you effectively?" A leader should never say, "So I can be sure you understood," because that puts the responsibility on the other person and results in defensiveness. As defenses increase, listening decreases.

I: So the leader should take full responsibility for the leadership.

SB: Absolutely. Even when they're receiving information. When receiving information, the leader should do essentially the same thing. They should say, for example, "Let me feed back to you what I just heard you say to be sure that I understood you correctly."

Take responsibility for understanding, communicating, and listening correctly from your perspective to be sure you understand. Leaders who get and give feedback and take full responsibility for it in that way tend to get a far better result than those who don't. In fact, sometimes eight times better.

I: That's amazing.

SB: It is. What's really interesting about the two types—good communicators versus poor communicators—is that leaders who are great communicators tend to say that they have really great employees, and leaders who are poor communicators tend to complain that their employees are incompetent. Again, what's the common denominator?

I: You work with a number of different niches and areas of specialization. How is leadership impacting those areas from the standpoint of what you see now?

SB: I work with coaches and entrepreneurs and people who are in leadership positions in large corporations, so from my perspective, leadership impacts everything—no matter what the area is. 88% of the population is looking for leadership rather than seeking to be a leader. Only 12% are seeking to lead, and less than 3% of the 12% seeking to lead does it well.

As a business owner myself, leadership is a critical component. It is for every business owner. If it isn't, it should be. Because I do work with business owners primarily, it's everything in my organization and in my business.

I: As a great leader yourself, how do you ensure your personal and professional leadership growth on an ongoing basis?

SB: I am always learning and looking for ways to continue learning. At the point we give up learning, it's time to give up lots of things.

I think every leader should have at least one good coach. I am really big on coaches, because coaches can see things that we miss. Besides that, a good coach serves as a guide, a sounding board, and an accountability partner. We can learn from anyone if we're open to learning, and I think coaching is such an important tool for moving forward.

LEADERSHIP OPPORTUNITY:

My mantra for many years has been to encourage leaders to get people-centric. Profits are always generated by productive people. Human ingenuity and human energy is the prime for the business pump. When people are engaged and connected to their work, you have that prime showing up every single day and priming the pump so that those products and services are getting out there easier, faster, and with greater flow.

The goal of business is certainly to generate a profit, but that happens a lot faster and a lot easier when a company recognizes that profits are generated by people, and when they see their people as their primary profit center.

Employees are generally considered a necessary expense, and that's only true if they're not led well, because what happens when people are not led well is that it leads to low interest, low interest leads to disengagement, and without the interest and the involvement of the people, there is absolutely no way to have a healthy, thriving business.

LEADERSHIP SUCCESS:

A couple of years ago a company called me in because the customer service department was completely dysfunctional. Their complaint level from customers was terrible. I found that there were a couple of things awry. One was that the people in the customer service department didn't know one another, they didn't communicate with one another well, and they didn't know the goals, values, or the vision of the organization. They didn't know how they fit into that.

Three weeks into the program and working with this company, they had done a complete turnaround. They had removed one individual who was stirring the pot, and they understood each other, they appreciated each other, and they were finally able to connect and communicate.

Three weeks later, the OD Director absolutely could not believe what he was seeing—happy people who were talking about ways to pull together, ways to improve their systems, and ways to improve their processes and procedures for serving their customers well. They changed their entire view of their role and of the customer. It was an amazing transformation.

Clara Noble
Lisbon, Portugal

Clara Noble fell in love with coaching after a successful career in international consulting and multinational corporate top management (finance and human resources). This dual-faceted experience of financial and human capital gave Clara a unique and practical view of leadership which is a key area in her coaching practice.

Born in Portugal in a family with strong French cultural influence, Clara has been married for twenty-six years to an English CPA she met at Deloitte and where she started her career after university. Moving into industry as a CFO at the age of twenty-eight, she asserted herself in spite of being both young and female in a male-dominated environment. Her creativity and multicultural experience has helped her UK, US, Australian, and Portuguese clients achieve rewarding excellence.

I: What is your speciality, Clara?

CN: I help executives, entrepreneurs, and small business owners gain clarity on their goals and the steps to achieve them by working on their mind-sets, communication, and leadership skills. This helps them achieve success and work-life balance faster and with less stress.

I: What is leadership to you?

CN: Leadership is a concept that has always been very present in my life. I am an only child. My mother was an only child and a high school teacher. My grandmother was the headmistress of a primary school in Lisbon, the capital of Portugal. We lived above the school in a fifteen-room apartment.

From my first memories of playing with my friends, I was always the one who decided what we would play, who would do what, and what the rules of the game were. I don't know why; it just happened that way.

In primary school, I decided what we would do on the playground and which homework assignment we would do first. You could say that my grandmother's position played an important role, but the fact is that when I went to high school with four thousand students, and after adjusting to being just a number—teachers used to call us by a number until they learned our names—my marks raised to the top three in every subject. In those days, unless you were totally unsociable, that placed you as a leader, even on the playground.

University was a strange yet rich experience because I went there directly after the peaceful revolution that ended the right wing dictatorship and opened the door to democracy. There was a period of extreme left-wing euphoria and political instability reflected in the fact that we had thirteen governments in seven years.

My first CFO position was in a Luso-American company at the age of twenty-eight, and I had a rewarding career in finance and human resources at the top management level until the multinational company I was working for pulled out of Portugal and I lost my job in 2000.

Many times during my career I was referred to as a "born leader." I was proud to lead by example. I thought that to lead people I had to know how to do their work and mine. I had to work twice as hard which was why I earned five to ten times more than those that worked for me. We never missed a deadline. I often worked twelve hours a day—and sometimes weekends too—to make sure of that.

Yet I see now that I wasn't a good leader. I often micromanaged, and although I inspired my teams and they were proud of their work, I was sometimes patronizing and I resented those few who put their personal lives first, leaving work unfinished. I obviously ended up taking care of what was left incomplete.

You don't see what you don't see. When I set up my consultancy company and had staff members working for me, I couldn't get them engaged because, first, it was not a prestigious multinational company, and second, they didn't buy into my dream. That was when I realized I had been talking to them as if they had the same values I did. My high IQ and so-called "natural leadership" proved to be quite useless.

That's when I decided to study coaching and became involved in BNI (Business Network International).

Coaching turned out to be my life's passion, because with technology and globalization dramatically increasing the speed of change, consultancy became frustrating and ineffective.

Traditional consultants don't challenge their clients' beliefs and paradigms. They don't usually explore their vision or how far they have drifted from it. Consultants present a technical solution in which the client usually has had little input and there is a low chance of succeeding because it will be imposed and not adequately followed up by the consultant as most clients don't want to pay support and implementation fees.

BNI helped to keep me sane by providing interaction with like-minded entrepreneurs and small businesses owners. Being chosen for the leadership team and later becoming the director provided me with experience and training in the type of leadership where there was no hierarchy relationship between members; it was an environment where you became respected for your ability to serve the group—an idea known as "givers gain." That path led me to understand how to be an intrapersonal leader.

I: What do you do to ensure your personal and professional leadership growth?

CN: I am a perpetual student. The problem in the past was lack of time. I am one of two partners that live and work in perfect synchrony. I've made all the proverbial mistakes. Those mistakes tend to include marketing too generally due to trying to help everyone and burning out by trading time for money without feeling much fulfilment.

Often we have been underpaid because we felt sorry for a client. This makes you realize two things: first, you have to choose a niche and be clear about what results you can bring to the table, and second, you are providing a disservice to clients by working for peanuts because they don't take the service you provide seriously enough and therefore don't get the full benefit of your expertise. This means that you either work exclusively for free for an agreed period of time, or you charge based on the transformation you can provide.

Once we came through that phase (a valuable step in our personal growth and in clarifying who would benefit the most from our inspiration), we started having more time for what is really important.

We started investing 10% to 20% of our time and money into our own education—reading, keeping up with trends via the Internet, travelling, attending live events, and interacting with experts primarily in the US and the UK. We loved every minute of it.

Investing in your own personal growth is a great way to improve your credibility as a leader. The awareness and knowledge you gain about yourself, the clarity of your values and your purpose, the discipline to establish goals and the strategy and timing to achieve them, the habit of questioning your own assumptions, and the ability to learn from the outcome of every action are all powerful outcomes of self-leadership.

As I mentioned before, being part of BNI has also been important, and because communication is key to the success of any relationship and even more so when it comes to of leadership, we joined Toastmasters International about a year ago. This experience has proved to be very effective in improving our communication and leadership skills.

Last, but not least, we always plan our holidays around our work trips which allows us to relax and immerse ourselves in natural and artistic beauty. This form of relaxation and self-care stimulates creation, and it is often in these moments that we have our biggest breakthroughs in regards to new areas of our business or how to help clients. There is nothing like designing a new leadership workshop while looking at the Grand Canyon or brainstorming a new idea while driving through the south of France.

I: How does leadership impact your specific niche or area of specialization today?

CN: I work with two niches: entrepreneurs/small business owners and executives. I work with the first because I've been a small business owner for the last ten years. I believe that having walked the same path as my clients helps me understand their challenges, and it is a step toward creating empathy for them.

For the same reason, working with executives was a natural choice since I was one myself for a large part of my professional life. I can feel my clients' pain and understand what they are going through.

"The relentless pace of change of the modern age coupled with the instability and uncertainty that results from it and from the economic downturn are the greatest challenges we face."

Corporate management has suffered many changes, and what is required from a leader today is very different from what was required ten years ago.

However, unfortunately most executives are still operating in "past mode" and waiting for the storm to calm down, not realizing that times have irreversibly changed and that the first and most important thing they have to do now is to change their own behaviours and beliefs. Accepting that the market is a moving, transforming train is just the beginning. You then have to start operating in the "Me, Inc." mode.

The way to catch up with today's reality is to work on yourself, which is the only factor you can really master and change. The relentless pace of change of the modern age coupled with the instability and uncertainty that results from it and from the economic downturn are the greatest challenges we face, and we face them as leaders in the professional arena as well as in our personal lives.

Leading effectively in today's world requires greater skills, adaptability to change, courage, and integrity than ever before. A leader must not only be capable of communicating and inspiring a vision to his followers, but he must also be flexible and prepared to continually adjust his tactics to get there while staying aligned with the company and his own values.

Constant innovation must be omnipresent in the mind of a leader in addition to a global perspective and an ability to develop strategic partnerships. Clarity of communication is essential to keep every stakeholder committed and fully engaged in each project.

In short, leaders need to think strategically, accept uncertainty, adapt quickly and constantly, and be alert for emerging challenges and opportunities. They have to build relationships based on clear communication, trust, integrity, collective strengths, and win-win opportunities.

LEADERSHIP OPPORTUNITY:

Imagine you could travel through time, and you leaped ahead to three years from now. For some reason, you had lost touch with one of your best friends. Write a letter to that person with the date of three years from now and tell him or her about your professional and personal life. What has changed, and how has it happened?

The objective of this exercise is to disassociate yourself from the present stress and roadblocks and to project into the future where anything is possible. Explaining how you got there usually results in more clarity about the options and the steps available to be taken in order to reach your objectives in your professional and personal life. This letter is an excellent tool to look into the future, open up possibilities, and create engagement and enthusiasm.

LEADERSHIP SUCCESS:

One of my clients was a small business owner. The business was experiencing financial strain due to the market and economic downturn, but it was still growing, and she had a team of consultants and a couple of admin people working under her supervision. She felt increasingly overwhelmed and found herself sabotaging her own work.

We soon came to the conclusion that the cause for her insecurity was that her father was a pathologic perfectionist who always found fault in anything she did. She was a very intelligent person, and she was willing to do any work I challenged her to do and was quick to understand the outcome and build from there.

One of the first things she started doing was a victory log, and through this she realized she was accomplishing more than she typically gave herself credit for.

She started running with some friends, participated in a mini marathon, and set the objective: to finish the race. A great win!

Building on the success and revelations she was having from running, she realized that she didn't have to be the best. She only had to finish the race and strive to keep improving her time. She accepted that the relationship with her father would only change to the extent that she changed her own response to his attitude.

She now lives a happy, balanced life and has just fulfilled a life-long dream by publishing a book for a nonprofit organization.

Gilles Brouillette, Ph.D.
Montreal, QC, Canada

Dr. Gilles Brouillette is a founding partner of the Transformational Learning Institute and the codirector of the Transformational Leadership Program at the Centre for Continuing Education of the University of Ottawa. His life work is committed to the study of organizational development and leadership training from a transformational learning perspective.

Gilles has been working with individuals and groups internationally for over twenty-five years. He holds a Doctorate in Transpersonal Psychology and numerous certifications including being a Certified Executive Coach.

His transformational coaching approach focuses mainly on vertical transformation. His commitment to learning, his expertise in personal and organizational transformation, and his authentic character offers the highest level of credibility in coaching and training senior executives.

I: How do you describe your development and transformational approach to leadership?

GB: I have been studying the process of transformation since I started practicing as a transpersonal psychologist, really looking at human beings from a developmental perspective. My study helped me to understand that we are in a process of continual growth and transformation throughout our lives.

I was curious to understand what is behind this process of individual and organizational transformation. I have spent most of my life researching that. What I discovered is that consciousness evolves through several stages of development that we go through as adults.

Before adult development research, we thought that all adults arrived at the same level of maturity. But that's not the case. In fact, research done by Joiner, Torbert, Cook-Greuter, and Wilber are clearly indicating that there are seven distinct levels of maturity/ consciousness. All of my leadership research has been oriented toward understanding those stages of development and, more importantly, understanding how we grow from the heroic/egoic state of consciousness to the post-heroic level.

"We are within a system, and we need to move from doing things for and by ourselves to doing things together in a deep spirit of collaboration."

One of our key discoveries was to find that most leaders today have hit a limit or some kind of developmental ceiling in their development. In fact, most leaders think, act, relate, and communicate from what we call a heroic/egoic level of consciousness. The tricky thing about it is that consciousness at that level is very reactive. It is not good or bad, but it is reactive and free or creative. There are two core stages of development at that level known as the Expert and the Achiever. The reason we refer to these levels as heroic or egoic is to stress the idea that the leader is coming from a sense of self-centeredness. It's the "I make things happen" mentality.

At the heroic/egoic level, the leader has not yet recognized that we are interconnected and interdependent and they are mainly looking to satisfy their own personal needs. The leader is in the process of establishing his own personal credibility. What is really surprising is that the statistics tell us that about 90% of leaders are not able to cross that developmental ceiling.

Beyond that level there is what we call the post-heroic/post-egoic level of development where only 10% of leaders are able to transcend the developmental ceiling. At this level, we have the Catalyst, the Co-Creator, and the Synergist. The core distinction between the heroic level and the post-heroic level is that at the post-heroic level, the leader is able to recognize at a very experiential level—not only intellectually—that we are within a system, and we need to move from doing things for and by ourselves to doing things together in a deep spirit of collaboration.

The title *Co-Creator* stresses the idea of moving into a collective intelligence, collective identity, and a collective way of thinking, and understanding that we are all interdependent and that we can only

achieve great things if we think and act from a collective perspective.

From a development perspective, what is really blocking people to access a higher level of leadership effectiveness is their level of consciousness, not their lack of skills. In fact, our whole leadership approach is articulated around the following core principle: the most powerful leverage to develop leadership effectiveness is to develop the leader's consciousness. As Bob Anderson mentioned in his article The Future of Leadership, "Great leadership requires higher order consciousness."

Now, to develop consciousness, we need to better understand our mind, and for that we need to explore and challenge our mental models. Mental models are the building blocks of the mind, and this is something we have spent a lot of time studying.

Basically, the mind has content and structure. Most research focuses on understanding the content of the mind, but I found very little research that leads to understanding its fundamental structure. If we really want to support the transformation of consciousness, we need to understand its basic structure. What is it made of, and how do we shift and transform it? So fundamentally, consciousness—at the heroic/egoic level—is made of a network unconscious mental models.

"Transformation is the capability to see your own thinking and to dis-identify from it."

Mental models are deeply linked to how the mind works. What we have discovered—and I need to acknowledge my colleague Mino Dallosto for some of these discoveries—is that our ways of thinking are governed by a core fundamental mental model which gives birth to the mental models we use to think when we are operating within the context of the heroic/egoic mind-set.

In other words, the way of thinking on the heroic level is based on a fundamental paradigm that is called the world of "OR." The world of "OR" is the structure of consciousness (a form) which gives birth to duality, separation, opposition, and the emotional field of fear. When thinking from that fundamental paradigm, leaders live in a world of conflicts and tensions where you need to look good, be right, and not show vulnerability. You have to be in charge, and your main focus is to protect or defend yourself.

One way to expand or transform consciousness is to shift from thinking through the paradigm of "OR" to thinking through the paradigm of "AND." That change in thinking represents a fundamental and very significant shift in consciousness. It opens the door for a totally new and more evolved way of thinking, relating, and leading. That paradigm of "AND" opens the door for thinking and leading from the post-heroic level.

The fundamental mental model or paradigm of "AND" is the core structural dimension of the mind that can give birth to experiences of inclusion, unity, interdependency, collectivity, partnership, and teamwork. All of these realities come from this fundamental mental model. In one of our workshops called Foundations of Transformational Leadership, we show leaders how to shift from thinking from the world of "OR" to think and lead from the world of "AND." That shift is often experienced as some sort of "awakening." This is our core strategy to transform consciousness and open the world of creative or post-heroic level of leadership.

Using this transformational methodology, we help leaders reach higher levels of effectiveness by shifting their fundamental ways of thinking. This process is based on the recognition that we "live" within the context of mental models which are literally shaping the world we live in, mainly the two core fundamental mental models of "OR" and of "AND." When leaders think from the "OR" mental model, they live in a world of separation/opposition, and their leadership style is mainly reactive and protective. On the other hand, when leaders embrace the world of "AND," they see the reality from a systemic perspective where all is connected and where everyone should win and be included. When that shift happens, leaders enter into a new creative and collaborative perspective. They connect with themselves and with others from a place of conscious intention. That conscious intention is to think and act as a collective system where everyone wins, where everyone is becoming more and more conscious, where everyone is aligned in the same direction, and where everyone becomes more effective.

I: Is this basically what you're referring to when you speak of transformation?

GB: Yes. Transformation is the capability to see your own thinking and to dis-identify from it. What you need to do is to separate thinking from consciousness.

The process of transformation requires that we see that we are thinking from a certain level of consciousness. That consciousness has a certain form, which is the level of development that makes the world appear in a certain way. If I am able to see it, that means I am able to access a part of my consciousness that is not packaged by that kind of structure of consciousness.

"Transformational agility is the capacity to start recognizing your ways of thinking, seeing your own mental models, challenging those models, testing, and evolving them."

We help people to move out from that place of conditioned consciousness to a place of seeing their own mental models. Once you have the basic methodology, you can start practicing and seeing your own ways of thinking and shift them at will. This is what we call a transformational agility, which is the capacity to start recognizing your ways of thinking, seeing your own mental models, challenging those models, testing, and evolving them.

The world as we all know it is becoming more and more complex, and we cannot really embrace the complexity of the world from an individual consciousness. We need to tap into a collective level of identity—a collective level of capabilities. We need to tap into the collective level of consciousness.

LEADERSHIP OPPORTUNITY:

Whenever you recognize any form of emotional discomfort, just stop and pay attention to it. Enter into the emotion, and be aware that the emotion is like a door to enter into a mental model. Once you see the mental model, look at it with curiosity. Explore it and challenge it. Be aware that the mental model is creating your experience in that moment. See if you could let go of it or even replace it by a totally new mental model that could open up a new uplifting emotional experience.

LEADERSHIP SUCCESS:

I have been in the business of leadership development for many years, but I never fully dedicated myself to developing a real transformational approach. Then, two years ago, I made the decision to create a new business partnership with two wonderful people and fully embraced a transformational perspective in leadership development.

We're a small company, and we've had a series of success stories. One of them, for example, involves two partnerships that came together. Early on, we sent our flyer advertising our services and a colleague who was already doing consulting work at the University of Ottawa saw a possible connection and made a call. A meeting was set and we went, not really expecting more than a conversation. The outcome was not only a formal business partnership with the Centre for Continuing Education of the University of Ottawa, but our Ottawa colleague became our third partner at the Institute.

We are now in the process of co-creating a transformational leadership program which is being offered to the leaders of the Federal Government of Canada.

This is just amazing. We feel so grateful for this opportunity that came into our life.

Lisa Hein
Seminole, Florida, USA

Lisa Hein is the author of *THE BOOK* "I'm Doing the Best I Can!" (They won't always be cute and adorable), in which she describes her journey through parentdom and shares valuable advice along the way. She is a motivational speaker and an internationally acclaimed radio show host of *Everyday Parenting*.

Lisa is considered one of the nation's top leading experts on the importance of parents being healthy and happy first. Her passion is to share her experiences and to, hopefully, inspire others to understand that good communication skills are just as important in the home as they are in the office.

I: Lisa, our children are our future leaders, and when we talked before, you said, "Parents have to plan from the beginning, because whatever behavior they start out doing is what they end up with." What actually inspired you to begin this journey? You've written a well-respected book, speak in front of audiences, and are in demand. Was that part of your background?

LH: Actually, no. This was one of those little gifts that just happened. Basically, I was a mom, and I just happened to be struggling. We had an amazing home life, and everything was going very well from my perspective—the way I thought it should be. We got along and the communication was great, but then there was a detour in the road that took place in those "high school years," which caught me so off guard that I found myself just "bedazzled," if I can say that word. I found myself asking, "What's going on? Why are these things happening?"

There were times at night when I would be very concerned, upset, and would get up and just start journaling my thoughts. It was my personal journey of trying to understand what was going on within our family dynamics and what was going inside my child's head. It was incredible to watch the changes that took place so quickly; one day you're friends, you're having fun, you're taking them to play basketball, and the next day it's almost like they're telling you, "I don't want to talk to you anymore." I've heard this from so many parents, and it really does catch you off guard.

I was just journaling my thoughts and really wanted to get these feelings out of me. Obviously my computer and I became very good friends at two, three, and four o'clock in the morning. During this time, I had a very deep faith in God, but had kind of turned my back on Him. After months of writing, I got a little nudge—a message that basically said, "Are you still mad at me? Don't ever forget, I brought him home every night."

It was a turning point in my life that made me realize that even though I wasn't where I should have been with my faith, God had never abandoned me, and that meant so much to me. Basically, He was telling me, "You need to share your journey with other people and let them know they're not alone, that kids change, and we can't take it so personally." We have to raise our consciousness and say, "That was then and this is now. What am I going to do for me?"

That's how it all got started. It was a journey I was on, and then I published a book! Since my book has been published, it's been amazing to see how many parents are hungry to hear some positive and sound advice. Many people have told me, "Your book isn't judgmental and is a true and down-to-earth story." All I did was put it out there. It was kind of scary.

I: It must have been a stretching experience to move out of the mom role and add the role of leader and expert in parenting. Your path has changed in the way you speak to audiences. Why is that?

LH: I realized that when you're talking about parenting, you're on very thin ice. Even though people know that there are issues going on, when it comes to your children, you can be a little standoffish. What I found was that people from all walks of life—everyone from CEOs who run Fortune 500 companies to individuals who are self-employed—potentially have the same things going on with their children. We want the best for our children; we want to create a beautiful life for them, perhaps one that we didn't have. We want to live our lives out through our children and to make sure they have everything they need to keep them happy.

"I decided that there's more to parenting than worrying about how I can make my child's life perfect."

I keep observing what's going on, and where we are today is like watching a dog chase its tail or a gerbil on a spinning wheel that never quits. We just keep trying to make our children's lives wonderful. We have equipped them with all this technology and the ability to talk to everyone else but us. Now it's even happening in elementary school where you see these young children texting as they're walking.

All I'm trying to say is, "Excuse me, we are out of control here!" There is very little communication going on in the house because everyone is busy communicating with everyone else, and that includes us. We get home, we check Facebook, we check our e-mails, we text our friends, we start preparing dinner, do some laundry, all with very little communication.

I decided there's more to parenting than worrying about how I can make my child's life perfect; it's about taking care of myself first! I found that many people are so stressed out, so overwhelmed, and just beside themselves because in addition to what's going on at work, they have to come home and oftentimes deal with children who are being unruly, disrespectful, and who don't want to be around their parents.

What's going on is extremely saddening to many people. It may be time to focus on the more important factors within the family dynamics. To find some peace inside, and to learn to listen to each other with such compassion that all we can do is inspire and support their thoughts without being judgmental. That's what all of us want, isn't it? We just want to be heard and not feel that someone always has to fix something. If we respect others' thoughts, wait until you see the repercussions and how happy and healthy you and your family will be! It starts within us first.

It's about making a shift in your way of thinking. It's about talking kindly and making a decision to raise our consciousness as parents, to be healthy, to achieve a new vision, new wisdom, and a new ability to calm down. Everything seems to be so intense these days. It's either black or white. Can we just find a little gray?

I'm not suggesting you smoke dope with your kids, allow them to drink in the house with their friends, or even aim to be their friend; I'm not saying that at all. What I *am* saying is to acknowledge that children today are so much wiser than we were. I'm sorry, but I was a little dork when I was ten or eleven years old. Today kids are on computers setting up programs, and they know where to go to get whatever information they want. I was playing with barbies. We don't understand the intensity that is inside our children today.

What we're trying to do is change everything. We decided we're not going to treat our children the way our parents treated us, and I don't understand why. I did this, and felt guilty after I did it. I decided to reinvent the wheel, because I wasn't going to treat him like a little robot; however, I went to the opposite extreme and paid dearly for doing so.

The more I saw the behavioral problem within my self, something started happening inside me. I said to myself, "This thing that was going on between us made me feel so unhappy at work, and then when I returned home, we're still being nasty to one another." I realized it had to stop. I had to focus on myself and learn how to respect who I was and set some boundaries. It was about learning to focus and respect myself. It was a major life lesson.

Many mothers have said, "I've lost *me*." I say, "Well, you have to find *you*, because without *you*, you're not much help to anyone. You're going from here to there and back to please everyone else but yourself." It's about learning how to fall back in love with yourself, how to respect yourself, and wanting to be healthy and happy.

My outlook on parenting took a little shift, and it's been such a blessing to be able to encourage parents today, because at times they just feel like they're being beat up. I've been asked, "If a child does something wrong, should the parent go to jail?" Absolutely not! Why should the parent go to jail? The *child* did something wrong, not their parents. They made the choice. If a child comes from a good home where the parents are trying to teach them good morals and ethics, right from wrong, and the child does something wrong behind their back, it's their problem, not the parents'. Why should the parent be responsible and held accountable? Is there a life lesson in getting in trouble for our children? It's time to let them deal with some repercussions!

We continue to make everything as simple as we possibly can for our kids, and yet we end up with migraines and being continually upset. We put ourselves under a lot of pressure, and there are many parents who feel that it's not fair. If I can encourage parents to be healthy, humble, grateful, and to take time to learn about their children in the same way they learn about their employees, their bosses, or anyone else outside of the home, then we will reach a point where we're going to have some serious stability in our families and in our homes.

I: You have a different perspective by focusing on the parents and their own quality of life. Would you share more about that?

LH: Like I said, we're doing everything we possibly can to make sure that our children are well equipped, so why aren't we doing that for ourselves? We tend to forget about ourselves. Why is that? Do we feel guilty because we're out of the house too much, because we have to work, or even because we're taking time for ourselves? It's like a catch-22: we either stay at home and give too much, or feel guilty because we're making time for ourselves. Let's find the middle of the road! It doesn't have to be so exhausting.

I heard something the other day that really touched my heart: What if we stopped presenting so much technology to our children and got back to learning about life? What if we got back to a place where we set time to take our children on nature walks or go down to the beach, inspiring them to feel the sand between their toes and discover amazing seashells? What if we could get them to experience those childlike thoughts and encourage each other to bring some new ideas or thoughts on how to make the family life more fulfilling inside our home? There has to be more than just slashing out demands and commands. Could some of the chaos we feel be caused from us not meeting each other's needs?

I: What do you do for your own growth in the area of professional and personal leadership, particularly with your family?

LH: To me, knowledge is bliss. I have surrounded myself with the most amazing people ever. Even though we may have issues with our children, I think it's important to take the time to seek the positive in everything. I've been so encouraged and blessed to know that everything I've been through was for a reason, and that reason is to inspire others to be all they can be. Things are not perfect in my life, but it is my goal to forgive and forget the past and accept and cherish what is in front of me. I take one step at a time, learn to relax, but most of all, I've learned to listen more. I don't want to ever stop growing.

LEADERSHIP OPPORTUNITY:

It's important that we learn how to communicate in a way that is nonthreatening, nonjudgmental, and that allows children to say what they need to say while you are listening. The key word here is *listening*! This may be the reason God gave us two ears and one mouth; we're supposed to listen more than we talk.

There was an article that I just wrote titled, *"If you really knew me, you would know that _____."* If your child was to tell you they're homosexual, they're having sex at the age of fourteen, or that they're playing a sport they don't really want to play because they're desperate for your approval, how would you handle that?

Learn to listen without feeling you must try to fix something. People are hurting—maybe because we're not listening to each other.

LEADERSHIP SUCCESS:

My favorite success story took place while I was doing one of my first speaking engagements. There were about four or five hundred parents in the audience. I was sharing my story and became a little overwhelmed. Here I was telling all these strangers what had happened, and of course all eyes were on me. I was really nervous, because I couldn't help but feel that they were sitting there judging me. Or were they?

I will never forget, when I finished my talk, this woman came up to me and she just stared at me with tears pouring down her face. I couldn't talk to her because I had people standing in front of me, so I grabbed her hand and we just held hands while I was signing books. As the line shortened, I looked at her and said, "Please don't leave." I finished what I was doing, and we hugged one another. It was the most noncommunicative situation ever. We didn't say much. She took my card, and then she walked away.

When I returned home, there was an e-mail probably six inches long. She told me, "Thank you for being here tonight. I was at my wit's end and couldn't fathom going on one more day. Because of your openness and honesty, you have given me a hope that I haven't found elsewhere. You gave me so much inspiration that I feel I want to continue living."

You don't have to be something you're not—just down to earth, open, and honest. You have no clue the impact you may have on people.

Jodi Orshan
Miami, Florida, USA

Jodi Orshan is a trained marriage and family therapist, certified life coach, and parenting expert with over thirty years of experience. Through her program, The Parenting Plan, she's developed a surefire three-step process for parents to create, nurture, educate, and lead their children to become caring, competent, and compassionate adults.

Jodi uses the highly acclaimed personal development tool, The Parenting Pyramid, so parents can successfully create the family life they've always envisioned.

I: What do you do to ensure your own personal and professional leadership growth?

JO: I'm so glad you began with that question, because I believe a good leader is someone who is enthusiastic, knowledgeable, creative, and always moving forward. Each and every day, I choose to move forward in my growth, and those are the questions I asking myself. Specifically, "What's my big dream for the day?" and, "What are the small tasks I need to do today to feel that I've had a successful day?"

I: Continuing growth is a big part of your own personal plan, and you actually have a formula for how to make that happen for yourself.

JO: I do, because we need to be the big dreamers and have ideas, and in the dreams—at the time that we create them—we need to have positive energy that flows and asks, "Where do I want to move, and how can I do that?"

I believe we need to feel our success every day. I need to be able to identify what I needed to get done today, whether I accomplished that goal, and if not, why? Was it due to something I misplanned or was it due to procrastination? I then need to ask, "What do I need to do to make tomorrow that much more successful?"

I: How does leadership impact your area of specialization? You're involved with parents and creating great leaders for our future. What does that look like from the standpoint of leadership?

JO: It's interesting that you ask, "What does it look like?" because it's something that I find parents don't recognize within themselves. A parent is the leader of their family, and whatever direction they choose to go in, that's where their family will go.

It is essential for each and every parent to know how to be a leader and to be comfortable in their role so they can define how they want their family to move and be successful in that movement, and to have their family grow and develop.

I: Today, with everything moving so fast, parents are faced with different challenges in this leadership role, aren't they?

JO: They really are, and so much of the time parents are reacting to a crisis. They're sort of always caught behind the eight ball. One of the things that I do when I work with parents is to help them become more proactive in their parenting by having them make a plan.

First of all, everyone has to understand what their goals are in life— their own personal goals and integrity—and what makes them, them. Parents need to define that for their family. Then, if they really know those and act on them every day, they will be in their own truth with their own integrity, and they will be able to move their family in the direction that they want to, often leading them in a positive direction and avoiding a negative crisis altogether.

I: That's fascinating and maybe something that not all parents, or even most parents, think about.

JO: I agree. It's actually unfortunate that most parents don't think about it. Parents are very geared to think about their jobs, their tasks, their community relations, and everything else that they need to get done, and the business of family just sort of falls in between that.

The priority should be family first. They need to be asking, "What do I need to do and what do I want my children to do to ensure our goals, standards, and values for our family are maintained?" Then,

"Hands down, parents need to have a plan, a purpose, and a direction—a goal in mind. A proactive parent will have the skills and knowledge to assess a situation, make a plan of action, and feel confident and competent to move their family in the direction they want to go."

everything else will fall in line after that.

I: Since this is really challenging in our rapid-moving environment, what leadership tools do you think parents need most today?

JO: Hands down, parents need to have a plan. That is what I was just talking about, parents being proactive parents, meaning that they have a plan, a purpose, and a direction—a goal in mind. Instead of floundering and reacting from one crisis to another, a proactive parent will have the skills and knowledge to assess a situation, make a plan of action, and feel confident and competent to move their family in the direction they want to go.

I: It's very reassuring to know that those kinds of tools are available. Will this be effective at any stage of parenting?

JO: Absolutely. Throughout the parenting process, parents often need to redefine and strengthen their skills. Parenting is never done. It never ends. Parents have to learn how to measure their success for their family in each moment and how that will take them into the future. They need to know what it's going to look like.

Most parents I know who have a plan based on personal philosophy, their integrity, their goals, their dreams, their hopes, and their actions are raising successful, happy families, and they're going through the process enjoying the parenting journey.

I: I would imagine that this is particularly important because there's a lot of definition set for everyone in the family to be able to participate in those goals.

JO: Yes. That's the beauty of this. You define yourself as a young family, and then you get to know your children. And while your tenets should really never change—you are who you are—the skills and the methods of how you do it will be based on your children as they come into your family.

I: How can parents hone their parenting skill set?

JO: First and foremost, they need to define who they want to be, and that is about making their mission statement and really seeing what that looks like specifically.

Second, parents need to honestly assess their current skill level and attributes they themselves bring to the family. Often, where you want to be and what you have now are completely congruent with each other, and that's fine, especially if you did an honest assessment.

Then the third step involves working—usually with someone—to get from where you are to where you want to be. Often, that means working with a parenting coach like myself. It might also involve a family therapist, working within groups, or utilizing self-help books. Often it's a combination of it all.

I believe that parents who understand the Parenting Pyramid and work through my program, The Parenting Plan, have much success, but there are lots of other ways of getting there. The key is for parents to know what they want, to truly assess where they are now, and then to make a plan to move from where they are into the future.

I: You've said before that parents need to be more proactive about their parenting. Can you explain why?

JO: Parents often just let everything come at them and hit them. It can start simply when the school year comes along and the teachers define the schedule for the year. The teacher is the one saying, "This is when your projects are going to be due. This is how we're going to be doing homework. This is what I want every family to look like and what you're going to do."

Already, the parents are starting out saying, "Oh my goodness! I have no time in my schedule because we have to read ten minutes each day and we're doing a project every other week. What am I going to do? How am I going to manage this?" They're already in panic mode.

For parents who follow me on my Web site and my Facebook page, they've already been following their summer plan. They have already been quietly going out and buying school supplies that are on sale and starting to stock up. I have parents looking at their personal schedules, their work schedules, their community commitment schedules, and clearing their calendar as much as they can for the first two weeks of school so they can be available, be there, and be with their children.

I have parents contacting the schools if possible. A lot of teachers do unofficially work during the summer, and they already have their first nine weeks planned out. Parents are contacting those teachers and asking, "What's our schedule going to look like? When are the first major unit exams and tests?" They're putting it on their calendars so they already know the flow for their family.

Look at your family's schedules, and try not to plan your kid's birthday party for the first weekend after school starts, when everyone else is going to be doing more back-to-school shopping and planning and might not actually want to come to a party in the middle of a Saturday. So plan that out.

We have parents responding this summer saying, "Of course! This makes perfect sense! If I just do a little bit of all of this now, I know I will be there, present, and available to help my children make their transition to their new grade much easier, because I won't be as harried, scared, or frantic, and I will be available for my children."

That's one simple, practical example of how to be proactive in your planning, instead of reacting to tears, crisis, and an *I can't get this done!* mentality. Instead, say, "Okay, we're going through that, you need these papers. Here we go, you need this, this is what you have. I'm here and available to help you through this. It's on my calendar, and I'm here for you."

Parents need to practice planned spontaneity too. Let children feel your surprise or the exuberance of a new plan, but have it planned it out so they're not overwhelmed.

I want to go back and clarify; notice how I had the parents prepping the whole summer. At no time did I say, "Have your kids start thinking about school." Let the *parents* go out and quietly get school supplies, have the *parents* start organizing their calendars, and have the *parents* start planning for the school year, but let the kids just enjoy summer. They only have a few weeks left. Let them play and run and create in their mind and enjoy their summer days.

LEADERSHIP OPPORTUNITY:

This is my favorite exercise for parents who work with me, and I have everyone doing this every night. First, they need to follow my number one rule, which is they need to know thyself. If you haven't already created your family mission statement, you need to do that.

Assuming you have your mission statement, the exercise I have every parent do comes at the end of each day and involves each parent asking themselves, "How well did I live up to my mission statement today? Did I live my life honestly and in integrity and up to the values that I've wanted to maintain?" They need to be specific, not just say, "Oh yeah, it was a fine day." They need to really ask, "What did I do that honored that mission statement?"

Then it is gut check time. This involves asking, "Did I miss the mark on anything? If I did, what can I learn from that?" Even more importantly, "If I really did, does it need to be corrected? How can I correct that tomorrow?" Each and every parent must say to themselves, "Today is done, and for all that I've learned, for all that I've gained, and for all that I grew today, I say, thank you—it was good."

What each parent has done then is they've taken the day, they've evaluated it, they take a deep breath if there are things that have to be continued, and they take it off their mind and put it on the schedule for tomorrow. Today is done. Take the gifts of that day into yourself, take a deep breath in and out, enjoy, and let it go. Then you can be at peace at the end of each and every day.

LEADERSHIP SUCCESS:

I have been blessed to work with many families, and I think one of the greatest things that has happened to me—and it typically happens during the summer—happened about ten years ago when I worked in my home city with a lot of families. My first group of young children and families actually graduated high school this June.

I got thank you cards and thank you letters from about a half dozen families, and just being in the community, I ran into or saw another dozen or so their parents, with tears in their eyes, as they reintroduced me to their kids by saying, "This is the first teacher who filled our family with hope and health and happiness." The parents were beaming with pride, and I was thrilled to share in that moment.

Raymond Perras, CIF, CPC
Ottawa, Ontario, Canada

Raymond Perras is a certified professional coach. He is the author of *AïM© for Life Mastery*, a handbook for creating Peak Performance in your life. As a Peak Performance Coach, he has developed a program designed to help clients raise their awareness and develop skills to get the best out of themselves and those they lead.

With more than twenty years working in the private and public sectors, he gained firsthand knowledge of how to deal with change and coach others in the development of organizational transformation skills. In the last eighteen years, Raymond has integrated his knowledge of the workplace to his extensive experience in the field of sports, resulting in the design of a unique program based on individual life mastery.

Communication skills, principles of empowerment, and the power of total focus form the basis of a proven strategy that enables people to align together to reach personal and organizational goals on a sustained basis.

I: From a leadership perspective, how did you come to be a performance coach from an engineering profession?

RP: I think it was a natural outcome of my family upbringing. I always felt that I had a knack for helping people grow. Later in life I realized that this wonderful gift was bestowed on me during the time that I spent with my terminally ill mother as an eleven-year-old boy, learning how to take care of my younger siblings after she would be gone. That lesson in nurturing has never left me.

Many years into my professional life I found that inclination getting stronger and stronger. Even though I was doing very well in engineering, I diverted into helping people engineer themselves.

I: That's such a beautiful way of putting it—*engineering themselves.* I know that sports have become a big part of your coaching. How is that a metaphor for people working together?

RP: Because I've worked extensively in business and in sports, I have found that sports serve as a metaphor for life, but it happens so quickly you almost miss it. In business, decisions are made, things are said, and people are asked to do things, but it's almost as though there is an infinite timeline for getting it all done. With sports, you have to perform almost immediately once a coach has instructed and passed on the knowledge and the scheme that should be implemented when the game is played.

Watching and being involved with sports—I started out as a player and then became a coach—I began getting more into the performance side and observing what was helping the top performers to achieve unexpected results. I think that the link was easy to make between sports and business. I brought back into business—both as a manager and later as a business coach and organizational development coach—some simple principles that apply in all situations; the common denominator is people.

Respecting those principles, you can help people produce peak performance at every turn. The idea is that you have to develop the awareness of that process and apply it consciously.

I: What are some of the biggest challenges leaders are facing?

RP: Let me reduce it to one massive challenge—communication. Information is key—it's boss. The more I work with individuals and organizations, the more I see how learning to communicate effectively through various modern technological channels and face to face is mission critical for success. Everyone has to have accurate information in real time so that decisions can be made at the level where they need to be made.

As a leader, a person has to be mindful of empowering people with **the right stuff, in the right amount, at the right time**[©] (Peak Performance). Today, it has to be fast because we all operate at "the speed of life" as Tom Peters once said. The faster you can execute, the better you can serve your client. That happens both in business and in sports.

I: I guess making technology our friend has allowed that to happen more now than ever. It may add additional pressure in order to make it happen, but it certainly has helped to make it happen, right?

RP: It is a challenge that society has to face and face very quickly. In the 1980s John Naisbitt wrote a book about the future, and he talked about how important it would be to develop the ability of adding high touch in communications because we were headed into a high-tech world. That book was *Megatrends*. When he revised the book in 2000 and called it *Megatrends 2000* about fifteen years later, so much had happened that was exactly as he had foreseen. More and more we're finding diversions between the technology evolution and the ability and capability of humans to work effectively with it.

A case in point: if you look around, more and more people's lives are directed by their cell phone. This point harks back to Orwell's book *Nineteen Eight-Four* where he said that robots would lead our lives. The robots are here in the form of our cell phones and all of the new technology gadgets. We need to learn to master that technology to be peak performing leaders.

I: That's such a delightful analogy and it's so true. Refocusing on the leadership question, how is a team, group, or organization a reflection of the leader?

RP: We have already pointed out that the common denominator is people; in business and in sports, it's all the same. I've worked with one university football team in particular for eighteen years—it's like a lab. I observe there how people behave and how the degree of success is almost entirely dependent on the leader. That's why I think leadership is becoming more and more essential. There are so many books that are written about it and the importance of leadership is highlighted and talked about so much.

If leaders don't "walk the talk," then people don't believe in or trust them. This distrust causes confusion. I can't help but think of Patrick Lencioni's book *The Five Dysfunctions of a Team* and how if a leader instills trust, gives trust, gives responsibility, gives authority, shares decisions, values people's opinions, and celebrates when they succeed, then confusion and disconnect will be minimized.

You have situations where you don't get the best out of an organization, team, or group. In many cases—as I find in sports where a game is played in minutes—what happens is that you prepare for a week, and then you lose it during the game because the coach doesn't do what is conducive to the continued performance of the team.

I: It sounds as if having a peak performance environment is critical for a leader to be able to bring his team to produce their very best as individuals and as a team.

"Getting the best out of a group has a lot to do with the leader creating an environment for performance . . . much of that has to do with communication."

RP: What I found is that you can have individual athletes—just like individual people in organizations—who find ways to get it done and even to excel in spite of the organization or in spite of the leader.

Generally speaking, getting the best out of a group has a lot to do with the leader creating an environment for performance; and as you probably know, much of that has to do with communication.

I: How can a leader actually enhance an environment to be one of peak performance?

RP: By respecting the six drivers of human beings. One main driver is that you've got to provide certainty. People have to know what's up, what's down, and what's sideways. If people don't know, they doubt, and when people are in doubt, they fear. Fear paralyzes people.

Beyond that, there's a sense of belonging that you must create. Sometimes that takes a little doing, but it's not that difficult if you show the way like Jim Kouzes and Barry Posner talk about in their book, *The Leadership Challenge*. When the leader shows the way in creating a peak performance environment, then everyone contributes and feels good about being there.

It's like a bubble, and when people come to work in that bubble, they're happy. They want to perform because they know they will be rewarded for what they contribute. They know they will be given opportunities to grow. They will have a chance to get recognition for what they have done, and variety is part of the daily exercise.

I: You have a new book, *AïM for Life Mastery*, that gives a simple formula with steps for how each of us can build competency and capacity toward true peak performance.

RP: In my coaching, I have found that you need to take time to simplify. We make things complex because we don't think that a simple approach will do. In this book I have developed a simple six-step process for individuals to create peak performance, because it starts with the individual.

Six Steps for Creating Peak Performance

Step 1: Learn to relax. You have to learn to quiet down bodily and mentally because that's how we perform at our best. If we're stressed, we can't perform properly.

Step 2: Remove negative self-talk. Once you have created an environment of calm, you should choose to talk to yourself in a way that will empower you to act, not in a way that stops you in your tracks. Change negative self-talk into *I can, I want, I choose.*

Step 3: Visualize your performance. This dips into my sports experience because all great athletes visualize their performance before it happens. Doing so relaxes your subconscious mind and helps you to look at things and answer the "how" as opposed to being stuck on the "why."

Step 4: Reduce fear. Gratitude focuses on the positive. The more you focus on what you have and forget what you don't have, the more you chase away false evidence that appears real (F.E.A.R.). Practice being grateful and fear will in time disappear.

Step 5: Practice. We cannot become peak performers if we don't practice. Just ask those who are top performers, whether that's in business or sports. They work at it diligently and continuously.

Step 6: Anchor these positive cornerstones of performance. Create an image of everything you develop in the way of self-talk and visualization and gratitude into one package. You can put yourself into that performance state of mind on command by reminding yourself how it feels when you perform at peak capability.

These six steps are simple and easily applicable. The key word is *work*. You have to work at it. I like to remind people that the only place you'll find *success* before *work* is in the dictionary.

LEADERSHIP OPPORTUNITY:

It all begins with the individual inside each of us. This is not a new concept. I find in coaching people that getting clear on who you are and where you're going is crucial to developing the ability to create peak performance.

A Life Successes Inventory will help you become aware of what you carry in abilities, knowledge, experience, and capabilities built on your life experience.

It's simple. Just take a sheet of paper and divide it into two parts. On the left side, brainstorm everything that you've ever accomplished that you are proud of; start from the time you were two years old if you want to. Just brainstorm. Write, write, write. Don't select and don't judge—even if it was helping an old lady to cross the street. List everything you've done that has made you feel good and that you feel you succeeded at.

Once you've brainstormed all of these successes, start looking at the right side of the paper and write down what made you do those things and what you felt about succeeding at them. If you go through that inventory, you'll soon see the evidence of what you're really good at. You'll see clearly what your inclinations are and what your drive is rooted in.

The key is to develop an awareness of who you are and where you're going. Doing a Life Successes Inventory works marvelously in determining how good you can be as a leader.

LEADERSHIP SUCCESS:

A woman who was an executive director of an organization had plateaued and was having some serious challenges with the organization. I coached her and then I worked with her and her leadership team. For her own benefit she left the organization; she was not in the right place and she found her niche elsewhere.

On the other side of things, because we did this work of developing awareness and developing a systematic approach to teamwork and leadership within the organization she had been with, that organization flourished. They grew their business and their numbers doubled in about two years.

Alison Forbes, Ph.D.
Edinburgh, Scotland

Dr. Alison Forbes is a change leadership consultant, coach, and physicist. Founder of Elevated Leaders™, an innovative leadership development practice, she helps corporate and entrepreneurial clients on both sides of the Atlantic achieve breakthroughs and create change that makes a difference.

Alison believes that connection to the underlying patterns of innovation, creation, and deep structural change in ourselves and our systems is vital to sustainability and meaning. She goes beyond the current systems thinking models to incorporate the human element. This enables leaders to connect to their inspiration and highest path of service, and to develop the independent platform, structure, and perspective needed to succeed in a personally sustainable way.

I: What are the greatest leadership challenges you see facing leaders today?

AF: I help leaders who can make a difference find the platform to succeed in the next stage of their career, business, or new leadership initiative.

There are three core challenges which I see a lot of in my practice:

Three Core Challenges for Leaders Today

#1: A Struggle for Influence—They need others to see that there's a need and priority for the solution being proposed. Unfortunately several factors—human and financial—can force the agenda elsewhere.

#2: A Difference in Values—The new consciousness is the greatest gift emerging from our organizations. It comes from certain individuals who are being called to step up, but they are hitting the boundaries of the old structures. A lot of the new paradigm thinking comes from a place of deep intuition, clear strategic insight, heart consciousness, game-changing innovation, and sometimes a deeply truthful emotion that touches on the heart of your soul's purpose. This can be hard to articulate in the language of many corporate environments.

#3: A Career Crossroads—Although they may be a little worn out with the day-to-day reality of their organization, part of the leader is being called to connect with their purpose. It isn't always obvious how they can find a professional pathway that fits them, and which they also know will work in the real world. So they feel stuck and doubtful about the best way to move ahead.

A pattern I see with these challenges is that they get triggered by certain kinds of proposals such as:

"Struggle is the clue that we are caught in structural conflict, and a freeing of perspective is needed to see it . . . You can't shift a system or solve a problem while trapped in the structures that created it."

- correcting strategy and delivery process
- sustainability
- making the organization more innovative, connected to purpose, or socially responsible
- organizational purpose and branding with integrity from the top down
- heart consciousness, bringing through the potential of the team
- organizational learning and making decisions from the truth

These leaders are moving us to a new paradigm and shift in values, not just bringing in any old incremental change. These changes they bring are aimed at helping the organization and the people in it become more sustainable, whole, and healthy.

I: These sound like good things, so what creates the struggle, and what is the solution?

AF: There are two different factors at play. First, you have the individual coming from the new paradigm. And second, you have the organization, which is really an organism that needs to change. When you couple these there can be struggle.

There is a conflict of interest and intention that is stopping them from succeeding—a structural conflict, you might say—which is often hidden and unconscious.

Struggle is the clue that we are caught in structural conflict, and a freeing of perspective is needed to see it. We need shift that out of our strategy so we can reach the outcome we want.

I: What is required in order to achieve this freeing of perspective?

AF: Organizations and many people in them are often mired in procedures, group think, and politics, and they can't step out of that box to make things happen very easily. They aren't ready. There has to be a readiness for the change being proposed.

You can't shift a system or solve a problem while trapped in the structures that created it. As leaders, if we can't see the clear path ahead and have the levers to deliver, we can't lead. We need to find an independent platform to lead from which is free and empowered to lead strategically and in a personally sustainable way.

Part of this is to recognize the struggle, and learn to take steps to see the truth of the structures with which we are dealing. This is easier when you get an outside perspective from a coach or wise advisor. But here are some questions you can ask yourself in order to do this:

- Is the organization ready for this change?
- What is really motivating you about this solution?
- Are the team members or other leaders and stakeholders at a level of maturity where they are ready to step back and make that shift?
- Are there bigger constraints around the solution that the organization cannot shift even if that is what they want?
- What would be needed for this to work?

The challenge and destiny for new paradigm change leaders isn't to try to fit their higher perspective and level of thinking into the old boundaries, but to build the bridge that lets the organization move its boundaries out to their thinking. This is both an art and a science!

And maybe for that organization it is only appropriate to go part of the way, and the full vision is really meant for a different vehicle in the future.

You need to look at the superstructure around what you are trying to do in order to see what is possible and find or create the structure that supports it. To create a transformation, you must remove the root of the problem, not the symptoms. But you need to have the right approach to do that.

"To create a transformation, you must remove the root of the problem, not the symptoms."

I: Can some of this challenge come from something within us rather than the organization?

AF: Yes, it often has to do with our own assumptions, motivations, and blind spots! We sometimes put forward a solution because of something we need to fulfill within ourselves, and it isn't always based on the truth of what is really appropriate for the organization. I've seen a lot of wrong or unnecessary solutions proposed, and the leader struggles because the solution is rooted in the wrong motivation. Or it is a case of the "right idea, wrong organization." They need to have a different vehicle to express that calling more fully.

We need to look deeply between the lines at these questions and be honest with ourselves about what is really going on under the surface so we don't waste energy or miss the right opportunity to make a real impact, rather than be mired in an organization that won't budge or one that can't fulfil the calling that is rising inside us.

I: How does leadership impact your speciality or niche?

AF: Before becoming a freelance change consultant in industry, and now a coach, I spent a number of years in experimental physics. For me, being a physicist isn't a job title; it is a way of looking at the world which has followed me through my scientific and industrial career.

What this perspective means is that we get clear by seeing past our blind spots and connect to the truth in ourselves, in our relationship to others, and our relationship to the system we are trying to change.

We need to see through the clutter and connect with the natural structure that will support our mission and position us to create the right solutions and thrive. We don't need to make it up; it's there already. We just need to get to the truth and find it. When we operate at this level, we not only deliver the personal thing we set out to do, but we are in harmony with a bigger shift for the better in the system around us as well.

I've brought this structural perspective into every role I've played in industry, and it has been the key to unlocking and lubricating the wheel of change in my own life and that of my clients.

I: What stops us from stepping into our full potential as change leaders?

AF: Aside from lack of clarity around how it will work, the main block is fear.

We're all being called to leadership right now. We all have a part to play in contributing to the bigger solutions. There is something our systems are crying out for, and we each hold part of that solution. If we don't step up, we leave a gap that makes it harder for others to have their impact.

We feel our call to leadership when we are compelled to step up or take the initiative, even if we can't articulate what is actually driving us. Our mission can bring conflict or hardship if we don't align it with the right approach, but it is also a place of real leadership power and energy when we do.

When we connect with the heart of the problem that matters most to us to solve, we are on our mission. And the closer our leadership platform is aligned to this, the more authentic and inspiring it will be both to us and to those we lead.

But it's scary to step outside the box and into unknown territory. We ask ourselves, "What is the cost?" It feels easier in the short term to stay where we are or step aside all together.

It is important to know how to build confidence in your next move step by step, and also to pay attention to the intuitive feelings you are getting about why it might not work so you fill the gaps and stay connected to your path.

The big shift for change leaders is to recognize that the struggle and fear they are experiencing is also their calling to find a higher point of leverage, which not only brings the right solutions to life more easily, but which are more personally rewarding, balanced, and sustainable as well.

LEADERSHIP OPPORTUNITY:

Making a successful transition in your leadership starts with asking the right questions and looking honestly at the answers. Consider the questions below and see what new truths emerge.

- What is your leadership calling?
- What do you know in your heart is the next step to make it happen?
- What blocks, missing pieces, risks, or obstacles do you see which would make you want to shrink back from that?
- Identify what pieces you already have.
- What support do you need to get the rest?

Allow this to provide you with an opportunity to connect to your heart and what you know is true for you, allowing the clear path to emerge.

LEADERSHIP SUCCESS:

This leader had a change initiative that he was really struggling to sell to stakeholders. It was what I would call an escalation structure. The more resistance he met with, the more he battled to convince them. Eventually both sides got locked into a political battle that he was never going to win, and it took a toll on him personally as well as professionally.

Together we got clear of the structural conflict and found the clear platform to support his full leadership potential. This has allowed him to connect with the leader he is destined to be and a strategic plan for his career path.

He successfully tested out new approaches in his original company, proving and delivering value, after which he could move into a fantastic new role in a company more aligned with his leadership platform. Better still, he is working on his ultimate goal of founding his own institute to develop and promote the new structures and strategies needed for organizational learning and sustainability. The lessons he learned in his growth process were vital in providing the insight and basis of this foundation.

He has a part to play and the structure in place for how it will work. And what was really lovely is that his new role allows him to spend so much more quality time with his family rather than struggling in the wrong situation: a changed leader with a changed life.

Karen Wright, MCC
Toronto, Ontario, Canada

Karen Wright is a Master Certified Coach based in Toronto, Canada and is truly a pioneer and global leader in the coaching profession. Karen works with top executives and emerging leaders in major companies. Her firm, Parachute Executive Coaching, helps organizational clients all across North America build leadership capacity. Karen is also a Certified Health Coach and creator of "The Complete Executive," a peak performance system for leaders.

I: What do you do to ensure your own personal and professional leadership growth?

KW: The one thing that I have always appreciated ever since I got into coaching—which was in the very early days, particularly in Canada—is that this is a profession that requires you to do your own work if you really want to succeed. If you are going to do well in this field and if you're going to be able to continually work with stronger and better clients, you really do have to do your own work. I have found this a daily exercise in personal accountability and professional development and learning. It keeps me on my "A game," as they say. I'm always mindful of learning and not getting complacent; being willing to be challenged is key.

I: So you're constantly in a growth mode.

KW: Constantly, and I do that in a number of ways. I've always read a lot and I love the fact that there are more books in this space and related spaces than I can ever hope to read in my life. I'm constantly on the lookout for the next big idea or the author who's bringing forward revolutionary ideas or ways that I can bring value to my clients and sharpen my own skills. Reading is a huge part of what I do.

I also work really hard to seek out clients who challenge me, stretch me, and make me bring my best skills into the coaching relationship. The clients I work with today are quite different from the clients I would have worked with ten or fifteen years ago because I have grown and changed as a coach. I'm attracting different clients, and I love that.

I: That's certainly a silent measurement of your own growth that speaks loudly.

KW: I think so, yes. I can feel it. If I am asked to work with someone who for some reason isn't a right fit, I really work hard to make sure that I don't take them on just because the client wants me to work with them or just because they showed up. It's one of the reasons I have an associate-based business, because that way I match the right coach with the right client and ensure that I am constantly putting myself in relationships with clients who will stretch me and who I can serve best.

The other thing I do is I associate with professional colleagues who keep me sharp. These people in the master coach community are leading the field with their thinking and their accomplishments. They're not afraid to put forward a different point of view and challenge the status quo. They constantly challenge me to be my best. There's no way you can get away with anything when you're in a conversation with another master coach.

I: What components about leadership attract you? What's happening there that you find yourself most drawn to?

KW: The whole subject of leadership is fascinating because you don't have to be appointed a leader in order to lead; that, in and of itself, is a revolutionary concept. My work is entirely about leadership—no matter what the client's title is or what role they're playing.

I like to describe my business as working with leaders of big organizations and big ideas. They don't have to be a CEO or a Vice President in a major company; they can be an entrepreneur with a huge vision and who is trying to build the infrastructure that will support the achievement of their vision.

I love working with people who have the capability to bring their vision to reality. Those people inspire me. They make me feel responsible to hold myself to the high standards that they hold for themselves.

I: A lot of us have vision, but making that vision a reality is sometimes very challenging. What two or three things do you feel are critical in helping that vision become a reality?

KW: You're absolutely right. There are probably four or five clients in particular that I've observed really closely. I've done so because they seem to be able to consistently create whatever the thing is that that they had envisioned. I've actually created a ten-part system that brings together all the things I've learned from these major clients and numerous other clients over the years. There are, however, a few characteristics that I think most embody what I believe is necessary.

Obviously, it's important to have a ton of physical energy and to have your own discipline around how you eat, how you exercise, how you sleep, and how you take care of your body and your physical energy level. You also have to understand what the components of leadership are; things like a fantastic network and great relationships help in bringing a vision to fruition.

"Having a reflective practice ensures that you are holding on to the vision as opposed to getting mired in the reality."

Another characteristic that I feel is particularly powerful is what I call having a strong, reflective practice. I have a client who spends a portion of every Sunday holed up in his office without technology just doing his planning, reading, thinking, and reflection on what has gone well up to that point and where the business is going. He's actually named that period of time as if it were an eighth day in the week. He and I are even collaborating on a book to share about that particular practice.

Having a reflective practice ensures that you are holding on to the vision as opposed to getting mired in the reality. There are ten total aspects of this executive performance system, but those are some of the components.

I: Do you have any other tips of that nature that you'd like to share?

KW: Have a business plan, have a strategic plan, have a life plan; know where you're going with personal goals as well as business goals. To have those plans recorded and to check in with the progress of those plans on a regular basis is crucial.

You need to understand what role your relationships play in your life. This is not even referring to your professional relationships, but rather to your personal ones, because none of us can be really professionally successful if we're not supported by people in our personal lives who help us to thrive and be happy. Relationships are a whole section of the model.

Networking is big. Make sure that you're reaching out into your network when you need help and responding to requests from your network when they ask you for help.

And have a plan for learning and growth too. You can start this by saying, "There are specific things I want to learn or get better at, so how am I going to do that?"

I: What are some of the major leadership challenges today?

KW: One of the things I spend a lot of time on with leaders is helping them understand how they need to communicate to their organization. Many people have gotten into some bad habits, and they've done so because it's a lot easier to send a quick e-mail than it is to actually sit down and have a conversation. To prevent this mentality, I link up the idea of overuse of technology and doing things efficiently. I connect that with what I think is missing in most organizations—the concept of giving and receiving feedback in a quality way. It's almost impossible to give someone constructive, solution-oriented feedback over e-mail.

That's the problem with the people who came into business when technology was already pervasive; they never really learned some of those foundational skills. And those skills do have to be learned. They've got to be developed, because otherwise it's really difficult to build trust with people when you don't have a good relationship.

Another thing that happens in relation to the growth of technology is that because so many organizations these days are built on knowledge and technology, oftentimes the people who end up in leadership positions come from that subject matter expertise or technical expertise background, and they are not always adequately equipped with the kind of people-leadership skills required to support a large team or large organization. That's another area where my business supports leaders in making changes within their organizations.

I: How does leadership play a role in your personal life?

KW: I believe that we as coaches—when we're trying to work with people to be their best and to work in alignment with their values—have to do our very best to walk our talk. That said, a long time ago I had to let myself off the hook when it came to being perfect. What I'm committed to now is being a constant work in progress.

I've developed a model called The Complete Executive, and it is the ten-part system I referred to earlier. I do my best to keep progressing through the different aspects of that model, because I am absolutely not there yet. I'm nowhere close to done, but I know that if I'm not always trying to improve myself or progress in some of the things that I think are important, then I won't feel comfortable doing that same work with my clients. You have to make changes where you think change will help you be a better person. I am a big believer in the integrity of walking one's talk. There's a little bit of pressure attached to this concept; it is self-imposed pressure, but I don't feel the need to be perfect.

I: How has this impacted you in your day-to-day living?

KW: I believe I have a higher standard for relationships now than I've ever had in my life because I know what's possible. I don't have a lot of tolerance for whining, blaming, or victimizing—and by victimizing, I mean self-victimization.

Using my kids as an example, the phrase *not my fault* is pretty much not allowed in my house. We all have a role to play in everything that goes on, whatever it is. I'm always asking my two boys to think about what part they played in whatever the situation was. I think that the kids of coaches are generally a little bit different anyway since we're always asking questions versus lecturing. My questions are always, "What part did you play? What could you have done differently? What have you learned?"

This relates to taking responsibility and Martin Seligman's definitions of an optimist and a pessimist. A pessimist believes that all bad things are their own fault, while the optimist believes that if a bad thing happens, it is an unfortunate circumstance that they have the ability to influence differently in the future. And you get what you focus on, right? That's one of the reasons that I think little tools like a gratitude journal are very useful. I keep one, and one of the things that I love is that at the end of the day I think back and ask myself, "What went well over the course of the day? What am I happy about?" It helps me sleep better at night.

LEADERSHIP OPPORTUNITY:

I read a blog called Great Leadership written by a guy named Dan McCarthy. I love his perspective. He's got a lot of experience working in the senior levels of HR in organizations, and he brings in a lot of different perspectives and points of view, and he's always a good source for resources.

I subscribe to Executive Book Summaries because they are fantastic eight-page consolidations of the best stuff in the major business books that are out there. I believe it's important for me to stay current on what my clients are reading.

On the more personal development side of things, I believe it takes courage to ask a really smart, successful person for guidance or for their opinion and advice, but I try to do that fairly often, and it is a big source of support for me.

I'm a big believer in looking around and saying, "Who's out there doing something really well that I think I can learn from?" and asking them to spare a few minutes and to allow me to ask a particular question. Most people are perfectly willing to help out. Just ask.

LEADERSHIP SUCCESS:

I'm really proud of what I've accomplished in the coaching space. I fell into it randomly, although lots of people say that there are no accidents. I worked to establish credibility by founding the local ICF chapter, by getting some media coverage, and by creating a local network of coaches.

My background in business and particularly in marketing was very useful. I was uniquely equipped at that time to do some of the things that I did to build the presence of coaching differently than people who came from a helping profession background or a consulting background. I feel proud that I saw the opportunity and used the skills that I had to create something that's lasted.

After a few years, it became clear that my start-up skills were not what was going to best serve the chapter to take it to the next level. I think one of the smartest things I did was get out of the way. In fact, the people who stepped in after me went on to create a massive chapter, and they actually established what is now an ICF-wide award, which is the Prism Award. That came out of the Toronto chapter. I couldn't have done that.

M. J. Jiaras, Ph.D.
Chicago, Illinois, USA

Dr. M.J. Jiaras is a principal and founder of Integrated Coaching Solutions as well as a seasoned executive coach and facilitator who blends practical and academic experience with widely regarded expertise and group dynamics. His unique combination of insight, creativity, humor, wisdom, and genuine warmth has enabled him for over a decade to help clients achieve superior results in their quest for leadership excellence. *Fortune* magazine voted two of M.J.'s coaching clients to their list of the nation's fifty most powerful executives.

M.J.'s knowledge of human nature plus over ten years of experience working with senior management allows him to assess each situation quickly, offer valuable insights, and provide a powerful plan for action.

I: What philosophy do you use to help C-suite executives truly reach their potential?

MJ: I use a process, which I call the Leadership Sweet Spot, addressing five interrelated factors to optimize an executive's effectiveness: Vision, Strategy, Strengths, Results/Action Planning, and Balance/Mindfulness.

One of the first aspects to consider, especially when you're dealing with C-suite executives, is vision. It is important to have a clear sense of where they see the company in the future and how they want to lead. From that visionary perspective, it is important for the executive to create and articulate a leadership credo or orientation based on their core values and beliefs. This will provide clarity and alignment, both for the leader and those they lead.

Secondly, we address strategy. What are the strategic drivers that need to be in place to realize their vision? This can be very complex for a leader. There are so many factors to take into account—market forces, internal politics, and short-term vs. long-term goals. Good leaders are able to take their vision and effectively implement a strategy that focuses actions and thought, positioning a company for success. Additionally, it is important for leaders to be artful in their leadership as they implement their strategy. This artfulness includes knowing how to navigate through the many motivations of others as well as the politics that are inherent in any organizational system.

With a clear sense of vision and the strategy involved, the next step is a plan of action to get results. At the end of the day, it's about getting results—both individually and organizationally. If I'm not helping leaders get results, I'm not doing my job. Ultimately, leaders will be measured by the results they achieve. To do so, it is important to have a clear plan of action with measurable results.

To foster these results and associated strategies, it is best for each leader to focus on what they do best—leveraging their strengths. Positive psychology in the workplace is built on the premise that if we leverage our strengths, we can be exceptional. While we must attend to developmental areas to not get derailed, the key to success is using your inherent strengths and abilities. Assessments are used to identify each individual's strengths and innate abilities. Once these are identified, we create a plan to optimize, leverage, and further develop their strengths.

Many times I'm hired to help people who have recently been promoted. If they're moving from an EVP to President, the skills and abilities they used successfully in their past job may not be the leadership skill set they need in their new job. I'm often brought in to help people evolve their leadership toolkit. This is something that can be achieved much more quickly and effectively with the help of a good executive coach.

The last piece of the leadership sweet spot is for people to be balanced and mindful. It is very difficult to be a leader in these turbulent times. Knowing that time is such a precious commodity, a key is being sure that you manage your energy to maximize how you use time. If you are not engaged in the moment, many moments can be lost. Therefore, the focus is much more on energy management vs. time management.

Additionally, for an executive to be their best, they must be mindful or reflective of what they do, how they do it, and the results they are achieving. With awareness and mindfulness, a leader can see

"A key component in this journey is the concept of free will—the ability to freely, mindfully, and purposefully choose new and more effective behaviors and practices. Helping executives to be more mindful and reflective is a key ingredient for success."

how they are leading, assess what is optimal, and be detached from preconceived notions of how it needs to be so they can skillfully align actions with strategy and vision—the Leadership Sweet Spot!

I: You've had a varied background; you've been a psychologist, a business owner, and even a musician. How has that helped you to be an effective leadership coach and consultant?

MJ: Being an executive coach for about fourteen years, I've had the good fortune to work with many excellent leaders and to see how leaders lead—both good and bad.

As a continual learner, each situation in each industry allows me to gather information that I can leverage in the future. I will not share the specific details of a situation, but instead talk about situational leadership. This knowledge base is invaluable.

Because the demands are so significant for these leaders, my job requires that I use their time well. One executive said I have excellent pattern recognition. I quickly get to the heart of the matter. What are factors, motivations, and desired outcomes in a given situation? Once identified, I help the executive think through what would be an effective manner to move forward, and what would be most valuable for the client and the organization.

Working as a psychologist, I understand human potential and the many aspects of the psyche. We all are human, which means we are complex. The shadow of a leader tends to show up at times, and I have an appreciation for the origins and value of the shadow. Additionally, we are creatures of habit, and understanding some of the internal wiring of these habits allows for more easeful and effective evolution of these routinized behaviors. Maybe the greatest value I bring is knowing how to create positive change in behaviors and actions.

A key component in this journey is the concept of free will—the ability to freely, mindfully, and purposefully choose new and more effective behaviors and practices. Helping executives to be more mindful and reflective is a key ingredient for success.

Additionally, I have run many groups over the years, and understand the unique nature and dynamics of each group. More importantly, I have an understanding of the nuances of group dynamics—from the impact of the leader to the anchor of outliers or naysayers—and can facilitate movement in a positive direction.

You noted that I've been a musician; I have been playing music most of my life. I started out as a musician, and I think it may differentiate me from most executive coaches. It has helped me to develop the skill of listening. Having studied jazz and jazz improvisation, I have learned the art of "comping" or accompaniment. The focus being on many different harmonic options and alternatives that will both support and influence the soloist or leader. It has fostered an understanding of how to promote creative openings for others. I also learned the different ways to turn a phrase, when to use a voice or voicing, and when it is important to take the lead.

One of the key things that I learned—and it feels like a lesson I'm still learning—is it is not where to place the note, but where to place the space that is important; understanding that space allows certain notes, concepts, and ideas to speak much more powerfully. Lastly, and maybe most importantly, being a musician has fostered a sense of fun and adventure that I integrate into both my work and life.

Additionally, being a husband and a father has been invaluable in my work. I've learned how to effectively compromise, where to set boundaries, etc. This has helped me tremendously.

I: Your background is amazingly varied and unique from the standpoint of the skill set that you bring to these leaders. What do you find are some of their biggest challenges, and how are you using your unique skills to help them with those?

MJ: I think one of the greatest challenges today—and I don't know if it's any different than it was yesterday or will be tomorrow—is how to do more with less. And that's applicable whether it's budgets that are being cut or industries that are changing.

The goal for leaders is to do more with less—to be creative and a visionary as they create results. It's a very difficult dynamic for leaders.

"The goal for leaders is to do more with less—to be creative and a visionary as they create results. It's a very difficult dynamic for leaders."

My job is to provide different perspectives to and for leaders. I take an agnostic point of view. I don't think the direction or focus should be A, B, or C, so I can walk in and provide multiple perspectives with and for the leader. I ask the questions that other people may not think of and/or don't have the courage to ask. Because leaders need to do more with less, time is precious and there is a need to add value in the moment. It's an instant-karma type of world. If I'm not adding value, I will not stay on their schedules. I help leaders to think through how be more effective and to do it easier and faster, and hopefully in the process to also have some fun. My goal is to create significant and sustainable results for my clients.

I: You've done so many wonderful things in this field with leaders; what do you do for your own personal and professional leadership growth?

MJ: A key element is to be a continual learner. I'm someone who is always looking at what could be a spark for the next idea. It requires a mind-set that is continually learning, evolving, and looking at things anew. I had someone who was more of a spiritual mentor ask me this question: "How do you think a new thought?" It's certainly not from doing what I did today. It's probably bringing in new information, new experiences, and new ideas, whether it's reading different things or staying current with technology.

Moore's Law says that in two years, technology will be 100% better. So if I'm going to keep technologically on the edge, I have to continually read and keep on top of ideas. This not only allows me to have the latest gizmo, which I generally have, but fosters a mind-set of continual learning. Additionally, I research what the new and interesting leaders are thinking about. How are they solving challenging business issues to lead companies successfully? It requires reading, having experiences, and continually looking at things from a new perspective.

LEADERSHIP OPPORTUNITY:

This is a simple yet powerful exercise. If you want to be a leader in your life, you have to know how you are leading in your life. This exercise leverages the mindful/reflective aspect of the Leadership Sweet Spot to focus your actions, strategy, and vision.

Start by committing to doing this exercise for one week. Each evening (or morning) reflect on the day and answer the following questions:

- Did I do what I said I was going to do?
- What did I feel good about today?
- If I lived today over, what would I have done differently?
- What had the greatest and/or lasting impact?
- Where was I the leader I want to be?

Write down your thoughts and reflections—just thinking about it is not sufficient. At the end of the week consider, "What did I learn about how I lead? What changes did I make? What changes do I need to make? Is this process of daily reflections something I want to continue?" This exercise will help you refine how you do what you do to optimize your performance.

LEADERSHIP SUCCESS:

This success story is about an executive who was promoted from an EVP to a President/COO role at a Fortune 500 company. This new role was a significant shift in responsibility and now had their peers reporting them. Especially with the COO role, there was a learning curve, with new responsibilities, new areas of focus, and a complex business. It required leveraging strengths and abilities and applying them in a new fashion—expanding their leadership toolkit. This included being involved more strategically than tactically, setting and implementing vision, and getting results.

In the new role, this executive has evolved the business model bringing the company into the twenty-first century. As the spokesperson for this organization, they have created positive shifts within the business community and press to create more value both internally and externally. They have recently been named as the successor to the CEO.

Ruth Littler
Perth, Australia

After graduating from nursing college, Ruth Littler has worked in the private and public health sector.

Moving across the Western Australia health landscape, she has done everything from dealing with high school blues as a school health nurse to the high-pace world of patient advocacy, coordination of a registered training organization, and managing a residential aged care facility.

From early childhood, Ruth has enjoyed teaching and naturally traveled into the career of training, counseling, and coaching. Realizing her strengths and passion for empowering others to shine, Ruth has commenced a coaching business and enjoys working part time as a project officer in aged care.

I: Ruth, how has your own leadership style changed, and why?

RL: When I first started nursing, the leaders above me were very autocratic, and there was an expectation to just do what you're told to do. I noticed that I used to blame the leader when things wouldn't go well. I also realized that my creativity was being stifled.

As the years went on and I sought management positions, I remembered an important lesson I had learned: when people are told what to do without a good reason, either they rebel, resist, or they were not very creative or innovative to begin with. I started reading leadership books and applied all the principles so that I was able to deliver results really well, and I tried to be as collaborative as possible.

Throughout my working career—which included counseling and training in addition to nursing—I've worked under so many different government changes and directive changes within organizations, all wanting the organization to be as lean as possible. This helps to manage risk and cut costs as well as comply with changes in legislation and policy. I saw something change, and the joy started to leave many people. People who were really good workers seemed like they were being squeezed and squeezed, and they were left with very little to give.

I started thinking that maybe that's not the way I wanted to be managing. I also noticed that sometimes really fantastic managers produce great results, have a great reputation, and seem to have their finger on the pulse of the organization, and they just get beautiful work done. Yet their staff on the lower rungs of the ladder, so to speak, weren't noticed; they weren't valued. Many times, I felt like that was the main reason why we had such a big turnover with staff, especially in the health area. This high staff turnover was a big problem, so I decided that my management style would be one of valuing people.

I also know how important it is to be accountable to taxpayers and investors for profitability of a business. However, I just feel that organizations haven't really learned the biggest lesson, which is to value their human resources.

To me, the words "human" and "resource" are just thrown around so flippantly, and yet human resources refers to the most valuable aspect of any company; it's almost like treasure. Think of it as treasured cargo that you have to handle very carefully.

That's how I think my leadership style has changed. We have to start leading while thinking about the community and thinking about the employees as part of that community. Whatever we do, the community will experience the effects.

For me, leadership now needs to build community, even if businesses or leaders have to make some really hard decisions. I had to make some tough choices by cutting down on staff and cutting down on hours. However, quality was reduced as a result of putting people on shifts where they were only working four hours per day.

I started seeing things that I don't think a lot of people see. I've seen staff members—especially men—run from one job to another. They may work a four or six-hour shift then run to another job so that they make enough money to pay their mortgages or their rent. Many of them could not afford to be sick.

I realized that those workers don't have the energy to attend training because all they want to do is survive and help their families survive.

So it's not just a leadership model that I need to use; I really needed to be looking at people as a part of the community as a whole. I've seen really good decisions made that are legal, but not necessarily ethical. This changed my leadership style from doing things just to get results to really looking at the people producing those results and valuing them.

"Leadership is about making sure that we nurture the environment and make it as positive as possible so that good fruit is being produced."

I think that is the greatest change in my life over the course of twenty years in this field. Human resources are assets and they are very precious. Leadership is about making sure that we nurture the environment and make it as positive as possible so that good fruit is being produced.

If the community is not built up, then I don't think organizations can exist. We don't exist in a vacuum; we exist in a community. That is the real reason I've changed my leadership style. I can actually say that I've seen people just thrown away and I don't like doing that.

I: I love when you speak to human resources being a treasure that needs to be handled with care. I think that applies in particular in healthcare because it translates to the quality of patient care. It must be very critical. Why do you say leadership is a way of life rather than a role?

RL: To answer this I'd like to give a little bit of background as to how I've come to this conclusion. As I said before, when I started in management positions, I just followed principles like steps to get results rather than to reflect on it and internalize it.

In the last decade, I worked in a situation with very vulnerable people in crisis—in high-conflict situations—and I found that I could get along with people when I was really being empathic toward them. It wasn't something I was just putting on; some of the stories I heard brought out every bit of empathy that I had, so it was a natural response.

However, the event that really changed my thinking about

leadership being a way of life took place at a performance management review. I was actually told that I was too soft and needed to disconnect from people. In that situation, I felt that to disconnect from people would be wrong. At the time, I didn't realize that compassion was not seen as an important part of leadership at all—at least not by the person who was managing my performance.

Eventually I thought to myself, *This is not right.* I still delivered successful outcomes and received great feedback from clients and staff, but deep down I knew that it wasn't a matter of being right or wrong. I just knew it was the right thing.

I felt very stressed because doing things that went against what I knew was right just wasn't part of my personality. I eventually left the job. At the time, I didn't realize that all the things that I had been criticized for were actually my strengths, including compassion, deep empathy, and simply being there for people. Being a comforting presence even in high-conflict areas did not take a lot of my time.

About that time, I attended a seminar presented by John McLean, who is the coauthor of *Lead With Your Strengths Wherever You Are.* He mentioned that leadership was an exercise, not a position. He said, "Leadership is not about me; it's about us." That quote has really resonated with me.

He also mentioned that leadership is a verb rather than a noun. For the first time, I connected leadership to a way of life, rather than a role to play. It's really not about being a service provider; it is about actually serving people. That really turned me around because I realized that it's not about what position I'm told to take or the role that I'm given. If I work from the philosophy that leadership is a way of life, then I know that I'm making a difference. That's what leadership means to me now. I'm making a difference to make things better.

Now, in seeing leadership as a way of life, I feel that I was called to serve. It doesn't matter whether I'm a trainer, educator, counselor, or coach, I value the people around me, and I strive to make the environment around me nurturing. I build community now. Whatever decisions are made, they are not intended to harm anyone. It is a freeing philosophy for me.

I also realized that by working from this philosophy, I know that if I'm making a difference, it's not just in my job—it's in my family, in the workplace, and in any setting. If I see something that needs to be changed, I do it.

I find that by living this philosophy, I'm speaking for people who don't have a voice. Also, from this perspective, I'm actually not able to accept complacency or corruption. I don't put up with that anymore because it's not part of the way of life I've now adopted. It's not about protecting my turf; it's about building up other people so that they can be better. And it's also sustainable. We're building up leaders to be who *they* are rather than to be like me or like someone else.

Based on this approach, exercising leadership is a way of life. It's easier to be accountable and to know when to ask for help because if I want to make a difference and if I don't have the capabilities or the resources, then I will ask someone else if they can help me to be able to do the job.

"*It's not about protecting my turf; it's about building up other people so that they can be better.*"

When I operate from this philosophy, leadership becomes a way of life. I'm always thinking of possibilities and opportunities and ways to build strength and empower others to be leaders, not to simply protect myself. I'm not worried if people excel and do better than me, because I am there to show others how to excel. I'm happy for them when they do and I celebrate their victories. That's why I've moved away from leadership being a role we play toward leadership as a way of life, and I enjoy it.

LEADERSHIP OPPORTUNITY:

I came up with the acronym BLEST to help me effectively lead. I operate from a position of knowing I am blest. I broke it up as:

B—<u>B</u>elief
L—<u>L</u>ove
E—<u>E</u>motions
S—<u>S</u>pirituality
T—<u>T</u>rust

It's not linear at all. It's really interactive. I found that the way to handle my emotions is to change my belief. I ensure how I act and live shows love for God, myself, and others, and that I follow my destiny and calling and trust myself. I choose "not to doubt my beliefs or believe my doubts."

LEADERSHIP SUCCESS:

In the aged care facility where I worked, I felt like I was burning out. Then I started to say, "I've got to change my beliefs. I've got to take care of myself and set some healthy boundaries." When I approached it by considering how wonderful my staff were and what a blessing they were to me, I was so respectful of them. I remember a staff member saying, "No one has ever _asked_ me to do things; I've only been _told_ to do things. You are the only one who _asks_ me to do things." That came after I changed my attitude and started using the BLEST acronym to guide my work.

I can also remember an employee who I constantly received complaints about regarding her manner. I worked with her and trained her rather than simply getting rid of her. After four months, she became one of our best workers.

I actually received a compliment that sticks with me to this day. In fact, it makes me emotional, because people never really liked this person. When I left the job, she said to me, "You're the only one who treated me like a human being." I thought, _I can't believe I heard that._ The greatest success story for me is that this person thought that I saw her as valuable.

Joan C. King, Ph.D.
Loveland, Colorado, USA

Dr. Joan C. King spent twenty years as a professor and department chair at Tufts University School of Medicine. Her rare combination of life choices—a Dominican Sister and a neuroscientist—coupled with her compassion for the human spirit gave her the knowing to lead her audiences to their own inner doorways of transformation.

Self-knowledge gave her life mastery in guiding women beyond their layers of inhibiting beliefs to a fuller expression of the magnificence of who they truly are. With her uncommon background, Joan was able to mix solid scientific knowledge with profound wisdom. Joan leads her audiences to the doorway of possibility in becoming the women they were meant to be.

I: We're talking about leadership, and I know you have both scientific research and practical knowledge that you share with women and men all over the world. You also share how to handle that knowledge to grow and foster leadership and creativity. Can you share a little bit about that?

JCK: Absolutely. Being a leader is an opportunity to bring forth your greatness. Because of the stresses, strains, pressures, and forces that pull you in multiple directions, leading often will reveal to you parts of yourself where may be weaker and parts of yourself that you haven't actually seen before. It's wonderful because it pulls you in both directions—a direction for your greatness as well as a direction to discover what parts of yourself that you might want to transform.

The basic thing about leadership is that you have to know who you are; you will not know it completely as you begin. I have had several leadership positions. It is wonderful to have vision as you begin your leadership position, but it will not be long before a lot of forces want to pull you in various directions so that you fulfill *their* particular desires.

That's where the stresses and strains come from. It's almost like you're a crucible in the fire. The reason you have to know who you are is because you need to know where your boundaries lie. You need to know what values are non-negotiable for you, and you need to be able to articulate a vision. No matter what your title is, you're not a leader unless someone follows you.

Leadership is the ability to articulate a vision—often one that others can't see—and to make it real, to make it achievable, and to make it desirable. It is your job to show the benefits because usually it will evoke change. Most people don't like change because change means moving toward the unknown. In today's world, the unknown appears to be very scary.

Leadership is that ability to be able to paint a clear picture about the benefits of where you're leading a group—and leadership is not just for the group; leadership is for you—for yourself.

"Leadership is the ability to articulate a vision—often one that others can't see—and to make it real, to make it achievable, and to make it desirable."

When I decided to leave academia, I had to lead myself into a new dimension of work. It was a dimension that would allow me to bring forth much of what I couldn't bring forth in the confines of the Dominican convent where I had been teaching all the chemistries at the college. I couldn't bring these things forth in the context of a medical school. I was teaching neuroscience and I was the chair of a department and head of a research center, but there was no place where I could bring all of me.

What I was looking for—and I had to lead and create my own pathway—was my own trajectory to a way to contribute to the world that would allow me to be all of who I am. Don't discount the fact that we're not only leaders in businesses, communities, and families; we are the leaders of our own trajectories in life. That is so important.

I: That is such an interesting perspective. Can you share how you were able to develop that?

JCK: I decided to trust myself. If I had a yearning within me for

more, I understood that there must be a reason. I trusted that and it allowed me to open up and see things in a new way.

As a neuroscientist, I'm always considering how the brain operates. The brain operates with minimal energy because it stores no nutrients. No neuron stores nutrients. Every other cell in the body stores glycogen that can be converted into glucose and used for energy, but neurons are so present in the moment that they devote all of their energy to communicating with other cells, so they store nothing. This means that their default state is to use the least amount of energy possible.

Oftentimes, when you want to make a change, part of why it's so hard is because you've already developed a set of neurons that are connected to each other, which we call a neural network. This is a manner of looking at the world a certain way. I had developed a neural network as a Dominican Sister. It was my identity, what my expectations were about, my behavior, etc. Later, as I went through graduate school and post doctorate fellowship and became a professor, I developed a new neural network about who I was, what my expectations were, and what my behavior was.

"I knew that there was a bigger way to play in the world than I had played before."

When I left all that behind, I left behind that identity. I wasn't traveling to the National Institutes of Health. I wasn't traveling to the National Science Foundation. I wasn't asked to give talks around the world as a scientist. That entire neural network was essentially no longer useful to me except, of course, for the skills that I had learned of being analytical and of being able to integrate information.

When I started to create a new neural network—and this is true for everyone who creates a new pathway—it took energy, because the nervous system wanted to go back to what it knew. In the beginning, you will find yourself wanting to slip back into old patterns. The problem with that is that if you do slip back into the old patterns, it strengthens those patterns and therefore makes it even more difficult for you to change and create a new pattern.

What I think is important in creating a new pattern, and what motivated me, was that I knew that there was a bigger way to play in the world than I had played before. I wanted so much to play in that bigger way in the world, so I kept my eyes open. I met a coach and that was exciting to me. A coach believes in people's potential—

in people having within them a greatness they haven't touched before.

I realized that even when I was a Dominican Sister and teaching chemistry, I was teaching it at a college for girls, and many young girls thought they couldn't learn chemistry. My role was to show them that of course they could. They had everything they needed and there were keys that would unlock that knowledge for them.

The same thing was true when I was in medical school and I was teaching neuroscience to medical students. Usually it's their hardest course; it's difficult for them to understand. Again, I had to reassure them that, indeed, they had the capacity, they had everything they needed to learn it, and that there were keys they could unlock to help them learn it.

Even though I was in domains that were very different than the new one I was exploring, when I found that thread of continuity in my own passion—my passion for people's greatness—that's what I followed. That's the thread that allowed me to start to develop a new neural pathway.

Many people in today's world are finding that change is not something they can choose or not choose; change is imposed upon them by the circumstances in our world today. How to approach that in a way that empowers them rather than in a way that makes them a victim is one of the important pieces of the puzzle.

I: It's as though getting down to an essence level actually assisted you in being able to continue on to something new and develop a sense of continuity from the standpoint of how the brain reacts.

JCK: Absolutely. It was also during my sabbatical and leave of absence that I discovered the concept and named it "cellular wisdom" because I needed a foundation for me to believe that all this power was within me.

Where did it come from? I certainly didn't look at it as egocentric. I knew that it was bigger than that and I wanted to play in the bigger world so I had to know what that was.

I looked back at all the years that I worked with cells in the laboratory—within animals or in dishes where the cells were grown—and the first thing you recognize when you work with cells is how exuberant they are. Their natural default state is to thrive. I began to say, "If that life force that makes these cells thrive is the same, then somewhere in there is all the wisdom I need."

So many people say, "Oh, I can't do this until I get another degree," or "I can't do it until I get training." But so much is within us. I'm not saying that within us already is a Ph.D. degree, but within us *is* the energy to pursue whatever we need to unfold that desire if the desire is really there. That knowledge about what cellular wisdom was gave me the confidence to open up to my true essence.

The first poem that I wrote when I left was *Who's There?* The main idea behind it was to consider who the person is if you take away all the titles, all the positions, and all the activities. Who is she?

That's when I invited my greatness to come forth and that confidence is what allowed me, over the years, to found Beyond Success in 1998. It has grown into not only a coaching company, but it has now grown an author of books, an international speaker, a coach trainer, a coach mentor in three programs, and a developer of advanced coach training in cellular wisdom. I didn't envision it in the beginning, but I envisioned a greatness of it. I allowed it to grow and I believed it could.

"Each of us is so unique that no one can make the contribution of another person."

I think that's the foundation of the kind of leadership that's necessary to take something from a nascent idea; everything we have was once an idea in someone's mind, but for many people, that's where it stays, and it never goes anywhere. Leading the development of an idea—whether it is in a corporation as a CEO or as the leader of your own life—demands a consistency of focus and the belief that it can unfold.

I: Something you've shared before is that when we do not share and realize our personal greatness, we are robbing the entire universe of that experience, and it leaves a hole in the universe.

JCK: It does, because each of us is so unique that no one can make the contribution of another person. If you decide not to make that contribution, no one else can make it. There's going to be a hole there. We need to know that greatness to be able to do what we are called to do in the world. That's why I'm so passionate about it, because we need everyone's contribution.

LEADERSHIP OPPORTUNITY:

I've developed a technique called the limbic stop. I envision a stop sign with a big word *STOP,* and above it the little word *limbic.*

Limbic is the name of the emotional brain—the limbic system. The way the limbic system is constructed, the particular emotion we have will go around and around the circuit, recruiting more and more neurons, getting stronger and stronger until you may find yourself the victim of horrible anger, jealousy, or what have you.

That doesn't have to be the case. If you begin to feel that emotional tug to go sliding down a place in which you are not empowered—in which you're the victim of emotion—immediately envision the stop sign just as if you were on a road and approaching a stop sign. Put the brakes on, because you *can* stop that emotional cascade.

LEADERSHIP SUCCESS:

A client of mine had studied for years as a part-time graduate student while also teaching in a major art institute in New York City. She was teaching as an adjunct professor with too much work, too little pay, and no respect.

It took her seven years to finish her degree, and at the end of those seven years, she said, "Joan, what am I going to do? I'm not going into academia, and I have a Ph.D. in art history and architecture."

I said, "I won't help you find a job, but I'll help you clarify what it is that you really want."

We spent some time in that process—and it took some time—and she came out wanting respect, to be able to use her expertise, to travel, and she wanted a flexible schedule.

Today, she is the Executive Director of a foundation for a painter, all of whose paintings are architectural, representing those paintings to galleries in New York, Milan, and Cuba. She is respected because she has a Ph.D. in art history and architecture and understands the context of what she is doing. She said to me, "Joan, I could never have envisioned this job."

We usually look for jobs that we try to fit ourselves into, and I would say when you think about what you want, find a way to articulate that and share it with many people. You might be surprised that a venue you've never thought of as possible comes your way.

Eve Agee, Ph.D.
Fayetteville, Arkansas, USA

Dr. Eve Agee is a best-selling author, certified life coach, medical anthropologist, and motivational speaker. She is the Founder of Transform Coaching Academy, and her coaching programs and training courses inspire thousands of people throughout the world to create abundant lives and to obtain careers they love.

Her best-selling book, *The Uterine Health Companion: A Holistic Guide to Lifelong Wellness,* was the winner of a 2011 International Book Award for Women's Health. In her work with groups and individuals, Eve provides an innovative, whole-person approach to self-discovery, healing, and personal and professional transformation that helps people more easily connect to their innate wisdom and power. Eve has served as a White House expert and received numerous honors and awards for her research on women's health and empowerment.

I: What do you think is the most important focus for our world today in the leadership arena?

EA: I think leadership is such an important focus right know because we're at such a critical juncture in our history. Having quality leadership is really imperative in helping us find the right path to evolve our way of living so that we and all the different species we share our planet with can really thrive.

Right now leadership is very important because strong leadership will help us come up with the solutions to the vast challenges we're facing today. I believe it's going to take a real free flow of creativity and people feeling safe to contribute to the dialogue so that all ideas are heard and respected. That idea is crucial to overcoming some of our biggest obstacles.

So much of the discourse about how to solve the problems facing our world isn't really a dialogue; often, it's more like a shouting match. A lot of people don't feel safe entering into this type of discussion. It's important for our planet that we create a situation where everyone can step into their leadership potential and help with what we're facing today.

People from different backgrounds throughout the world have so much to offer one another and so much to offer toward our collective future. Our differences can provide wonderful insights that will lead to solutions if we can begin to listen to one another's ideas and let go of our fears.

One of the things I see often with clients is that people are actually afraid to step up and become the leaders they're meant to be. They are scared to make their largest contribution to the world because they feel like it won't be welcomed or their contributions won't be celebrated by their communities, their families, or the world.

One of the best ways we can inspire more people to become leaders is to help them feel comfortable making their biggest contribution. This means actually helping them develop the attitudes that they need to feel safe going ahead and becoming the leader that they can be in making the contributions that they really want to make.

The more we can do to help people release beliefs that they're not safe making their biggest contributions, the better off we will all be. People need to be able to see how much the world really needs every one of us and all of our contributions.

We can start doing this on a personal level by acknowledging and celebrating leadership contributions with our circle of friends, our families, and with our colleagues every day in an effort to make the world a better place. We can also focus on surrounding ourselves with others who encourage us and who are very supportive of our own contributions.

One of the things I think is really helpful is to start a tradition within your family or with your friends to acknowledge and celebrate one another's successes—even the small ones. It's something you could do every night at dinner, or simply once a month with a friend or a group of friends. Just get together and talk about all of the different contributions each person is making. Allowing other people to acknowledge our accomplishments allows each of us to see how we are contributing to the greater good. This shows us how we are all leaders in different areas of our lives and in different areas of our communities.

If you have children, I think it's wonderful to help them learn that the contributions that they make to improve our world and to improve other's lives are meaningful and important. I think helping our children become more comfortable taking on leadership roles and doing even small things to make a difference in the world is really important, because the younger generation is going to be such an important part of continuing our global transformation.

I: What you suggest sounds so simple, and yet it's such a powerful way to make an impact on the world. What else can people do to develop strong leadership skills?

EA: One of the things we can all do right now is to try anything we can that will enhance creativity and inspiration to come up with the solutions that are going to transform our lives and our world. We are facing a lot of challenges all around the world. We're going to need some new ways of doing things in order to learn how to create the best world possible from where we are right now. There's always more inspiration, creativity, and ingenuity when people feel safe and free creating outside of the box.

"By transforming failures or mistakes into learning opportunities, we free ourselves to be able to make the leaps in human ingenuity that we're capable of making."

One way that we can help to instill a sense of comfort for children when it comes to taking on leadership roles is by teaching them that it is safe to make mistakes. It's normal to sometimes experience failures as kids grow and attempt new things. If we're going to find the solutions we need, it's going to take a lot of experimentation and creativity. We all need to be comfortable with the fact that some of our attempts may not go exactly how we want them to, but they are going to give us new answers, and they are going to point us toward the right way and help us find the way to go.

In my coaching programs, oftentimes we see people who are afraid to step up and try things because they've been taught that they might fail. So it seems like a big risk to take. We need to reinvent our attitudes and our way of thinking about failures and mistakes. Instead of thinking of failure as something dangerous that should be avoided, it should be thought of as a way to learn. By transforming failures or mistakes into learning opportunities, we free ourselves to be able to make the leaps in human ingenuity that we're capable of making.

There are so many different things we can do to free up our creativity and start opening up to completely new ideas and new ways to craft the path forward for our planet. A good exercise to help people do that on a personal level is to start being very gentle with yourself when you make a mistake; observe your own beliefs about failures and mistakes and creativity.

Start to notice if this is an area where you're hard on yourself. If you notice that you end up being pretty self-critical when you make a mistake, consider letting go of those beliefs and adopting new ones that will help you see what you've learned from that mistake. Those situations that you thought of as failures may be a great path toward learning something very valuable.

I think any way we can free ourselves up to start letting go of self-judgment and start celebrating our successes will help us be more creative and more equipped to find the solutions we need for our world.

I: What are some of the ways to help people claim their leadership potential so that they can make their biggest contribution?

EA: It's important for us to envision a bright future for our world. Throughout our history, people have been able to band together and manifest many amazing things. As an anthropologist, when I think about our world's situation, I put it in the context of human history.

We've done some amazing things as humans. One of the fundamental steps toward creating the leadership that our world needs right now—both on a personal level and on a global level—is to form a collective vision of what we want to create. We need everyone to step up to become leaders—each in our own way—in order to establish this collective vision.

When John F. Kennedy announced the goal to go to the moon, he gave people a clear vision that they could imagine in their minds. There were specific action steps that people could support and work toward. I think, right now, one of the main things that is missing for us is that vision of a really bright future for our world.

So many people I speak to on a personal level feel rather hopeless.

Just look at the news and various stories in the media. In many ways, people feel powerless about what they can do, even though there's so much that each one of us can do. I think, in large part, it's because our collective imagination has gone to a very dark view of our future.

"A major role of great leaders is to point us toward where we want to go and to help define the steps that are needed to get there."

Albert Einstein said, "Imagination is everything. It's the preview of life's coming attractions." Literally every amazing thing we've ever created as humans was first imagined in someone's mind. Our collective consciousness has tremendous power. Right now, our collective consciousness, for the most part, is envisioning a very dark future for our world. We need leaders who can help us shift that focus and provide us with a concrete vision of a bright future. A major role of great leaders is to point us toward where we want to go and to help define the steps that are needed to get there.

The more we can do on a personal level, on a national level, and on a global level to shift the dialogue and to start to focus on how we want our future to be will be very helpful. Once we do that, we can envision and define the steps that are needed to create that.

If you think about the last few hundred years of our history, whenever humans have faced real challenges, the people we really considered to be the greatest leaders were people who emerged during those darkest and most difficult moments. Those people have been able to help their followers see a better future. They helped people see that a better future is possible, and they motivated people to take the steps necessary to create that vision.

We don't have to wait for one special leader to emerge; each of us can be that leader by talking to our friends, families, colleagues, and communities about the vision we want to create for our world.

When you look at history, most people who became leaders were normal people who felt the call to create something they really wanted to see happen. We can become those leaders, and we can speak up for those who don't have a voice. The more we can do to start getting connected to this vision of the future that we want to create, the more we're going to be able to connect with the personal power each one of us needs to make that kind of change.

LEADERSHIP OPPORTUNITY:

Let's create a daily celebration of ourselves. Daily, sit down to acknowledge four different successes you've had that day. It could be anything at all from recycling to being kind to someone to really listening to someone. It could be a success at work or taking the time to meditate or exercise—any kind of personal care.

Acknowledge that success and then recognize yourself or acknowledge yourself. Generally, we're pretty quick to recognize those things that we consider failures or mistakes. We are usually pretty quick to criticize ourselves, and we don't frequently acknowledge our successes as much.

Acknowledge those successes, recognize yourself for creating them, and then give yourself time to really feel that. Take a few moments to breathe deeply and feel how good that feels in your body. Maybe let yourself share it with a friend—someone who is going to be supportive—if that feels comfortable.

You can also create a success journal by writing down your successes. It's really important to go ahead and actually let yourself feel it. You can also create a gratitude journal or write gratitude points in your success journal.

LEADERSHIP SUCCESS:

A client came to me about two years ago, and at that point he was very ill with an undefined illness. He had never been able to get a definite diagnosis. He spent quite a bit of time at the Mayo Clinic.

He healed himself using the techniques I teach people to do, including combining guided imagery and conscious breathing with coaching, along with other techniques from mind-body traditions. He has improved his health so much that he is now going to become a coach and share these tools with people who have chronic diseases and chronic pain throughout the world.

This is someone who could barely sit up for thirty minutes a day, and now he's enrolled in a coaching program I'm going to teach. He's going to become a coach and share his own healing experience with the world. That's an incredible success.

Stacey Chadwell
Las Vegas, Nevada, USA

Stacey Chadwell is a small business success coach and media personality for *Expert Insights* radio show, *Write Now* radio show, and *Profiles of Success* radio show. She is also an interviewer for *Insights* and *PUBLISHED!* magazines.

Stacey has interviewed visionaries, top business leaders, and others on the rise. Stacey helps others successfully start their own journey to be seen, heard, and known.

I: You're certainly a leader in your field and have interviewed some of the great leaders of our time. Could you share some of the things you do personally for your own leadership growth?

SC: The leaders I've interviewed read. I also read books in my arena, as well as books on marketing and sales, because I think that's important. Some people are natural salespeople, but it always helps to keep reading and keep learning. As I read more and more, I'm surprised to see the things I read coming out of me; I find myself saying and doing those same things I've been reading. I constantly fill up my reservoir of education.

I also like to journal. I like to write down my thoughts and how I'd like to use them. The more I'm reading, the more I grow, and I love sharing information with other people. I love helping others to be their best. Once I've read something, the growth aspect is in applying it and then sharing it. I think it is so important that we keep sharing.

Then, basically, I find that I need to step forward and take action. I step forward with it because I've never known a leader to step back. They step forward—always.

I: That's such a good point. You're in such a creative field. What do you do to spur yourself on and lead with creativity?

SC: That's a very good question. I think journaling helps a lot.

Sometimes I'm just inspired. If I wake up at four o'clock in the morning and I have a thought in my mind and it has to come out, I sit down and I write.

It's funny because I've interviewed so many people who write books, and that's how quite a few of them do it. Authoring a book is not as methodical as I thought it would be. Some of them simply write when they're inspired. They sit down and pour it all out. I also find it best to write when I'm inspired.

I: You homeschool your children, so you are actually serving in a number of leadership roles for our future leaders everyday—your daughters. What would you like to see for them as future leaders?

SC: I really would like them to have an open mind. I would like them to embrace the entrepreneurial spirit and see my example. I'm at home, but I'm also working.

I also want them to have the ability to think for themselves as leaders. It's very important to me that they don't learn to follow what everyone else tells them: "Get in line, stay in line, don't talk," and all of that. I would like to see my daughters be able to develop their own entrepreneurial spirit in order to be leaders in their own right.

I: Was that part of your decision to homeschool them? To prepare them to be leaders?

SC: That certainly was part of it. When my daughter Avery was ready to start school, we found that the school systems really aren't built for everyone. In her case, she was ready to start school at age three. By the time she was five she was reading on a fifth grade level. She needed to have the freedom to learn at her own pace, so I decided that the best step was to take her out of the system. I had her in a private school, but that wasn't working either because they want to keep all the kids together. That doesn't necessarily work for everyone; some people need to spread their wings and fly.

She had her own pace, and it wasn't ever going to meet the school's pace for learning. They could move her up, but within a couple of months, she would be onto the next grade level. Some systems are so entrenched that it's very hard to fight against them. I thought it would be easier to bring her home and let her learn and become her own person instead of being disenchanted, which is how she had started to feel.

I: What have you noticed in her from the standpoint of her growth as a potential leader? What are the traits you see in her that you're most happy with as a result of your choice?

SC: Anyone who meets my children wants to know how they became such strong girls. The first thing they ask is, "Where did they get that from?" I say, "I don't know." They have no problem telling people what they think in a respectful way. They step forward. They're not reticent to stand back in the shadows. Both of my daughters are strong willed in a positive way.

I think that's probably going to help them more than anything else in their lives. They can rely on themselves and feel confident in that. One's academic life is just one small part of a bigger picture. They're very active, social, friendly, and they love to get to know people. They don't have the kinds of boundaries typically seen in kids their age.

My daughter Katie is soon to be seven and is just as comfortable talking to my older daughter Avery's friends and hanging out with them. They adore her. In fact, my older daughter's cheerleading teacher has asked Katie to help teach Avery's class because she's the kind of person who steps up and says, "This is how it's done."

I think that's a skill that's going to be very good for them in their lives because they've faced some things and they now know they can depend on themselves and how to do that.

I: That ability to depend on themselves and to step up and step out is fantastic.

SC: I'm hoping that my daughters choose to have their own companies and to follow their passion. My oldest daughter, at eleven, loves to draw cartoons. She loves art. If she was given an opportunity to do what she likes to do, she'd be more than happy working in an environment where she was drawing for someone else. And I could see easily my youngest rising to the top and being CEO of a company someday.

I: What do you see might be challenging for them, either now or later, in being able to accomplish that?

SC: The most challenging thing if they were to go into an established corporation would be that it's not theirs. It depends on the corporate environment though. If the culture is good, then they'll be able to speak and be heard. I think it might be hard if they're not heard, if they get in and they're used to being able to grow in their own way. I think that might be the only thing that I could see that would be frustrating for them, that feeling of, _Hey, I wanted to contribute and you weren't listening!_

I: A sense of not being heard is one of the challenges that a lot of people are already facing.

SC: Yes. I've heard that it's something that's coming up a lot with the Millennials. They want to be a part of the process. I'm raising two of my own, so I'm sure it's going to come up. One of them has gone to school and has experienced it and absolutely does not want to return. The other one would like to try it out, so she might get to find out.

I think that because they are headstrong. it may be frustrating and they may choose to go their own way at that point. I could see that happening.

I: You interact with leaders all the time from all over the world through your broadcast show and media interviews. Can you share about how some of our top leaders demonstrate these abilities to step up and step out?

SC: There are several things I've noticed in talking with all of these people. Here are a few key steps these leaders are taking that help to place them as leaders in their fields.

Five Key Steps Leaders Take to Step Up and Stand Out

#1: Leaders read to gain knowledge and insight into their own arena as well as other arenas. This is something that is so important and it's something that I do too. As I mentioned earlier, the leaders I talk with all read books written about topics specific to their arena as well as books on how to promote and market themselves. Most of them read at least one book per week and probably more than that, and they're not just focusing on their own area.

#2: Leaders invest in themselves and in their own growth. One thing I always hear is that these leaders are constantly investing in themselves. They go to seminars and events in order to make sure that they are constantly learning and staying on top of the game.

#3: Leaders share what they know. They come up with their own thoughts and ideas and share them with others. They like to share what they know.

#4: Leaders aren't afraid to be seen. The willingness to step out and be seen by others separates these leaders from others around them.

#5: Leaders ask questions. In college I kept getting asked to be on this board and that board in just about everything, and I didn't know why. I started paying attention, and I learned that it was because I asked questions. In response to that then, others would say, "Okay, you're in charge." I was thinking, *Why am I in charge? I just asked a question!*

Leaders read, they invest in themselves, they share what they know, and they're not are not afraid to be seen or to ask questions. Those are some of the hallmarks of the leaders I've come in contact with

You'll never learn everything; there's always more to go out and learn. Leaders understand that. They don't think they know it all. They understand that there's more to learn, and they are constantly learning. They're lifetime learners and they love it, they're passionate about it, and they dedicate themselves to it.

To them, it's not work, it's what they love. Not one of them has said, "I have a job." Instead, they have a *passion* that they pursue and they enjoy doing so every single day.

LEADERSHIP OPPORTUNITY:

John C. Maxwell said, "Leadership is influence," and I can't think of a better time when everybody has access to being influential. Get out there. Get on social media, get your voice heard, and be seen. Inspire others, help others, step forward and take action, and you too will be a leader.

It doesn't matter what you do. You could be a parenting coach, a thought leader in the business world, or a homeschooling mother—it doesn't matter as long as you're reaching out, helping others, and sharing your knowledge.

LEADERSHIP SUCCESS:

When my daughters were three and seven, and right between their birthdays, my husband came down with a type of leukemia that they told me would kill him. He had a 20% chance of surviving for another two years, but that was all. Basically, they were telling me he had a death sentence and only had about a year to live.

He was in the hospital for thirty-three days, and during that time I had my daughters stay with his mother so I could be there and take care of him. At the same time, I realized, as I mentioned earlier, that going back into the school system would not be a good fit for my daughter. At that point she was doing middle school level work, and there was no way I could put her in a second grade class with her own age group.

I had to figure what I was going to do. Basically, I found myself sitting there figuring out how to go on.

The doctors told me my husband was going to die. As gently as they could, they impressed upon me that it was going to happen. I had to make a plan because I had to figure out how I was going to be home with my girls and educate them while still making enough money to take care of all of us, not to mention taking care of my husband and providing him with the best last months he could have.

He received all of the treatments, but he wasn't getting better. Then they found out why. They got the pathology report, and it turned out that the type of leukemia he had was one of the most deadly in the 1970s because the treatment itself would kill patients. Now, however, medical professionals knew that if patients simply took Vitamin A, they were 95% curable.

One doctor with a forty-year career and another one with a twenty-year career came rushing in to tell him that he could be cured. He said, "Okay." He looked at me and asked, "Why are you crying?"

I said, "They told me you were dying, and now they just told me you are going to live. We just won the lottery. I'm sorry, but I went ahead and planned my whole life without you because I had to."

This is my daughters' success story as well, because they were aware of what was happening, they knew what their dad was going through, and they never let it hold them back. They never used it as an excuse for anything.

Ann Farrell
Winfield, Illinois, USA

In 2006, Ann Farrell retired as a corporate executive to launch her own successful executive and leadership coaching firm, Quantum Endeavors, Inc. In her career, she remains the only woman to rise from entry level to top of the house in the 150-year history of the Fortune 200 Company where she has held three executive positions.

Based on her own experience of success and her passion to support others to live their greatest lives doing their greatest work, she has developed leadership coaching and development programs so impactful that they are now used by more than fifty corporate coaching firms. In addition to the impressive list of client companies that she and her team serve directly, Ann also mentors other coaches to coach for success in corporations and organizations. This increases the ripple effect of Ann's ability to share what she feels so grateful to have had the opportunity to experience.

I: You've enjoyed a lot of leadership success in your career in and in your life. What are the keys to personal and professional leadership?

AF: It starts with The Three A's: awareness, alignment, and authenticity. I believe that the quality of one's leadership is directly correlated to the quality of one's relationship with these three keys.

Leadership is a lifelong journey. Each of us is like a great big rose—every time we think we know ourselves, we look inside and we always find we are "more." Every time we think our consciousness is where it needs to be, we quickly see, know, and feel that there's even more waiting for us to learn and see, be and do.

Let's look at each of these keys more closely:

The Three A's of Effective Leadership

Awareness: This is where I believe leadership starts and what I am referring to is the awareness of what's important to us—our values, our strengths, our passion, the difference that we want to make, what inspires and even what bores us, what we love, and what we hate—that makes us into great leaders.

Alignment: Once we have awareness, our mission is to get *aligned.* The job of leadership is similar to what a chiropractor is to the spine. When leaders are aligned, they have access to their own personal power. When our spines are aligned, we can stand tall have the strength we were meant to have. Alignment in leadership is about making sure we know the truth about ourselves and that truth, when it's aligned, enables us to leverage all that we are on the inside and project it out in how we behave and in what we do.

Authenticity: Once we have awareness and alignment, it is then that we have a responsibility to stand in that with authenticity, to put us out in the world, and to hold ourselves accountable to fully stand in our strongest personal power by revealing ourselves. That can be very scary. It's so much easier to be someone else—sort of a play actor—but to me, being real is the key to personal and professional leadership. It is the ultimate integrity.

I: Authenticity is always unfolding and growing as well, isn't it?

AF: It is; just when we think we know who we are and what we are capable of, life sends us another challenge. That is our leadership journey.

I: How do we sometimes get in our own way when it comes to quality leadership?

AF: Ever since we were little and we were told what it looks like to be good or see behaviors get rewarded. We are encouraged to play or be a certain way—to "role play" versus be who we really are.

We get in our own way the most by trying to be what we think other people expect us to be or want us to be. It happens a lot in organizations where leaders look up and say, "In order for me to be a strong leader in the organization, I have to lead like *that*." This is where the epidemic of "imposter syndrome" comes into play. People are always afraid they're going to get caught or be found out that they're really not the person they are pretending to be, and it's

125

because they are playing *roles* versus playing *real*.

Losing sight of the fact that our strongest leadership is that which is real for us can be dangerous. Once we show up as ourselves and start getting real, that's where our power and the opportunity to really be in the service of others is at its best. It's hard to do. We get messages from a very young age that there's a certain way we're supposed to act. Letting go of that takes courage.

The biggest gift we can give to ourselves and others is to encourage them to be authentic and real.

"When we look beyond our own gifts to see everyone else's, we start honoring their authenticity and appreciating what they bring to the table."

I: How do we enable ourselves and support others to reach true, full leadership potential?

AF: The truth is that we all possess the personal power that I keep alluding to. It isn't power that we should use to exert over others, but it's power that lets us stand confidently and with humility. It is in this instance that we are most impactful. How we enable ourselves and others is by embracing and supporting The Three A's.

Encourage it! We all have a superpower, and once we are aware of what our superpower is, then it truly becomes a gift, not just to us, but to all those around us. When we look beyond our own gifts to see everyone else's, we start honoring their authenticity and appreciating what they bring to the table. When we bring our different superpowers together, we can make big movements and big differences.

One of the ways that we can encourage others to reach their full potential is by treating them the way they want to be treated and not the way *we* want to be treated. It's a twist on The Golden Rule; we need to ask ourselves, "What is the best way to inspire, support, and encourage them to fully show up?"

I: You do so much in the arena of leadership, and you've accomplished so much in your own career. What do you do to ensure that you're growing professionally and personally?

AF: My biggest growth both professionally and personally has come from finding the gifts in adversity. My entire career as the only woman in a male-dominated organization and male-dominated industry might be considered all uphill, but I had a blast.

"It's the tough times that really take me to task and make me a greater leader, because I'm learning every day that there's so much more for me to learn."

Over the course of a six-month period in my life, my marriage went through crisis, my father—for whom I had been the caregiver over the last five as he lived with Alzheimer's—went into hospice and passed away, and within two months following his death, I was diagnosed with breast cancer. Life keeps bringing me opportunities to more fully honor my values, remain aligned, and be authentic in the face of bad times and good times. It's the tough times that really take me to task and make me a greater leader, because I'm learning every day that there's so much more for me to learn.

Now, on the other side of that six month period, my marriage is strong, my dad's in a much better place, and my health is better than it's been in a long time.

I: That's amazing. Thank you for sharing that. What are some of the big challenges that are facing the coaches you work with and some of the individuals in leadership roles in corporations now?

AF: One of the biggest challenges is that people are looking for people to be like them instead of appreciating the fact that we need all kinds. We need diversity of thought, leadership style, and beliefs; it's a must, not a want.

There's a reason that it takes a village to do big things. None of us have everything that is needed. None of us, alone, have all the superpowers, but if you amass enough of us and you appreciate the different power that each individual brings to the table in their different, great, and perhaps even eccentric way, then you have everything you need to do the really good stuff.

Organizations still think in terms of "fit or fix" versus authentic. It's as though all leaders are supposed to fit into a very narrow definition of what they are expected to be. Often we have to go through a personal transformation before we are willing to reveal ourselves. It would be so nice if it was encouraged from the beginning. There's a thought—let's just each encourage and support each other to just start there!

LEADERSHIP OPPORTUNITY:

Here is an exercise you can use and play with. This is one of my favorites. I use it with coaches and with clients, and it reaches right to the heart of who you are as a leader.

I call it "real play versus role play," which is language I use a lot in my leadership model. You begin by simply writing a description of who you are and how you want to be as a parent, a partner, a manager, an employee, a friend, a daughter/son, a sister/brother, etc. Write one for each role in your life.

> *"This is about your best, biggest self tapping into that great leader within."*

Once you have written all of your separate descriptions, the challenge then is to write a composite description of who you choose to be where you show up. This is about your best, biggest self tapping into that great leader within. Ask yourself, "What would it be like to be this great leader in all that I do? What is the power in aligning all of my gifts as the real me versus stepping into the different roles that I now play?"

For example, when I have a leader who is really struggling with authenticity in the workplace and doesn't really know what their "great leader within" is, I always start by asking them, "What kind of parent do you want to be?"

The last portion of this exercise is to identify the red flags of being "less than." Whenever you feel that you're about to step into a role and you find yourself saying, "I have to be a leader now," or "I have to put on a suit and I have to go to work," or "I have to show up in this certain way," or "It's time for me to be the parent—I have to step up and put on that stern voice," just remember that in doing so you are diluting your power because you don't have access to all your gifts in that space.

Pull back to who you really are, access your "great leader within," own your superpowers, and make the difference you are meant to make!

LEADERSHIP SUCCESS:

I call it a composite, because yes, it's mine, but it is also a story I see every single day.

I am a short female at five feet two inches tall, I am warm and friendly and very relational. I went to work every day in an environment with men taller than six feet who were primarily authoritative leaders who were very much in command and in control.

I started in the corporate environment when I was only nineteen years old, only two years out of high school, and definitely still forming. I had the feeling every single day that I didn't fit and that I was the one that had to figure out how to be like "them." Let me also say, there were no female role models for me to look to either.

I struggled to find the way for me in the very beginning. Obviously it's impossible for me to turn myself into a tall man; that was never going to work. I had to find my own way. I stumbled through self-discovery and authenticity. Finally I said to myself, "I'm just going to be me. I'm just going to have fun. I'm going to love people and what I do. I'm going to lead from the heart." That was what felt real for me.

As soon as I started doing that, I started to create success and receive recognition from my organization. It was as though everyone was saying, "Finally! That's what we've been waiting for you to do!"

My and my clients' success stories come when we finally understand that no one else can tell us how to be great. It comes from us being willing to do the work of The Three A's to bring the greatness that is inside each of us out and into the world.

Each of us has to unlock the key that will make that happen, and when we do, we find our own success story after success story. It unleashes incredible personal power that elevates us and all that we do!

Terry Zweifel
Manzanillo, Mexico

Terry Zweifel is a leading expert in innovative aerospace design for major defense and commercial aircraft, including Lockheed Skunk Works on the SR-71 and programs with NASA. He was Chief Engineer for a major aviation company and a Senior Engineering Fellow with Honeywell.

With twenty-three patents to his credit, Terry has led teams and spearheaded some of the major programs that are making air travel safer for the world. He is also a creative artist whose work has been featured in major publications and books. Terry's passion lies in fostering talent on the rise to greatness.

I: From your perspective, what makes a great leader?

TZ: In my area of expertise—engineering—first of all, it's very important that you select personnel for your team who are going to work with you. You need people who work well together, yet have the required expertise to accomplish the program's objectives.

In general, a leader acts as the coordinator of the team, guiding the general direction to accomplish the goals of the program without stifling any creative ideas that may make the outcome of the program better and more efficient. Perhaps just as important, a leader has to be a buffer between the team and others—including upper management—to ensure they aren't interfering with the day-to-day work necessary for the program. Oftentimes there is a tendency—which I personally try to avoid—for management to try to micromanage everything. The leader should try to let the team members do their thing while keeping management's confidence up in regards to the team's competency.

I: What are some ways people can stop micromanaging?

TZ: Probably the best thing to do, at least in my experience, is to become very familiar with management. In other words, build up trust so they have confidence in what you're doing. The minute they lose faith in what you're doing, they're going to be all over the program, trying to make sure that they know what's going on and pushing their ideas.

There's a bit of the Peter Principle that goes into it where they think they know what they're doing when in fact they don't have all of the necessary information. It's important that you build up confidence with them so that they feel sure that you know what you're doing.

I've been on both sides, and I know how it feels. There's a tendency as a manager to start thinking, "Are these people doing the right thing?" That thought process makes you want to get in there and thrash around, whereas usually—if you have a confident team—it's better to rely on the leader to make sure things are going smoothly.

I: In a leadership role in a project situation, you're actually operating almost in a liaison capacity between the upper management the team reports to as well as the team members you are guiding to do the project.

TZ: Exactly. You become a buffer to protect your team, so to speak, from all of the input that comes from the outside. There may be people questioning judgments that the team has made and how effectively they're doing things. You have to assure everyone that things are going well, and hopefully they are, of course.

I: How do you bring the upper management leaders into the loop?

TZ: One of the first things is to avoid having meetings over and over. As a leader, you should go into a meeting with management and give them a very thorough briefing of where you are, what you're doing, what potential problems you see, and how those are going to affect both the schedule and the budget of the particular program. Again, you don't do that daily; it's needed maybe a once a week. It's simply a tool to let them know that you're doing what they expect.

I: You believe that we each have greatness within us. Can you share a little bit about how you've fostered that greatness in others who are on the rise?

TZ: A good leader should be a mentor, and I've always tried to be that. I had mentors who helped me through my early years, giving me the experience necessary to proceed. I try to share that with the team members with whom I work. Bounce innovative ideas off of them, see what their reaction is, and then listen to what they're saying. Once you've done that, review it and give them some constructive guidance based on your experience. You need to ask, "Will this actually work, and is it a better solution than what we have now?"

Of course, if their ideas are good ones and result in more efficient productivity, then give them credit where credit is due. Praise never hurts.

I: That's for sure. You said that you've had some mentors who have left a lifelong impression on you.

TZ: Actually, yes. There are moments when the light comes on, so to speak. One of those moments took place when we were having a big discussion about who was at fault for a particular problem we were having. We were all pointing fingers at hardware people who were blaming the software people who were blaming the system people, and we just kept going around in circle.

The manager stepped in and said, "Stop it. It's my fault. I'm the manager. If we're having problems, they're my fault. Let's start fixing those problems right now. It doesn't help us at all to be pointing fingers at each other. What matters is getting this job done."

That always stuck in my mind as the way to do it. Ultimately the leader is responsible for problems that occur. And the leader is the one who has to sit down and get those problems solved.

I: So it's basically, "Let's not dwell on the past. This is what we're looking at now. Let's move forward and fix it and make it a positive result in the end," correct?

TZ: Exactly. And that also applies if, for example, you've spent a great deal of time going down the wrong path. There just comes a point where you have to say, "This isn't working. Throw that out and let's move on." You can't keep trying to make something that's not working work. It's not going to happen.

I: Rather than being remorseful continuing to try to push it, when another solution is obviously required, you just move on and find the appropriate solution.

TZ: Right. You start from that point. It doesn't matter how much you've invested before—how much money has gone into it—if it isn't working, move on to something else, and start at the beginning, and say, "We're starting over."

I: What are some of the major challenges that leaders face?

TZ: There are a lot of challenges, but probably one of the biggest is that there's a certain myopia that occurs during phases of a program. We get so involved in day-to-day activities that we tend to forget what the overall objective of the project or the program is. It becomes blurred, and you end up spending a great deal of time working on things that are not that important.

As one of my mentors said a long time ago, "You're separating the wheat from the chaff and concentrating full time on the chaff. Let's get back to the wheat."

I personally like to step back periodically and look at the program from a different perspective. This helps to avoid what I call "designing shock absorbers for square wheels." In other words, oftentimes we find ourselves sitting there working on something that is not solving the basic problem. We're trying to bandage it or come up with some weird idea for how to solve the problem. But by stepping back and looking at the big picture, so to speak, we can redirect a team's activities toward the best way to solve the problem without resorting to bad solutions and wasting a lot of time.

"It's hard to be a leader if you're not keeping up with the technology and problems that are facing you in your area of interest."

I: How do you ensure your own personal and professional leadership growth?

TZ: Just keeping up with it takes quite a bit of time in itself. Aviation computer systems change rapidly, just like the technology of home computers is evolving all the time. New techniques and designs are constantly emerging. It's important to keep aware of what's going on and what problems are arising. It's hard to be a leader if you're not keeping up with the technologies and problems that are facing you in your area of interest.

I: You recently worked with a company where you mentored some very young engineers. What are some of the things you had to call up in yourself in order to work with what might have been decades of separation from the standpoint of age, mentality, and the way people are currently operating in the workplace?

TZ: I never really found the age difference to be any kind of a challenge. Maybe I still think like they do, because we didn't have problems like that. I was obviously more experienced, but I was aware of the changes that had come along, so I could fit right in with what they knew coming right out of school. I wouldn't say there were any major problems that I experienced in regards to the generation gap, so to speak.

I: Was there a certain respect for that knowledge and the fact that the passion for technology pulled you together as a team, despite any difference in age or learning experiences?

TZ: It wasn't any question of respect. I respected their ideas and their competence—they were very bright individuals—and I listened to what they had to say.

Conversely, I shared my experience. There was a certain amount of knowledge gained on my part from the College of Hard Knocks; you learn a lot as you're out there doing. I was able to share that with them. There was a mutual respect built up.

Many times they'd have a clever idea or way to do something and say, "Hey, we could do it this way," and we'd find out that, yes, their idea worked great. They would get the credit and the respect of the other team members and myself.

You've got to listen to what your team members have to say. Some of the ideas won't work in the real world, but sometimes they'll come up with a very clever idea that saves time and is more efficient; it makes life easier for everyone.

No one knows it all, no matter how much experience or how many decades you've been at it. There are things you're not going to know that they may know—maybe because of the technology that's changed that you hadn't kept up with or what have you. It's important to be open-minded and to have that real fluid interchange with your team members.

LEADERSHIP OPPORTUNITY:

I was very fortunate that a lot of people who mentored me listened to my ideas to see if I had any input. They weren't hard and rigid old-school types. They wanted to find the best way to do things because they understood that ultimately that would make them look good. They were focused on getting the job done more efficiently, on schedule, and within budget. Here are three tips I can share from my experiences learning from those mentors:

Tip #1: Keep the goal of the program in mind. Try to avoid distractions that come from outside that may lead you off on some other path that you shouldn't be going down.

Tip #2: Avoid constant meetings. This seems to pervade today's business world. If you're going to have a meeting, have one meeting that results in decision-making, not just discussions; meetings should be for the purpose of deciding what to do next.

Tip #3: Check in periodically. It is important to strategically review your program as well as make sure you are protecting your team and praising their accomplishments.

LEADERSHIP SUCCESS:

I was asked to review a company's computer system for airline safety, and after looking at it a while, I saw that the basic design concept was flawed; it wasn't going to work.

The company had invested several years and millions of dollars in this concept, but they couldn't get the FAA certification, which is necessary before you can put equipment on a commercial airplane. It's an example of designing shock absorbers for square wheels. They were trying to make a flawed design work while missing the basic point and not understanding the principles of what they were dealing with.

We assembled a small team of about half a dozen people, created a new design, and certified the system with the FAA within a year. What was more important to me than that was the opportunity I had to mentor young engineers and the personal satisfaction that I had hopefully contributed some small part in their subsequent success. Many of the engineers I've mentored are now Vice Presidents, division heads, and department managers of major aviation companies. I take some pride in that.

Ann Van Eron, Ph.D.
Chicago, Illinois, USA

Dr. Ann Van Eron is Principal of Potentials—an international coaching and organization development consulting firm—with over twenty-five years of experience coaching leaders and teams all over the world to fully develop their capabilities. She specializes in creating environments where people have open-minded and productive conversations for greater results in any situation and anywhere.

Ann has developed a proven process to understand and work effectively with people with different perspectives—which includes everyone. Ann's clients include Fortune 100 companies; government and nongovernment organizations; healthcare, consulting, education, and privately held organizations; and executive coaches. Ann provides leadership development and teaches executives how to be effective in coaching their teams. She supports organizations in creating cultures of respect and open communication that facilitate achieving goals. Ann is an executive coach and leadership development expert.

I: After over twenty-five years working with major organizations all around the globe, you're in a wonderful place to share with us some of the most critical challenges you see for leaders and organizations today. What do you feel are some of the most significant of those challenges?

AVE: I think it's a difficult time for leaders. Clearly, both leaders from organizations as well as individuals in their own personal leadership roles are facing turbulent times with massive technological, economic, and social change. The challenge is that the rules are just not clear anymore. Leaders are being required to be resilient, to be flexible, and to be able to implement change quickly and efficiently, which isn't easy. At the same time, people are weary of change; it takes a lot of energy.

A big challenge I see that corporate and organization leaders are facing is that they can't rely on their positional power. People are less open to automatically following the person in charge. Individuals in positions of authority have to use influence. To do this, it's critical to create an environment where people are engaged, where people feel open, and where someone listens to them. It's critical that leaders really listen to people and hear all of the very different perspectives.

This isn't easy, because a lot of times I find that leaders think they're listening, but they really already have in mind where they think things should go. This means that they aren't really hearing all of the different perspectives or valuing or respecting those perspectives. This is critical. No matter at what level or in what part of the world I work, I find that I'm always encouraging leaders at all levels to create an open environment. To do this, they must lead by inspiring an open-minded environment where people feel engaged. This requires listening effectively and letting people know that they've been heard—and then listening some more, actually. Two-way dialogue is essential.

This is a complication because leaders say, "We're so busy. We don't have time." However, they can't afford _not_ to engage in this type of listening. When they listen and create this kind of open and respectful environment, creative solutions naturally emerge and commitment is developed. I've seen it happen time and time again in all different kinds of organizations, whether it's manufacturing or financial services; it happens on all levels. I've spent a lot of my time in recent years on creating open-minded, respectful, and engaged environments. When leaders and others "assume positive intent" and listen to one another, innovation becomes the norm, and efficiencies and synergies are identified. Less energy is wasted and people can even have fun as they realize results.

Emotions are contagious, and a lot of people—because of the nature of where we are in the world—have a lot of anxiety and fear. We have four generations in the workplace, and everyone sees the world differently because of their backgrounds and their experiences. I work in many multicultural environments, and the people in those environments all see things differently. People in the field see things differently than those at corporate headquarters.

Often there's a lot of tension and an "us versus them" mentality among those with differing perspectives. People end up spending their energy pushing for their point of view or not feeling respected

> *"The key is creating an environment of trust . . . There needs to be an understanding that people have the freedom to be creative and innovative."*

or valued. This use of their energy depletes them and takes away from working together toward a shared vision. With dialogue, roles and responsibilities can be clarified and alignment created.

The key is creating an environment of trust. Right now, given the uncertainty in the world, we feel most certain when we are creating collaborative relationships and working together to create a mutual trust. There needs to be an understanding that people have the freedom to be creative and innovative.

I: Certainly you know as well as anyone how challenging this is in current conditions. How do you go about supporting personal and professional leaders to be open-minded and to create great results?

AVE: I have developed a process that I've been testing all over the world for many years. All of us naturally make judgments. We do this because of our history and how we organize. It's very easy, especially in a stressful environment, to lock in to thinking that we're right.

What happens is that we hold on to the perspective that we're right and thus reinforce it even more. That's when we need to catch ourselves and realize that "we don't know what we don't know." If we can catch ourselves in judgment and shift into being curious and open-minded, then opportunities emerge. When we understand that it is the human condition that we all see the world differently, we can be more open to understanding others and being empathetic.

The process I have taught all over the world is called OASIS Moves™. It is a practical proven five-step process that encompasses all of the elements of becoming self-aware and effectively communicating for results. It's about catching ourselves so that we can become aware of our assumptions and emotions and what we are observing. In addition, it helps us to be open and curious to what others are observing and experiencing. Finally, the process supports finding common ground and developing solutions with others. I have introduced OASIS Moves™ into many organizations. People report that the moves are easy to remember, create an understanding environment, and support open-minded conversations. Years after learning OASIS Moves™, people report they are still using the process with great results.

Catching ourselves in judgment, stopping, and then shifting to this open OASIS state takes some practice, but with intention, it becomes easier. In fact, as we shift into being more open, then we can take in more data. We can understand other people's perspectives and also share our own perspective to find out what is important to each of us. Then we can more easily create options and solutions. Each of the moves takes practice to build the skills of effectively communicating.

I also focus on the issue of respect. It's an old word, but I think all of us have a need to feel valued and respected. When we feel that people aren't open to our differing perspectives, we tend to feel not valued.

What's interesting about respect—and I see this a lot as I work around the world in different organizations—is that each of us have different definitions of what respectful behavior is. Of course, this is based on our background, our experience, our childhood, and the environment in which we were raised.

A simple thing like considering whether we should say hello seems obvious to many us; we think, "of course," but other people have had different experiences, and this sort of greeting may not have been emphasized. A simple thing like not saying hello makes people feel disrespected and then that carries over into all other aspects of working together.

In almost every system I've worked in, whether I've worked with a team, a large organization, or even a small group, I help people to identify what behaviors are important to them. Sometimes it's a simple thing. One manager expects people to wait outside for an appointment, whereas someone right next door in the same organization says, "No, if you have an appointment with me at eleven o'clock, I expect you to come right into my office."

It's hard to know how everyone sees things. What usually happens is that people don't discuss these things. Then the person who expects people to wait outside figures that the person who just walked in is rude, and that impacts how they interact with him going forward. Over time, a lot of tension can be created. We don't even think to talk about some of these things related to respect because we assume everyone should know. We need to create climates in organizations, in families, and communities where we can talk about what's important to us, understanding that it may not be important to someone else. As we understand these differences, we can be more responsible and agree on actions that support everyone and help achieve shared goals.

I: Does this process support this level of communication?

AVE: Absolutely. I've tested OASIS Moves™ for the last fifteen years all over the world. It is basically how humans work. We naturally make judgments and we naturally consider other people to be wrong. We need to catch ourselves so we can shift into this open state. Recent brain research supports each element of the OASIS Moves™.

Emotions are contagious. Research on emotional intelligence shows that if you shift your energy and become open, then other people experience that, and that shifts them as well. It is hard for people to become aligned around a shared vision, especially in turbulent times, when people don't feel comfortable talking together and listening to one another.

How do we ever break the ice and shift behaviors? By introducing this process, people can share with each other and say, "This is what I'm noticing. This is what I'm experiencing. What are you experiencing? How can we create something together?"

I: What do you do to ensure your own personal leadership growth?

AVE: I've always been committed to my own personal and leadership development. To me, the most important thing in my work as an organization development consultant, an executive coach, or working with teams is my presence. I make sure that I am fully engaged and create an environment where people can work together toward exciting visions and achieving their potential.

I'm an avid learner. I always participate in leadership and personal development workshops and groups. I have a daily practice of reflecting on my goals, becoming centered, and writing. I exercise and focus on health. I study and read and am always exploring an area. I try to practice what I preach and I have a personal coach.

And finally, since I have the great opportunity of traveling around the world, I stay curious and take a lot of photographs. I reflect on leadership issues with friends and colleagues and I'm always open to learning different perspectives and enjoying life fully.

LEADERSHIP OPPORTUNITY:

One of the keys to being an effective leader is self-awareness. There was an interesting study reported in the 2007 _Harvard Business Review_. They asked about one hundred top leaders what they thought the most important factor in being a successful leader was, and they almost unanimously answered, "self-awareness." Most new leaders reported that they didn't have time for this. Actually, leaders can't afford not to develop this critical skill of noticing and making choices for effective emotional intelligence and the ability to effectively communicate. Begin by making it your intention to simply notice your response to differences and pausing before taking action.

LEADERSHIP SUCCESS:

I worked with a Fortune 100 organization. They had low engagement scores and their results were declining. People were fighting each other, competing for clients, and hurting the organization. It was an "every-person-for-himself" environment.

I started working with the executive team. They were unaligned and struggling with each other. This was happening throughout the entire organization. I see this often. The same thing happens in families; if the parents are fighting, it impacts the whole system.

I started with the top team and basically led them through my OASIS Moves™ process. I encouraged them to talk with each other. I supported them in listening to one another, speaking, and sharing their perspectives. We worked on creating an open-minded environment of respect. We got them focused on a shared vision for the organization and how they wanted to work together.

They began to work with their teams. We gave everyone this process of how to talk with each other, how to listen, and how to be open-minded. We had people identify what respectful behavior was for them, and within a short time, the whole culture changed. The next year, they had very high scores in engagement and they came up with some very innovative, creative ideas that moved the organization forward with greater market share and positive results.

I see this in many organizations where there is competition in the organization and we are able to shift the perspective so that people begin working together in service of achieving an aligned vision. It's critical to help people assume positive intent and to help them focus on how they can work together toward a common goal.

Teresa Ray
Fayetteville, Arkansas, USA

Teresa Ray is President and Founder of NWA Executive Coaching Solutions. She is an advocate for emotionally intelligent leaders who build energizing work climates and strive for effective communication and motivation. Her clients are developing and maximizing their leadership capabilities, communication, and emotional/social intelligence skills. These clients are learning new approaches to creating positive organizational climates while leading and motivating individuals and high-performance teams.

Teresa is also an adjunct professor at the University of Arkansas, facilitating courses in leadership. Prior to founding NWA Executive Coaching Solutions, she served as an Associate Director of Executive Education at the Center For Management and Executive Education at Sam M. Walton College of Business, University of Arkansas.

I: What is the most common challenge facing leaders today?

TR: The title of this chapter is *Trust Me, Trust Me Not,* but the full title would be *They Trust Me, They Trust Me Not*. Trust is the issue I find bubbling up to the top in most of the organizations I work with. I have a mental image of leaders roaming the hallways leaving trails of flower petals on the floor as they try to figure out if for today, those they are leading trust them or trust them not.

There are multiple reasons why organizations have been fractured in this economy. Those reasons include job loss, decreased profits, a high unemployment rate, decreased sales, increasing costs, and sometimes it's simply due to the insecurity that results from watching our own government leaders struggle with decision making. Although trust can be easily broken across the organizational chart in a normal economy.

Having a bad economy facing organizations today is like tossing a cinder block to a person who is already swimming and saying, "Hey, why don't you carry this along with you too." It doesn't help.

Leaders are constantly challenged to build and maintain a trusting environment. Trust isn't something that you just ask for; it's something you have to earn. I often hear comments in organizations such as, "We just need to start trusting each other." Well, it's not that easy. It doesn't work like that. We don't order trust like we would order a hamburger, and it's not as easy as a group decision to wear jeans on Fridays.

"Leaders are constantly challenged to build and maintain a trusting environment. Trust isn't something that you just ask for; it's something you have to earn."

John Maxwell writes about trust in his book, *The 21 Irrefutable Laws of Leadership.* He refers to it as the Law of Solid Ground, with trust being the foundation for effective leadership.

I couldn't agree with him more. And he's right—there are no shortcuts. There's no substitute for a trusting organization where employees work together in a positive climate. In this type of environment, employees will produce more, feel more valued, and have a greater sense of clarity regarding the direction of the organization.

I: What are some of the factors that cause trust to be broken?

TR: Under normal circumstances, without these added pressures, you have the human factor. We all have to work on building and maintaining trust and a trusting environment because we're human. You have feelings, and no matter how many times you hear someone say, "You need to leave your issues at the door, this is just about work," you're one person, and so you carry all of that with you.

You have feelings, and when someone doesn't keep their commitment, when you hear someone talking about an issue that you usually get consulted about at work, or when someone brings you news about a decision being made and you know that's your swim lane and you probably should have been included, any of those things which exist in all organizations start to build this idea that you can't trust others.

Then you start trying to fill in the blanks. *Why wasn't I consulted? Why wasn't I talked to? How did this happen and I didn't know?* Leaders are responsible for all of that kind of interaction, so if you ignore it, it begins to fester. It manifests itself in the form of disrespect. You start to notice people not respecting one another.

If left unattended, broken trust can create a cancer in an organization. These are normal behaviors we have with each other without any added pressures at all. We have to constantly keep ourselves in check. This is especially true for leaders, because you're being looked to as an example.

I: It's obvious, from what you have shared, that the issue of trust is very important. It's the underpinning and the power behind a leader getting things done within an organization. What does it take to build and maintain this trust?

TR: I'll tell you what I tell my clients, which is that trust is the end result. Trust is the end result of behaviors. We have behaviors that lead us to either trust or not trust others. All of those behaviors lead us to the end result, to the answer to the question, "Do I trust you, or do I not?"

The spoken word is valuable, but we know from research that no matter whose words you follow, actions are always going to trump what is said. People are always watching to see what happens. It's one of the reasons why I've included the exercise at the end of this interview for the readers' consideration. It is critical that people take the time to reflect in order to become emotionally intelligent leaders who are self-aware and who understand the impact of their own behaviors.

I: What do you personally do in order to grow your personal and professional leadership?

TR: I'm constantly seeking and participating in training for myself. I believe in the theory that a coach needs a coach. I don't think there's any leader out there who doesn't need someone they can rely on. I have many coaches and mentors I rely on and who I stay in touch with in order to constantly work on improving myself.

My goal in my company is to help people. That is why I'm in this business. There is no greater satisfaction than to help someone else excel in their career and in their life. If there's something out there that I can learn to add to my tool belt in order to help my clients,

I'm always seeking that.

I: It seems that you work across a number of different types of industries and organizations. Is there anything you're finding that's prevalent when it comes to current challenges in leadership or that is impacting any of the companies that you're working with now that you also see occurring across the board?

"Trust is the end result of behaviors. All of those behaviors lead us to the answer to the question, 'Do I trust you, or do I not?'"

TR: The challenges are across the board, but each industry is a little bit unique. You can imagine how the federal government agencies I'm working with are feeling with the push and the pull of what's happening with our political leaders who are struggling with making decisions. It affects everyone's job. No one is safe.

Those in the corporate world or small business world are feeling the pinch too. They are in the pressure cooker. There are challenges in every organization; that's kind of the nuts and bolts of why I do the work I do. I want to help them discover how their unique qualities can survive in the current economy or even in a "normal" economy, although I'm not sure that I have a definition for what "normal" is nowadays.

I'm driven by those challenges; it's why I do what I do. I'm motivated by their efforts. People that are reaching out to say, "Help us. We want to do better, to be better, and to survive this." I think I have the best job in the world.

LEADERSHIP OPPORTUNITY:

Behaviors lead to trust. Some of those behaviors include giving someone the benefit of the doubt, seeking clarity, a shared understanding, keeping commitments, aligning words with actions, doing what you'll say you'll do, apologizing when mistakes are made, sharing information, being transparent, trying to make work issues and decisions not personal, trying to work out differences one on one before they escalate, speaking up in meetings, sharing ideas and concerns in the larger group (not in the hallway later), and clarifying roles and responsibilities when people are in doubt.

Those are just some descriptions to guide you into a framework to think about the behaviors at your workplace that lead to trust. You can add to, change, or take away from that list.

Create three columns. In the first, list the behaviors you believe lead to trust. Then go to the next column. There are three different scores you can give yourself for every one of those items. Be honest. Here are the three scores: if you always do it, give yourself a 3; if you do it most of the time, give yourself a 2; if you never do it, give yourself a 1.

Stop there for a minute. Trust and how you behave starts within you. Now look at those scores and ask yourself, "What do I really do well? What do I excel or exceed at? What is successful for me that I should keep doing and possibly influence others through it?"

Then, take a look at areas where you think you need to step up. Have you had those hallway conversations because you didn't want to speak up in the meeting and give your thoughts? Did you escalate something before you really tried to work it out with someone else? Did you seek clarity, or did you just complain? What are you doing that you can do better?

Then, go to the third column. Now give your team a score and decide what the word *team* means for you. Is it a smaller group that you work with all the time? Is it the larger organization? Who are you rating? Define that for yourself.

How is your team doing when it comes to every one of those behaviors? This isn't to say that you go to them and say, "Here's where you're messing up." Instead, take a look at what your team does really well. Does the team as a whole do something better than you rated yourself? If so, there's some growing you can do there.

Does the team not do as well on something that you think is really important? Then the question becomes, "How do I encourage and influence my team to have these behaviors?" It's only through your actions and behaviors that you begin to solidify and build trust so that you can maintain it.

In larger organizations—and at times when an organization has been very broken—we've had group sessions where people will brainstorm behaviors. We get them all written down on a board and then break them into chunks.

I don't think there's any more important time than right now for people at all levels to step up and be leaders. The title *leader* alone doesn't make you a leader. The act of leading comes from everyone at some point. Organizations are held together by the skills and the strengths of those people.

LEADERSHIP SUCCESS:

Recently, in a larger organization, we went through this trust model and built it for the organization. We had everyone sign up to it, and it was an enormous success.

When you can get a large group of people—approximately forty people—together in a room and decide, "This is what we're going to do, and we're going to behave this way, so that everyone who works for us sees us behave this way," it's a catalyst for changing the climate in an organization and changing the culture and how it feels to work there for everyone.

For those people to come together and do that was tremendous for their organization. Of course, it goes without saying that it impacts their bottom line as well as the things we often overlook, like turnover. If someone doesn't feel good where they work, they're going to leave. That doesn't mean that's a good way to weed out the bad people—your good people will leave first.

The cost of turnover and retraining—that hidden number we don't talk about a lot—is extremely high. I know there are a lot of studies out there that attach a number to it. I don't have one for you because there are too many different ones, but we do know that it's costly (both time and money).

If you have to take your eye off of the strategic ball, you're not watching where the organization is going, you're just trying to survive.

Joyce Odidison
Winnipeg, Canada

Joyce Odidison is the world's leading Interpersonal Wellness Expert and has devoted the last two decades of her life to creating interpersonal harmony with programs such as creating Interpersonal Wellness Coaching and Armistice Day at Work. Joyce's unique approach is evident in her innovative Interpersonal Wellness System Model and Quotient Assessment Instrument.

She is an engaging keynote speaker, mediator, coach, and group facilitator who has helped numerous clients obtain optimal levels of interpersonal skills to work well, live well, and play well. Joyce is the training director of IWS Coaching Institute and President/CEO of Interpersonal Wellness Services Inc., a firm that provides organizational and employee learning and development strategies for workplaces and groups.

I: Joyce, tell me about your passion for interpersonal wellness. Why did you choose to make it your business focus?

JO: Have you ever been in a relationship where the other person drains your energy? They get upset easily, are constantly on the attack or defensive, are often irritated and moody, and as a result, those around them are always on guard—scared to approach or respond to them. I would describe this type of person as interpersonally unwell. The phrase, *walking on egg shells* would reflect the reality of this relationship.

The state of being interpersonally unwell is a very common situation—even more than I had ever thought possible. Many people are working hard to create healthy relationships and failing miserably because they are focusing on fixing the other person rather than getting well enough to contribute to the wellness of the relationship.

These people are recognizable because they have failed time and time again to make a go of their relationship, and now they are bitter. A conversation with them usually reveals their bitterness and disappointment with life and "other people." They see themselves as victims of those they believe have failed them, such as a current or ex-friend, spouse, coworker, in-laws, or even their job. These are interpersonally unwell people who will not be able to have a successful relationship until they first get well themselves.

Interpersonal wellness is a state of being interpersonally well enough to positively engage with another person and contribute to the wellness of the relationship even in less than ideal situations.

"It is common for those in interpersonally unwell relationships to make excuses for inexcusable behavior."

Becoming interpersonally well allows us to reach our full leadership capacity in all areas of our lives. It requires a high state of awareness of one's self and one's own level of wellness. It truly is the key to optimal wellness that enables leaders to live well, work well, and play well.

I: How can I know if my relationship is interpersonally unwell?

JO: There is often conflict in interpersonally unwell relationships, resulting in frequent disputes about minor related and unrelated issues. One or both of the parties are often apologizing, making amends, arguing, and defending themselves, their thoughts, their feelings, and their actions. They question their judgment, become unsure of themselves, think poorly about themselves, and become resentful of the other person. In some cases, they grow to become agitated and fearful of displeasing the other person, and they often become critical and judge each other harshly.

Often clients describe the relationship as draining, wearing them down, emptying them of who they are, suffocating, oppressive, and most times frightening. This kind of relationship is interpersonally unwell, and someone in such a relationship needs to get help or get out.

I: What if the other person in the relationship is not like that all the time? What if most of the time they are okay?

JO: There are stages of being interpersonally unwell. It is common for those in interpersonally unwell relationships to make excuses for inexcusable behavior. Those in such relationships become worn out, and their self-esteem depletes. Their thoughts and beliefs about themselves and their self-worth are gradually worn down. They undergo a gradual personality change in order to survive in the relationship. They eventually become interpersonally unwell. What they are indeed experiencing is the loss of their own wellness capacity.

I: You mentioned that interpersonally unwell relationships are more common than you had thought possible. Can you tell me where you encounter this kind of relationship in leadership?

JO: Unfortunately, interpersonally unwell people are everywhere. What draws attention to them is their lack of ability to contribute to the wellness of any relationship. They can be found in the workplace, on teams, on boards, in our communities, and often in our homes. Some are also good at faking it at work and unleashing at home or vice versa.

I had an encounter at my church recently with such an individual. I was sitting in a seat he vacated earlier, though I did not know that at the time as I was only there temporarily. He made it an unpleasant experience for me and everyone close enough to hear. I must say that I was actually quite shocked and appalled by the behavior of this grown man. Would you believe that I was momentarily speechless? The energy he exuded was so palpable and ugly I needed some time to call on my own positive energy to deflect his.

I really wasn't expecting this kind of blatant attack at my place of worship and it stunned me for a bit. My natural tendency is to counter attack, but here I was looking at the embarrassment of his wife and the other people sitting in the pew and those in front of and behind us. How very unpleasant. I can attest that I would not want to have too many dealings with this person. My clients often think that I don't encounter these challenges, but I do. I can assure you that interpersonally unwell people are lurking everywhere.

I: What can we do? How can one become interpersonally well enough to contribute to the wellness of their relationship?

JO: We are creatures of habit, meaning as we practice certain actions, they become character traits. This makes it more difficult to change our behavior without an encounter such as what one experiences while working with an Interpersonal Wellness Coach.

Becoming interpersonally well takes commitment, awareness, a high level of responsibility, and consistency to change some of the more ingrained habits and traits. This is something I encounter very often.

Becoming interpersonally well is a personal journey that occurs through awareness, responsibility, and skill development in areas such as responsible communication, conflict management, negotiation, and collaboration. It also requires one to expand their thinking about wellness to encompass all areas or life dimensions, such as spiritual, social, emotional, occupational, intellectual, environmental, financial, and physical.

I mentioned my natural tendency earlier because it's important to note that regardless of our personality type, natural tendency, or style profile, we can learn interpersonal skills and have the interpersonal intelligence to become interpersonally well. This equips us to contribute to the wellness of our relationships.

I: Am I correct in thinking that this requires perspective change and a major paradigm shift?

JO: Yes. Interpersonal wellness asserts that each of us can attain the level of wellness we desire in our life relationships. Only then can we be the kinds of leaders we are intended to be. Anything less robs us of our full potential and detracts from our greatness.

None of us are perfect, so any of us can become interpersonally unwell at some point. Our job is to ensure that it does not become a chronic problem that robs others of their own wellness. This is a fundamental aspect of understanding interpersonal wellness.

The interpersonally well relationship does not have a manipulator and a victim; each party shares the responsibility of assessing their capacity to contribute to the relationship wellness. This involves addressing real issues in a timely, respectful manner, being honest about your intentions for the relationship, knowing the kind of relationship you want, and comparing that to the personal values of the person you plan on having that relationship with.

I: This sounds like a very freeing and liberating concept.

JO: Yes, it is a very freeing and liberating concept. It takes the responsibility of an interpersonally unwell away from either party and makes it a collaborative effort. It also means that each person has the responsibility to make a decision whether they want to

"Becoming interpersonally well takes commitment, awareness, a high level of responsibility, and consistency to change some of the more ingrained habits and traits."

continue committing to the relationship's wellness. There is no cheating involved in this kind of relationship.

The level of personal wellness that each party maintains will determine their ability to be self-aware and to positively contribute to the relationship. If one is tired, then they should arrange to take a break, not snap at their partner. This kind of personal responsibility for self and action is not the norm, but it is essential to prevent us from becoming lazy and interpersonally unwell. It calls for all of us to develop Responsible Communication (RC).

I: Tell me more about the practice of Responsible Communication.

JO: Responsible Communication (RC) is a term I created to help my clients and coaches understand without doubt what we are working to attain. RC means one is well aware of their needs and takes responsibility to articulate their needs in a manner that will encourage others to help. It requires practicing stating your purpose and listening as well as knowing when to apologize if you are misunderstood or if your words cause hurt. It is not about manipulation or sabotage; it's about respect, negotiation, and collaboration.

When we are in an interpersonally unwell relationship, not only are we frequently upset with each other, but it is not good for our nerves or our health. It impacts our breathing, heart rate, pulse, blood pressure, stress level, and our immune system. It is critical that we see our wellness as more than just physical exercise and nutrition.

Interpersonal disharmony is the number one cause of most of our stress and stress-related diseases. In order to develop wellness, we need to unlearn many bad habits and begin fresh with a life scan. This requires looking at areas of our life that otherwise we may seldom consider.

LEADERSHIP OPPORTUNITY:

One goes about creating interpersonal wellness by assessing, developing, and maintaining their wellness in each dimension. Begin by segmenting your life into the following eight dimensions: spiritual, social, emotional, occupational, intellectual, environmental, financial, and physical. Then ask yourself the following questions as they relate to each area:

- How well am I doing in this area of my life?
- How are my realities in this area of my life impacting the wellness of those around me?
- Is what's happening in this area of my life good for my overall wellness?

I developed the Interpersonal Wellness Quotient (IWQ) instrument, and use it to help clients gauge their current level of wellness and what they want to attain. It is comprehensive and gives a quick, easy reference for the development and maintenance of one's wellness. It presents a roadmap to help clients work on the areas of their lives including self-esteem, personal style, culture, core values, beliefs, religion, faith, integrity, balance, hope, vision, and trust. (See the _Complimentary Resources_ for access to the IWQ.)

LEADERSHIP SUCCESS:

A client of mine in a leadership role informed me that she feels like a bear when she gets home from work. She doesn't engage in great conversations or spend quality time with family members, and is often even short with family members, because she has a great desire to be alone.

Upon further reflection, it was discovered that this very intelligent, beautiful, and caring woman gave far too much of herself at work, and as a result, there was nothing left for her family. She had very few structures in place for her own wellness. She exercised sporadically, indulged in binge eating, and became a vegetable in front of the television when she got home.

After completing the IWQ, she was able to set a goal for herself. As a result, she built in structures in her work days, assigned set times to respond to e-mails, and encouraged staff to set appointments with her assistant. She now feels that she has the wellness capacity to lead her department and her life more successfully.

Sharon McGloin
Kansas City, Missouri, USA

Sharon McGloin is the President and owner of Experiential Alternatives, a training and coaching company that focuses on personal growth and development as well as a variety of seminar topics from team building and conflict resolution to compassion fatigue.

She is also the Vice President of Performance Improvement at Marillac, a residential treatment center and psychiatric hospital for emotionally disturbed children ages six to seventeen.

Additionally, Sharon is an adjunct professor at Avila University in Kansas City and has taught on leadership from the inside out. Sharon is a lifetime learner and enjoys being a catalyst for others' growth and learning.

I: How do you help clients and leaders find the words to put with their experience and give meaning to what they're experiencing in order for them to become their most authentic self?

SM: Most of the time people have an experience and they don't really think about that experience very much, or they are sitting around thinking about something and coming up with words, but they don't have the experience to match it.

I try to sit down with folks and talk about what is going on in their lives right now—what kinds of experiences they've had—and then address how they can identify the words that match those experiences. I do that in a variety of ways. I may sit with folks and ask them a series of questions. I may encourage them to journal and to write out their thoughts.

Sometimes I encourage folks to take a retreat, and I hold some retreats at times. We'll sometimes offer a day-long seminar or a weekend retreat and take time to really dig into what's going on in their personal lives and examine their beliefs. This allows them to have the experience to go along with the words.

I: Based on what I'm hearing you say, looking at the internal is the key here it seems. Why do you feel people are so afraid to examine their shadow side and dig deeper for reflection?

"Most people carry around with them a great deal of fear . . . That fear can take over."

SM: I think most people carry around with them a great deal of fear. A lot of folks have limiting beliefs about themselves, such as: *I'm not even sure why I was placed in this position, I don't think I'm good enough, I don't think I'm smart enough,* or *I don't deserve this.*

It's amazing to me how many people have these limiting beliefs; most started when they were very young. When these people sit down and ask themselves, "How can I be more authentic in my life? How can I take the time to sit back and reflect about what's going on in my life?" it's a little scary, because they're going somewhere they've never gone before.

Often, when people begin to do that self-examination, it also requires some changes in their life. Sometimes those changes— although they're going to be really good—are going to be really scary. Those changes may require giving up people, places, or jobs in order to actually make that change and to dig in a little deeper.

What happens is that fear can take over and people stop. They don't keep going, they don't dig in, and they don't reflect about where they really are in their lives and where they want to be. I've seen that happen quite a bit.

I: Of course, without doing that, they can't really discover their life's purpose. You are a leader in the arena of helping people live in their purpose. How do you act as a catalyst to help them to do that?

SM: Let me tell you a story about why I chose the word *catalyst.* I had been working on my purpose statement for about five years. I came up with a purpose statement, and then I attended a training session with Jack Canfield. I went through his Train the Trainer program in order to teach his book *The Success Principles.*

We did an exercise about purpose, and I realized when we were working on this exercise that at that moment my purpose was to act as a catalyst to empower others to live in their own purpose.

"I can't make people change, but I can help them understand what their purpose is, why they are here, and what it is they want to do."

I can't make anyone do anything. I can't make people change, but I can help them understand what their purpose is, why they are here, and what it is they want to do.

A lot of times it's simply about asking the right questions. It might be by a little push and a little shove or maybe a little nudge. Maybe I should call them "nudge statements." They are used to push people out of their comfort zone a little bit, and then again, they go back to the shadow side.

I: When people remain in that comfort zone, they don't grow. I've heard you say that you help people experience this journey as an adventure. It's really an awesome thing that you're doing for people to deliver them into this new territory and help them determine what their real purpose and focus is all about.

SM: I've been having a great time doing just that. Most people want to grow and to change. I think the majority of people really do want to take a look at themselves and, if we can get past that fear and they can keep going, it's awesome to watch them have that "Aha!" moment. That's when they realize, *I am worth this. It is possible for me grow and change.* It's when they discover that they don't have to live like "this" anymore.

One of the questions I always ask people is, "When are you going to be sick and tired of being sick and tired?"

I: You speak to authenticity a lot. What does that mean to you?

SM: Authenticity, to me, means showing up to your life. It means coming to the table every day with who you are, whether it's the good, the bad, or the ugly. You have to approach your work, your personal life, your friends, your relationships, your colleagues, or whoever it is that you're interacting with on that particular day by coming into your life, showing up to your life, and being present.

I heard a great phrase recently. Someone said to me, "Did you know that the word *listen* has the same letters as the word *silent*? And in order to really *listen*, you have to be *silent*." When you are in your authenticity—when you are showing up and being present— you're listening. You're there. You're being real. People know that what you're talking about is real. You're coming to the table in your most authentic self.

I: When we're not living in that authenticity, we're actually robbing ourselves and the world of who we really are and the fulfillment of all that we can be.

SM: One of the things I talk about is compassion fatigue. A lot of people are caregivers. They give and they give and they give. In leadership roles, a lot of times leaders are the ones who work late, work overtime, and continue working. They give and they give and they get tired. They don't stop; they don't know when to stop.

It's important to understand that in order to be present in your life, you have to set clear boundaries about where you're going, and you have to do some of that inside work as well.

I: If we don't have that, we won't have it to give.

SM: Absolutely. When you do that, you are happy. You are grateful. You know the old phrase, *Is the glass is half empty or half full?* We need to approach life as though the glass is half full. In fact, you should probably approach life as if the glass is completely full by saying, "I feel full. I feel grateful. I am happy."

Another great phrase that I have heard is, *It takes just as much energy to be miserable as it does to be happy, so why not be happy?*

I: That is beautifully put. What do you do to ensure your own personal and professional leadership growth?

SM: I do quite a bit in that arena and I always have. I've always been a seeker. I think people who are seekers are looking and listening and reading and watching. I read all the time. I look for books that will help me grow as an individual.

I attend seminars, as I mentioned. Not only did I go through the Train the Trainer program, but Jack also has a week-long seminar called *Break Through to Success*. It's a personal growth and development seminar. I did that and I have to tell you that it was transformative. It changed my life. It was seven days of digging into my own stuff.

I believe that, as a leader, you shouldn't ask people to do anything

"As a leader, you shouldn't ask people to do anything that you're not willing to do yourself."

that you're not willing to do yourself. You should be doing self-examination at times. If you're going to ask the people you supervise, manage, or lead to do self-examination or to look into their own selves, then you have to be willing to do that as well.

LEADERSHIP OPPORTUNITY:

I have a great exercise that I use when I'm doing a seminar. It is called the Line Exercise and was originally developed by Jack Canfield. Here is how it works:

Let's say that there's a group of fifty people in a room. Everyone lines up across from each other and sits down in chairs, so each person is facing a partner across from them. We ask a series of questions, and we begin with the question, "Who are you?"

You might think that's a really easy question to answer, when in fact, it's a pretty difficult question to answer because you can say, "I'm a woman. I'm a mother, I'm a sister, I'm a friend." You can stay at the surface, or you can choose to go a little deeper. Generally, people start out by staying at the surface.

The next question is, "Who do you pretend to be?" That takes it down a notch, and now we're getting a little bit deeper.

Then, we move through more questions, such as those listed here:

- What is missing in your life?
- What do you want?
- What do you care about?
- What are you confused about?
- What is your purpose?

When I was doing this exercise recently, I came across a really great resource, which was a book called *Community: The Structure of Belonging* by Peter Block. He has a series of questions that he uses in organizations when he's working with developing leaders. I took some of those questions and added them to my exercise. To give you an example of some of those questions, he asks:

- What are the crossroads you are facing at this point in time?
- How much risk are you willing to take?

- What doubts and reservations do you have? (This is a great question!)
- What is the no or refusal that you keep postponing?
- What have you said yes to that you no longer really mean?
- What forgiveness are you withholding?

As we go through these questions, they get deeper and deeper and deeper. The last time I did this exercise, I had to get some tissues for folks, because it evoked some deep feelings for people. They really began to think about what is missing from their life, who they really are, why they're here, and what their purpose is.

LEADERSHIP SUCCESS:

Awhile ago I taught a weekend class at Avila University in Kansas City, and I was using the book called *Leadership From the Inside Out* by Kevin Cashman. In it he talks about seven areas of mastery, which are Personal, Purpose, Interpersonal, Change, Resilience, Being, and Action. When I designed the class, I focused mainly on personal mastery because I felt that was really important.

I watched one of the students in the class as we went through the exercises, because I had a series of experiential exercises that I used that matched each of the areas of mastery. I watched her bloom; she just opened up like a flower. I called her recently and I asked her if she would meet me for breakfast, because it had been about a year since the class took place and I wanted to see what she did with this and how it had impacted her life.

We sat down, and I said, "Tell me about which one of the areas of Mastery you felt really impacted you?"

She said, "I really identified with Personal Mastery, because it was about being authentic." Up to that point, she hadn't really considered the idea that she wasn't being authentic. But there was something about being true to herself that really impacted her, and she now has deeper relationships because of it.

Juracy Johnson
Ensenada, Mexico

Juracy Johnson is an expert in self-growth. She has studies in Life Coaching, Holistic Coaching, NLP, and is currently studying Business Coaching to help others develop their full potential.

A National and International Workshop Leader from Mexico with an MSc in seismology and a passion for life and self-discovery, Juracy is the author of more than one hundred scientific and self-help articles.

"As a cancer survivor since 1993, I made a choice: I absolutely refused to be a victim. I love life and I am grateful for the support I received from my husband, my family, and my friends during that difficult time. I love people, and helping them reach their dreams is one of my goals."

Currently, Juracy is a coach, a professor at the State's University, and also a caregiver to her husband who sustained a traumatic brain injury in 1999. She coaches and offers workshops in Mexico and Latin America. She also participates in conferences regarding natural hazards all over the world. She is the Founder of Mujeres Con Propósito (Women With a Purpose). She has been offering workshops and coaching services since 2003. "I a passion for helping people overcome their challenges and guiding them into having a joyful life," states Johnson.

In Mexico, there are no support groups for caregivers of adults with brain injuries, so Juracy is starting a foundation. "Thank God my husband has me to love and support him, but not everyone has the same opportunity. Caregiving is the hardest and most rewarding role of my life. We can all be survivors instead of victims no matter how hard the situation

seems to be. We just have to learn to live life differently and keep loving and enjoying it."

I: What are the greatest leadership challenges you see today?

JJ: People are surrounded by information about the world facing chaos at this time. A lot of us are reacting to that information by letting it guide and drain our emotional, physical, and spiritual energy. Just as we have the ability to feed ourselves with negative energy, we also have the amazing power to create by transforming that negative energy into positive feelings and actions. It is simply a matter of deciding which energy you want to give and receive.

You've got to be MORE than the situation that presents itself in your path of life, have focus in your heart and values, and then lead accordingly. That is why it is so important to surround yourself with like-minded, positive people who are driven to action. You can start by joining a Facebook or Yahoo! group, or even a Web site to find more people who want to give positive energy into everyday situations. You just have to decide which energy you want to give out. It is how you face everyday challenges that makes the difference in your life. The key is to always stay strong while remaining calm when challenges appear in your path.

I: What does leadership mean to you?

JJ: To me, leadership is conducting your life by your own principles and values while on the path to success. It is my belief that we come into this world with all the information we need to support ourselves and other people and to become whoever we want to become. This is called the "self." Sometimes, as we are growing up, certain situations occur that do not allow us to release the leader we have inside of us. We need to rediscover that leader and believe in ourselves to achieve what is ours by birthright. This is a good opportunity to hire a professional life coach or self coach who can help you motivate yourself to greatness.

I: In your opinion, what are the main qualities a leader must have or develop?

JJ: One of the main qualities is communication. A leader has to be able to be a good communicator to themselves and to others. Leaders must be able to express their thoughts and ideas with confidence and enthusiasm in such a manner that the audience interprets and adopts the message as their own with the same intention in which it was transmitted.

Another great quality is charisma—a special kind of magnetism that makes people's presence noted.

I: Is one born with charisma, or can any person acquire it?

JJ: It is my belief that some people are born with it and all others can acquire it. Remember, you can be all you believe you can be if you take action! A good start for developing charisma is to smile! A smiling face is an attracting face.

Other qualities of a leader include being a good listener (a part of the communication process), understanding people, integrity, sensitivity, and having a strong spirit, among others.

I: How does leadership impact your specific niche today?

JJ: My niche is directed to empower women to live their life as full as they will allow their potential to develop; sometimes this involves taking gigantic steps, other times it means taking baby steps. That's fine! Each one of us is delightfully different, but so is the sunrise! Sometimes it takes a bit longer for the sun to come out because the fog will not let us see it. Other times, it seems that the sun comes up earlier, bright and shiny. But the sun always comes out!

It is important that women feel safe and confident. That is why I have founded Mujeres Con Propósito (Women With a Purpose). It is an association to help Latin-American women push themselves beyond their limiting beliefs to reach their goals.

In Latin America, many women are still afraid to move ahead and become leaders in their lives. Some feel overpowered by the strong image they have of men, while some fear that if they are perceived as strong leaders, they won't be loved. This could be due to past experiences or because they were brought up to think that men are supposed to be the breadwinners and women must stay at home or settle for low-paying jobs that allow them to come home and make a home-cooked meal. They don't realize that they can take care of their families and still maintain a great paying job if that is what they truly want. They can also make a decision that would largely improve their quality of life if they are living in an abusive situation by moving out of that "status of comfort" that is causing them harm.

I support women so they can rise above those feelings of fear by building up their inner strength and self-esteem through a powerful and positive process of coaching and empowering workshops. I travel throughout Latin America when I am called, and I am so grateful to live the unique opportunity to assist people to regain control over their lives, to open their hearts and love themselves, and to transform their ideal into reality while enjoying the journey. Everyone deserves to shine!

I: What do you do to ensure your personal and professional leadership growth?

JJ: I keep myself up-to-date with the new theories and practices of personal and professional development and remain an active member of associations with the highest levels of training and experience such as The Coach Exchange (TCE). This is where coaches can exchange experiences and knowledge in a very professional and friendly atmosphere in order to grow as leaders and to guide others in the most ethical way. I also continue to advance professionally by taking courses and workshops with internationally recognized personalities while developing my own techniques that help my clients to carry out their personal, professional, and organizational goals.

I keep up-to-date with current situations that might be of interest to people by reading and sending surveys. Something that is very important to me is having daily quiet moments to develop strength and to be centered within so that I am ready and have the energy to serve others. People enrich my life, and I am always learning from them too!

I: As a coach, caregiver, and mother, how do you manage time? What would you suggest to other people who are transitioning between the job they have and the life-job they love?

JJ: Each day, very early in the morning, I set up my priorities—the main one is advancing on my next book—and from there I take it down to things like going to the store to buy oranges. As the day progresses, I might have to change my schedule depending on the aides—if they come to help me with my husband or if they fail to show up—and I do it with love.

I take control of my circumstances, and if it means that I don't advance on my book, that is fine with me. I enjoy the time I can spend with my loved one. We might watch a movie or do some physical therapy. I know there will be more opportunities for me to continue writing the following day or the next. As a mother, I have always supported my daughter, and now she is studying for her BSc degree in the field she has always dreamed of, but she is in another state. We communicate frequently, and I am very proud of her and of her achievements.

While transitioning between careers or jobs, it is important to put the same effort to one as well as the other. Treat them both with love; if you've been in your old job for a lot of years, start collecting pictures of your family and souvenirs you've received at the job you are trying to leave in order to help you shift slowly into your new opportunity. There might be some days when you will not be able to sleep eight hours or you will eat at a fast food restaurant. I am not encouraging you to do that, I am just recommending that you love yourself and accept that you are working very hard at this moment; you are making some changes to progress in order to have the life you want. Give yourself a pat on the back even if you didn't have the time to exercise that day. Avoid criticizing yourself for not being able to do all that you wanted to do today. You will get there and you will succeed because you are focused on your dream, you are persistent, and you are taking action!

LEADERSHIP OPPORTUNITY:

Feel pretty and able because you are! If you don't feel that way for the moment, your clients, coworkers, and others will sense that and take their business elsewhere. Hire a life coach, a self coach, or attend a workshop to help you realize you are smart and beautiful!

Lift your spirit! Avoid watching negative news and listening to negative people. If you are with someone at work or at a social meeting who is criticizing someone or is in a negative mood, gracefully excuse yourself from the situation.

Role play. Focus on the present character: if you are spending time with your family, give them your full attention; if you are working in a project, reserve time for research and use that time only for that project.

De-clutter. Get rid of things you don't need or love. Do you absolutely, definitively, surely love that painting? No? Why is it stashed in your closet? Sell it or give it away. Only keep the things you really love or need. This will save you time when you need to clean your office, home, etc.

Have a small, sacred place just for you! No matter how small, it is for "me-time." If you can't find even a corner for you to enjoy in your own home, find a small, quiet coffee shop or library where you can go at least once a week to be by yourself, either reading a book or writing one! This will help you engage in your life purpose.

Allow your spirit to have control. Meditate for at least fifteen minutes a day.

Change the way you express yourself. Use the word *situation* in place of the word *crisis.* Instead of telling yourself, "I am losing time," say, "I am investing time."

Hush the negative internal dialogue. Fill your thoughts with whatever beauty you are seeing at the moment. Focus on how magnificently green the leaves on the tree are or how pleasing the feeling of the sun is on your shoulders, etc.

Remain grateful. Be thankful for the people who support you, for your lovely pets or plants, for the beautiful sky, etc. Embrace all the beauty that surrounds you and give thanks.

And last, place cups of love, feathers of peace, and seeds of prosperity in your heart to make your journey easier.

LEADERSHIP SUCCESS:

Female leaders are increasing in number! Great examples are Dilma Roussef, Laura Chinchilla, and Cristina Fernández who are leading Brazil, Costa Rica, and Argentina respectively. Paula Santilli is President of PepsiCo Beverages in Mexico, and Mariela García is General Manager of Ferreyros in Peru. While these are some of the topmost examples, there is still a long way to go to ensure gender equality. The first step is to change the limiting mind-set many women have. It can be done. These examples represent role models indicating that women can go as far as they decide to.

Many women have not realized that they are already leaders by managing roles such as a mother, daughter, wife, and cooking magician, making miracles with any small amount of money. They plan, organize, participate, and resolve situations that arise every day. And this doesn't include the fact that they might be studying or working outside the home as well. As women play these different roles, they are developing a new set of skills they didn't even know they could have!

Laura Pedro
Camas, Washington, USA

For over twenty-five years, Laura Pedro has helped leaders of Fortune 500 companies stimulate breakthroughs in their businesses. Working primarily with senior executive teams, her clients tap the power of human commitment by simultaneously addressing strategic business issues and the leadership and culture issues that surface during implementation.

Laura is living proof that the leadership principles she teaches actually work. Beginning with an unknown startup, she and her partners built that company to become part of a nine billion dollar consulting firm, where she was Vice President.

Her present company, Alder Associates, LLC, fully integrates strategy and transformational capabilities to help its clients achieve their most ambitious goals.

Laura's latest initiative, Lead and Flourish, is dedicated to developing women leaders, encouraging them to "play full out" at a time when the world needs more women leaders.

I: Can you tell us a little bit about the source of leadership and helping women play full out?

LP: One of the most dangerous misperceptions that we have is that leadership is a trait that exists in certain people and not in others. Just as I have blue eyes and you have brown eyes, we think that one person is a leader and another is not and never will be. That's a very disempowering assumption. It's much more empowering (and true) to think of leadership as a set of conversations to be mastered.

The reason I say that is because I think it's important for everyone— women in particular—to know that real leadership begins when someone is willing to say or do something to obtain an outcome that other people want too; it's taking a stand for a future that supports the common good.

Rosa Parks didn't have the authority to change segregation laws in the southern United States. She wasn't militant in her attitude, nor was she the kind of eloquent, charismatic person that people think of as a leader. She was tired and sore from her work, and when she was ordered to give up her seat to a white man, she refused. When the bus driver threatened to call the police, she said, "You may do that." When the police asked her why she refused to stand and let the white man have her seat, she told him, "Because I don't think I should have to." One woman's simple act in 1955 was the catalyst for sweeping change that moved a whole country closer to living its ideals of freedom and equality.

"Real leadership begins when someone is willing to say or do something to obtain an outcome that other people want too; it's taking a stand for a future that supports the common good."

All of us have things that we care about deeply, and when we look out into the world, we see places where something is just not working. What is really needed is for all of us to step up, to take on something we see that could be better, and to help other people embrace that possibility. That is how we move in the direction of a more workable world.

Another point is that when we think about the source of leadership, it's really important to recognize that leadership requires that we get out of our own way. What I mean by that is when we think about something we want to change or something that is important to us, often the very next things we think of are the reasons why not. We're afraid that we're not capable or that we'll look foolish or fail. We may tell ourselves, "There are real leaders out there who should be doing that."

We have to be able to recognize those fears as fears. Leaders aren't stopped by their fears. They keep looking out into the world to see what's working and what's missing and stay focused on that for which they stand.

I: What are three key competencies that are required to truly be a leader?

LP: These are not in any order of importance because I think they're all equally important.

Three Key Competencies Required for True Leadership

#1: The Willingness to Always Be a Learner—You need to have enough humility to learn and be coached by the world, because when you're taking on something new, you don't have the experience to know exactly what will happen when you try your first step. You can't say, "The last time I tried this, I did it this way, and it worked great. I'm going to do that again."

Breakthroughs are facilitated when we are willing to be coached. Even when we are open to coaching, we tend to be selective about whom we will allow to coach us. Sometimes it's an expert or a mentor. Are we willing to be coached by our team members or subordinates? Taking it a step further, are we willing to be coached by the world?

Being coached "by the world" means that we are committed to taking feedback, no matter where it comes from and no matter how it is delivered—even by someone who is criticizing us—and make it useful to help us be more effective in achieving that to which we are committed.

#2: The Ability to Listen and Engage Other People—Any leader who is taking on something that he or she wants other people to participate in needs to be able to listen and engage other people. It's as though your job is to give away your vision without giving away your ownership or your responsibility for the outcome.

"Your job is to give away your vision without giving away your ownership or your responsibility for the outcome."

What I mean by giving away your vision is to begin by articulating what you think is important—what you stand for—and then allowing the magic to occur when other people take that on as their own vision and begin to add nuances to it. They make it better, and together you will have so much more impact than you could by yourself.

#3: Resilience—You need to be clear about what you're committed to and know that there will be setbacks, because you don't know exactly what's going to happen as you launch this initiative. It's important to use those setbacks as the source of invention instead of allowing them to be the things that stop you.

I: How do you take that resiliency and use it to stay on course? As you said, that can be hard sometimes.

LP: It really can. As a leader, people are counting on us to exhibit grace under pressure, and we can develop the discipline necessary to do so. There are three parts to using major setbacks, whether at work or at home, to get to the next level. The first is to honestly confront the circumstances and really look at the facts in the matter. The next thing is to focus on your commitment rather than reacting to the circumstances, and the third is to then look at what is possible.

I'll share a story from my own experience that centers on the notion of being clear about what you're committed to versus the interpretations that you have that could stop you. It was the biggest lesson I've ever had about this principle.

My son was twelve years old and he was diagnosed with leukemia. At first I was in shock. All that there was to do was to put one foot in front of the other and make sure that he got to the doctor and so on. For the first week, they had him in the hospital and they were trying to induce remission. After that, he was treated on an outpatient basis and we would go back and forth to the hospital almost every day. About two weeks into that, I woke up one morning and that old song lyric, "Is that all there is?" was going through my head.

I realized that I was really depressed. When I looked deeper, I realized that what was depressing me was a feeling of helplessness—that there was nothing I could do to make sure he got better. I thought that was a mother's job—to make sure that her children were safe and taken care of and living a long and healthy life. As I looked at the situation, I could see that the truth was that I couldn't guarantee that he would get better. Then I asked myself, "Okay, given that, what am I committed to?"

I realized that what I was really committed to was that he have the best life he could possibly have as long as he was alive.

When I shifted my focus to giving him "the best possible life," it was a miraculous experience that gave me a pathway to actions that I couldn't see before. After doing some research, I learned about the role of laughter in healing. I learned about the role of diet when people are going through chemotherapy, etc. I had to shift my own relationship to the circumstances because I realized that my depression wasn't going to help my son at all. It worked because he's thirty-seven years old and a father now.

I want to talk for a minute about the biggest enemy of leadership. The one thing that will kill leadership faster than anything else is resignation. It's that feeling of helplessness, hearing yourself say, "This is just the way it is and it will never change. There's nothing I can do about it."

We all fall prey to it from time to time, but it's important to realize that there are some antidotes to resignation. One is curiosity—the spirit of inquiry—learning from what happened, rather than resisting it. The adventure of experimentation is so important in leadership because leadership is about birthing something new.

Another thing that I feel is equally important is gratitude—taking stock of what you have. When I was little, I hated going to bed at night because I didn't want to miss anything; life was an exciting adventure every day. Unfortunately, as we get older we tend to lose touch with the wonder and mystery of life. Gratitude can help us stay in the present, remain in touch with how great our lives really are, and continue that experience of joy, wonder, and excitement.

Third, it is crucial to take stock of what you're accomplishing along the way. Sometimes leaders get so focused on what's next and what's missing. It's important to see those things, but it's equally important to celebrate our accomplishments.

LEADERSHIP OPPORTUNITY:

At the quantum level, matter is a potentiality that is manifest in relationship to the rest of life. In the same way, each of us is a unique expression of possibility in the world, and the world needs us to fulfill that possibility in action.

Take a moment to ask yourself the following questions and then act on your own commitment:

- Whether in the work I do or in the world at large, what possibility do I care about deeply? What do I think needs to change?
- What would it look like for me to take a stand for that possibility?
- Am I willing to confront whatever could undermine my leadership?
- With whom could I have a conversation that will begin to make my initiative real and concrete?
- Whose support do I need to make this successful?

This chapter has focused on the way of being that sources leadership, and these questions can help you generate that way of being. Now get into action and do the things that need to be done!

LEADERSHIP SUCCESS:

An example of resilience: I was working with a new product introduction team, and they were committed to getting a new product to market faster than they'd ever been able to before.

They were about two-thirds of the way into their nine-month goal, and they found that one of the electronic devices was incapable of transferring electrons fast enough to be able to give the device the level of performance it needed, which was a really big breakdown. They found themselves up against the laws of physics.

Most people would have just said, "I'm sorry, I guess we're not going to make it," but one engineer was just absolutely committed to doing everything that she could do to find a way around this problem. She engaged the team and they realized, _If we slanted that channel, the electron wouldn't have as far to go._

They cut the time to market in half. They were successful because she was dogged in her commitment and flexible in her strategy.

Michael Simpson
Provo, Utah, USA

Michael K. Simpson has over twenty-five years of practical experience in business and management consulting, leadership development, and executive coaching. He has consulted, coached, and advised some of the world's best leaders and companies. In his role as a consultant, advisor, and executive coach, Michael has partnered with C-level and senior executives to improve their business results and leadership performance. Some of Michael's key clients include Frito-Lay, Marriott Corporation, Nike, John Deere, Procter & Gamble, Kroger, Nokia, Verizon, New York Life, Prudential, and ExxonMobil.

Michael's expertise is in the area of one-on-one executive coaching, clarifying strategy and goal execution, executive leadership team building, talent and performance management, and improving human potential. He's been a Senior Consultant with FranklinCovey's Global Delivery Practice for sixteen years. He has been on the faculty for three years with Dr. Stephen R. Covey and Dr. Ram Charan and FranklinCovey's Executive Leadership Summit. Michael is also the Global Director of FranklinCovey and Columbia University's partnership with their Executive Coaching Certification Program. He has certified leaders worldwide in the executive coaching methods and tools used by FranklinCovey, Columbia University, and the International Coach Federation. He is also the coauthor of *Unleash Talent, Coaching for Greatness,* and *Seeds of Greatness*.

I: What are the critical breakdowns and barriers that you see when it comes to organizational and team execution?

MS: If you go to business school, study finance, or even as you move up the ranks within an organization, you're primarily trained on how to address finances, how to look at things from an MBA's perspective, and how to craft strategy targeting formulation, planning, and analysis. People aren't trained in how to address the execution of goals; however, strategy is the easier job—execution is the more difficult aspect of leadership.

In their book, *Execution: The Discipline of Getting Things Done,* Dr. Ram Charan and Larry Bossidy state that 70% of all strategies fail because of what they call the "execution gap." The execution gap is the inability for leaders and teams to execute on what is most important. Most leaders became infatuated or enamored with the problem of execution, and the research shows that 70% of leaders and teams consistently fail to execute on their most important goals. People don't fail to execute because they lack vision, passion, are lazy, stupid, or defiant; they are busy with what they call "the real work of the day-to-day" tasks and priorities.

At FranklinCovey, we leveraged execution research from Harris Interactive and McKinsey & Co, and used our own internal global execution research from a survey called Execution Quotient (xQ) in which we assessed approximately 350,000 leaders worldwide. We focused on why leaders and teams fail to execute on their most strategic priorities. The data showed that there are four critical breakdowns common across all teams and organizational levels.

Four Critical Leadership Barriers

Barrier #1: Not Knowing the Goals—When teams were asked, "Do you know the goals of the organization?" 44% responded, "Yes." But when asked to match those goals with key measures and timelines, only about 15% could do so.

The number one breakdown is that there are either too many goals, the goals are not clearly communicated, they are written in a format that is not measurable or too broad, they are too vague, or they are simply not cascaded effectively down to the front line.

Barrier #2: Not Knowing What to Do Behaviorally—If people don't have absolute clarity on the most important goals and priorities, then many don't know what to do to achieve those goals. Surprisingly, only 15% of people actually focused on the right actions and behaviors that would drive to goal achievement.

Many people are working hard in the fury of the day to day, but most are just working on those things that are most urgent and not necessarily those things that are most important.

Barrier #3: Not Keeping Score—Many leaders and teams are tracking measures and metrics that move, but they are primarily focused on lagging measures or indicators which are tracked after the fact and are too late for any real course correction. It is analogous to driving a car down the road while looking through your rearview mirror. Many people disengage from their game of work because they don't know what game they're playing, they don't effectively engage the "players" in the game, and the "players" don't know what they would proactively do to effectively impact the score. About 88% of leaders and teams didn't keep score at all or they didn't do it in a way that was driving proactive behaviors to influence the right results.

Barrier #4: Not Being Held Accountable—Many people and teams were held accountable to the right goals, measures, and metrics, but accountability got slippery, permissive, or weak because leaders were only holding their teams and subordinates accountable for goals each month approximately 26% of the time. Accountability was viewed as coercive, abusive, punitive, and as a method of creating a fear-based culture to get results. Under this guise, results were short term, but this approach ultimately drove the wrong kind of culture, values, and sustainability for effective commitment and lasting change.

Another underlying barrier to successful execution that kept showing up in our research was what we termed "the whirlwind." The whirlwind includes all of the urgent tasks found in a person's day-to-day job. Some call this "the real work" needed to maintain the operations and includes urgent activities that keep you from operating on your most important strategic goals and objectives, including meetings, phone calls, e-mails, interruptions, administration, and other daily demands of time, resources, and energy. Flawless execution is not simply accomplishing a goal; it is accomplishing your most important goals in the midst of a one-hundred-mile-per-hour whirlwind.

The nature of change is dynamic, constant, and swift. The whirlwind is not going away. Global financial crisis has led to a psychological downturn with most organizations simply seeking to survive. Leaders need to address key factors, such as strategic direction, competitive threats, strategic partners, leveraging talent, improving quality, costs reduction, innovation, renewal, research and development, and investing in new opportunities for profitable growth. If we get myopically drowned with all of the short-term urgencies and distractions, it is difficult for the organization to succeed over the long term.

Leaders will always have more good ideas and opportunities than capacity to execute. There's lots of good, but success is about differentiating between what's good and what's truly great.

I: How can teams solve this execution gap?

MS: The Four Disciplines of Execution™ help organizations cascade their top goals and measures. These four basic principles of execution are a behavior-based strategy for change. They are logical, sequential, and work in all situations. For the past eight years, I have applied The Four Disciplines of Execution™ within many organizations, and I have seen how this process applies in various industries. It is transformational.

The outcome offers absolute clarity to define goals and measures that are directly aligned with the organization's top goals. Once embedded, they offer a framework, a set of principles, and a language for executing strategic goals with consistency. Each team member knows the key performance measures as well as how to drive the desired results within their respective functions.

The Four Disciplines™ of Execution Overview

Discipline #1: Differentiate between the good and the great; focus on the wildly important goal. If you have between one and three goals for a team or an individual over a one-year period of time, you can accomplish one to three goals. When goals start increasing to between four and ten goals, the level of accomplishment will drop to between one and two. If your goals jump to more than eleven to twenty, you literally won't be able to accomplish any goals. That's why this approach doesn't work.

You have to narrow the focus. There should be no more than between one and three strategic goals per team or per person at any time. Leaders and teams need the discipline of sequence, priority, and narrowing the focus.

You need to get goals cascaded down to where execution actually happens—you need to have clarity at the organizational or war level. Then you have to cascade it down to divisions, functions, cross-functions, or team levels. The lower-level goals have to help drive the parent or upper-level goals. It is essential to deconstruct the goals down to functional teams and individual contributors.

The goal also has to be written in a measurable language in what we call the "From X to Y by When" format. Without clear, valid lag measures in your goal statement, the same goal will mean one hundred different things to one hundred different people.

Discipline #2: Act on the right lead measures or leading indicators. This discipline helps leadership and teams identify and isolate the right consistent player behaviors, best practices, key targeted actions, and how-tos that drive toward goal achievement. This is the Golden Rule of execution. This discipline propels teams, leaders, and individuals to understand and identify what's most predictive and influential in terms of behaviors to drive your goal to successful completion.

Discipline #3: Create a compelling players' scoreboard. Most people disengage from a game or a goal if they don't know what game they're playing, if they don't know if they're winning or losing, and if they don't know what to do each week to impact the goal.

A player's scoreboard helps engage and motivate players to win. The scoreboard should be simple to understand and visible to all. It must have visible both the stated measures for the goal and the right weekly or daily behaviors to proactively drive the goal.

Discipline #4: Create a weekly cadence of accountability. The weekly accountability review engages the team in a nonauthoritative, nondirective, and noncondescending way. It offers a check-in to create peer-to-peer transparency, openness, and accountability. In the session, the leader acts more like a supportive coach, asking the players to do the heavy lifting and having the players make commitments. It's a brief time to report back and see what the leader and team members can do to remove barriers and advance the goal each week.

The weekly accountability session is offered for twenty minutes—same time and same place—to help spotlight, review, plan, and act on those big rocks to help stave off and fight against the intense demands of the daily whirlwind.

When leaders are able to execute their plan in a disciplined way, to set the right strategic choices and priorities, to hold people accountable, and to do it in a respectful and collaborative setting, they find great clarity of purpose and contribution.

LEADERSHIP OPPORTUNITY:

Leadership is not about being perfect; it's about building leadership influence through modeling the right behavior, focused performance and results, creating a high-trust culture, and helping to align and unleash talent. This can be done effectively by holding leadership conversations that can ignite the passion and unleash the power within those you lead. Greatness already exists within all people. It's our job as leaders to help bring that greatness out.

Begin holding leadership conversations today—formal or informal, short or long. Look for opportunities to turn a normal conversation into a leadership conversation. Begin abundantly calling out those things that can be a game changer for others, linking a critical business need and their vision, passion, strengths, and possibility.

LEADERSHIP SUCCESS:

I partnered on a consulting and coaching engagement with Neil Pryor, the Senior Vice President at Frito-Lay in the U.S. Northeast Region, to explore his business needs, his key strategic priorities, and challenges. I asked, "What's going to be a game changer for you in your business?" He chose to focus on revenue growth in their high-margin business called Single Serve Flex (SSF).

They needed to increase their SSF units by 15% year over year. While they had some key areas that sold SSF well across the board, they were not consistently doing well. We brainstormed how each district team would need to drive the goal to achievement.

I took Neil and his leaders through the intense process of prioritization and rank ordering the right lead measures. We came up with three: 1) Focus on the top ten accounts. 2) Have perfect displays and racks every time. 3) Own the space about ten feet from the cash register in order to help drive unit sales. They established a weekly cadence of accountability and provided weekly reviews to monitor, track, report, and improve results.

By following The Four Disciplines of Execution™, Frito-Lay Northeast Region went from number six to number one in the U.S. in SSF unit revenue growth. Defining strategy is critically important. A bad strategy executed well will simply lead to failure more quickly. The real challenge is to create a culture of focus and flawless execution. If you can execute, you can do anything.

Sylvia Lafair, Ph.D.
White Haven, Pennsylvania, USA

Dr. Sylvia Lafair is a business leadership and communications expert as well as President of Creative Energy Options, Inc., a global consulting company that optimizes workplace relationships.

Her book, *Don't Bring It to Work*, has won multiple business book awards, and she often is quoted in leadership blogs as well as in the *Wall Street Journal, Forbes,* and *Fortune* magazine. She has years of experience with all levels of management as an executive coach, conflict resolver, and team builder. Her retreats for women in business—based on her book, *Gutsy: How Women Leaders Make Change*—are in high demand.

Her state-of-the-art program, Total Leadership Connections, is now in its tenth year and has transformed the lives of thousands by showing people the power of increased workplace productivity utilizing her "Results Through Relationships" principles. She delights audiences with her storytelling ability and capacity to make sense out of office politics.

I: Can you share with us two or three of the most important core competencies for being a great leader?

SL: I think the key core competency we all have to look at is to be a leader who knows him or herself. Without that, we are going on scavenger hunts with very little to help us, and we see the results of that in leadership everywhere—people are avoiders or they become persecutors and act like bullies, then things don't get done.

Knowing ourselves is a lifelong process. What does "knowing yourself" mean? It means learning to observe, understand, and transform our behavior so that when our buttons get pushed, we don't react inappropriately. If we know ourselves, we can stay centered and be effective.

Another competency is compassion. Seeing the tugs and pulls that another is experiencing and having the observation and social intelligence skills to relate to it, understand it, and offer support, coaching, and mentoring.

I: Your work is so paramount and focused on actually coaching and training great leaders. What do you see that is missing in leadership training programs today?

SL: There are two things that I think are really clear. One is what we just talked about—there's really no training about the internal, personal part of us. There's personal power and there's positional power. Sooner or later, positional power will get people in trouble if they haven't looked at themselves. In leadership training, we need to give people the understanding of who they are and their relevance.

The other thing that is critical in leadership training is to really understand how systems operate. Engineers recognize that idea on the physical plane; we need to know it on the mental plane as well. It's how things connect.

We need to begin to look at how changes in all cultures are adapting to what we live in daily—challenging times. That's not going to change. We're in a speed race and we need to be exceptionally fast. We also need to know how to connect the dots. That is an important part of understanding how the economy fits with the emotions of people, how we make decisions, and what has happened in the past that connects with the present. This helps us to create a better future.

I: In your opinion, can you be an integral part of a team and also lead?

SL: Let me answer this one with a story. We were doing some team building, if you will, working with one of the major orchestras in the country. We were invited to go on their summer tour through Europe. I heard Dvorak's Seventh Symphony fourteen times in twelve days, which was very interesting. I watched the orchestra members walk out of different concerts saying, "This one was better," or "That one wasn't good," or "This one wasn't on cue," and so forth. My ear isn't that well-tuned; it all sounded wonderful to me. So I finally started asking, "What was the difference?"

> *"It's all in the timing. Knowing when to speak up and when to hold back is one of the most important talents a leader can develop and enhance."*

The difference was the conductor. When he put his hands up and when he put his hands down things changed. It was nonverbal, but they all paid attention. What I took away from that is that it's all in the timing.

With leadership, you are part of the team. You can't be totally separate, because you're there. Your presence is there. It's silly to say, "I'm not part of this," if you are the leader. It's all in the timing. Knowing when to speak up and when to hold back is one of the most important talents a leader can develop and enhance.

That's how you can be part of a team and have your input, but there are times that, as the leader, there are several things you need to be mindful of. One is that in a meeting, the leaders go last. They wait. They don't share all of their ideas even if they have the best idea; they wait until the others have spoken. If a leader speaks first, people will align around their thoughts because they want to please and to be accepted. Occasionally you'll get a naysayer, but usually it stifles the dialogue. If the leader goes last, of course, what they have to say is important. It's all in the timing.

I: What is the leader's responsibility as a mentor?

SL: When we work in the business world, we tell the people we're working with to please remember this: *Work is not a rehab facility!*

I think there are times we forget that when we're mentoring. It is a leader's responsibility to mentor, and he or she will usually have a team of direct reports. But there's a very fine line. The key here is that you mentor, and mentoring, for me, is really about asking questions and leading people to their own new understanding—their own "aha" moment.

If someone is having an issue that has to do with something at home, such as a sick spouse or a sick child, you do talk about it and ask how they're handling things, what they need, and what could be done differently. Of course, if it's above and beyond your area of expertise, you need to have someone available that they can go to for assistance. The mentoring that you do takes place by asking questions.

If someone doesn't get it, then you have to look at things like a performance improvement plan, and that's a whole other issue.

Giving and getting feedback is one of the biggest responsibilities that a leader has as they mentor. My theory is that the more you ask open-ended questions and accountability questions that people have to answer, the better you are as a mentor.

I: What are some of the key areas for leaders to pay attention to so that they don't burn out?

SL: There are a couple of major things to consider when it comes to leadership and burnout. One is—and we're going back to the beginning of what I said—knowing yourself and knowing when to take time. It is also important to have someone you can talk to.

I believe that the most successful leaders are those who have an advisor—today we call them coaches—who they can go to when they're starting to feel that they're falling down the rabbit hole. As a leader, it's important to spread around the successes in terms of having other people take part in what is happening.

Leadership in the twenty-first century is more about collaboration than the individual. In the old days, the Lone Ranger or the Superman or Superwoman would do it all; today it's about finding ways to get other people to help when we feel we have hit our wall. People are there and can help.

It takes a lot of real security in one's self for a leader to ask for help, and I think that's really key. It's different than pointing your finger and delegating, "You do this, you do that." Instead, saying, "I really need some help here," is critical.

I: What do you personally do to ensure your professional and personal leadership growth?

SL: I believe in vacations. A vacation can be two hours to vacate and to empty your mind and think about something totally different. Instead of picking up a leadership book, I will pick up a good, juicy novel. I love words. I love the way words are put together. I will read something from Isabel Allende or someone who has a great capacity with words. That, for me, indirectly empties my mind.

I take a lot of walks. I'm a really good walker. Or, if I'm at a point during the day where I feel that I'm at my limit, I will close the door, say, "no calls," and sit and do some deep breathing.

> *"Leadership in the twenty-first century is more about collaboration than the individual . . . it's about finding ways to get other people to help when we feel we have hit our wall."*

I'm very fortunate because my business partner is also my spouse and we're pretty simpatico in terms of giving each other room. As a female, if I'm really at that stress point and I feel like crying, I'll cry. It's a good release.

LEADERSHIP OPPORTUNITY:

In my book, *Don't Bring It to Work*, I have pulled together the thirteen most common patterns in the workplace that we acquired from what we learned in our original organization—the family. I haven't seen this research anywhere else in the way I have compiled it together.

Here's what happens: When stress hits the hot button, we revert to patterns we learned as kids in our original organization, the family. When stress gets really high in the workplace, sometimes we kick back to what we originally learned for security and survival. If your boss is behaving like a baby, he or she is, and if you're acting like a thumb-sucking toddler, you are.

I would like to suggest going to my Web site www.sylvialafair.com and taking the Pattern Aware Quiz, to find out which patterns you have the biggest propensity to operate with. There are thirteen of them. I can make a case for each one for myself, but there are really two or three that are the most common for each of us.

There are two exercises to help you begin looking at your language when you're in that stressed place. What we do is we go to "always" and "never."

For example, I was with a colleague who knows about this concept, and I was super stressed. I was talking about someone else and I said, "She always does that. Every time I ask, she always does that."

My colleague said, "It sounds like you're getting locked into a pattern." I took a deep breath, I closed my eyes, I put my hand on my stomach, and I thought to myself, *Let me go back and find an* _earlier time when this "always" or "never" feeling was in my consciousness._

It only takes a few seconds to do this. You can usually go back to an earlier time when the stress was that great, and you can begin to connect the dots, seeing how that past situation is affecting the present situation.

Doing this eases the present situation. You find new ways to work with it. When I talked about how this person "always" behaves that way, it was because there was a lack of accountability. I was able to look back into an earlier time in my life to see how that happened with someone else and how it made me feel disenfranchised, which was how I was feeling with the current situation.

LEADERSHIP SUCCESS:

This success story is about a woman from Ghana. She and her husband had moved to Atlanta, and I met her when she was in process of moving back to Ghana. About four years ago, she came to do our "Total Leadership Connections" program (TLC).

After returning to Ghana, she flew back and forth to Pennsylvania to complete the program. Through her time in "TLC," she began to see how the disenfranchisement her mother experienced had impacted her own behavior. She realized she tended to stand back when challenged by a man.

In the fourth and final session of "TLC" she made a major decision to run for Parliament to become a voice in the government.

At that time there were very few women in public service. I was concerned and thought, _I hope this doesn't become a major disappointment for her._ She was very clear that she had looked at how patterns from her past had created the stop points in her present behavior.

My husband and I spent two weeks in Ghana campaigning with her and giving it the best shot we could. It was an exciting time and I'm proud to report that she did win! She is now a Member of Parliament, and her voice is being heard in very positive ways.

The added beauty to all of this is that she set up a scholarship in her mother's name in the town where she grew up, to enable girls to attend college and have their voices heard also.

Linda Cobb
Melbourne Beach, Florida, USA

Linda Cobb is widely respected for the coaching and training services she provides to healthcare leaders and their teams. Her joint focus on self-discovery and awareness of others helps executives grow through transition, make tough decisions, and co-create meaningful results. Linda is the author of *Directions: A Guide For Life,* a flipbook of tools and insights for busy executives who need "at a glance" learning as well as visual reminders on their desktop.

Linda is a personnel psychologist, and a graduate of Coach U and the Arbinger Institute Coaching Mastery Program. She holds certifications in Neuro-Linguistic Programming and Trauma Debriefing among others, and is a registered corporate coach and member of the International Coach Federation.

"Coach Cobb" currently offers life and leadership coaching, executive team coaching, assessments, and seminars. She works extensively with healthcare executives and her goal is to help caring leaders emerge in this industry with the creativity and clarity of purpose to reverse the poor health of our population.

Linda states, "Leadership's biggest challenge is people, and people's biggest challenge is change. Leaders who help people master change will create lasting positive results."

I: Can you share about the personal responsibility that we, as leaders, have in order to fulfill our purpose?

LC: Absolutely. Most of us don't recognize, or are not aware of, how we actually obtain the results we get in our lives. It's very key to understand the fact that we're continuously co-creating outcomes with others. How many of us would take better care of ourselves if we knew that someone else was depending on us? The nature of leadership is that you are affecting others all the time, and it has everything to do with the results that you get in your own life.

I: Your goal is to help leaders discover their higher purpose and direct change for themselves and their organizations—to actually create a force for good in the world. Can you speak to that role, particularly in the arena healthcare? How do you work with them to help them become aware of the energy they possess?

"Human energy is a lot like electrical energy. It has enormous power and its uses are infinite, but only when it's part of a connection."

LC: Successful leaders know how to focus their own energy pretty well to achieve goals; that's how most of them got into leadership positions, and most of them have learned along the way that results are created through people. It is a Management 101 concept. Yet many of them have a blind spot about how their own energy affects other people and the results they get through others.

Once we establish that they want to maximize the power of human energy in their organization, I begin with a couple of simple questions. One is, "Are the results you're getting where you'd like them to be?" From there I ask, "What is it like to work for you?" That one often stops the discussion because, honestly, many leaders don't know. They've never been asked that question, so it gives us a place to begin.

Often, that leads us to discussing former bosses and what it was like to work for that person, whether they trusted that leader, and why or why not. I ask, "Did you give them your best performance?" If it wasn't their best performance, we talk about why that was the case. This helps them begin to see their own leadership from the eyes of those who report to them.

From there, I coach them on how to focus their own energy in a way that connects with the energy of others in the organization. I do that by using the analogy of a circuit board: Human energy is a lot like electrical energy. It has enormous power and its uses are infinite, but only when it's part of a connection. I let them know that there's a process they can implement to harness and direct human energy in their organization and that there are practices they can put into place that will continuously strengthen those connections and sustain that internal environment.

The circuit board is a good analogy because it too has a specific purpose, design, and parts, and it requires energy to function. The leader designs and maintains that organizational circuit board, and

if any connections are broken, the whole thing breaks down. It is their job to ensure that the circuits keep flowing. I challenge them to become that master Chief Energy Officer through series of steps they follow.

I: What do you do to ensure your own personal and professional leadership growth?

LC: I am a continuous learner. Lately I've been looking at a lot of the sports coaching material because, in working with leaders, they're typically pressed for time. They need very efficient practices. I found a lot of wonderful tools while researching in the sports coaching arena.

An interesting thing happens in the workplace when contrasted with the sports world. In the sports world, athletes spend roughly 95% of their time practicing and about 5% of their time actually performing. Conversely, in the business world, we spend about 95% of our time performing, and about 5% of our time practicing.

My goal with leaders is to help them install practices with their teams so that they practice as they perform, because that is how the current workplace operates. It's wonderful when we can go to an off -site retreat, get with our team, and really practice, but that opportunity is very rare. We have to have tools and true practices— just like any athletic team—that we practice on a daily basis. In fact, in the current workplace, we must have practices that create the performance we want. Therefore, the practices and tools must be very effective.

I: Your specific niche and area of real interest is healthcare. Could you share a little bit about how leadership is impacting that area of specialization?

LC: I think very creative approaches are going to emerge out of the crisis we're in right now. Quite honestly, most of the healthcare executives that I have been in contact with are very aware that it was headed for a train wreck—that this was certainly on the horizon. There's absolutely no doubt in my mind that creative things are going to spring out of this.

As we know, it's a very heavily regulated environment. What I have seen consistently with the leaders that I work with in healthcare—which again are the seekers—is that when people aren't seeking solutions that help the greater good, they are not as creative.

There is a real desire to turn around the health of our population. It's been going on for a while, but the strength and commitment is very strong—people aren't leaving the healthcare arena even though it's very difficult right now. They're really rising to the occasion and coming up with very creative solutions.

One thing that I think is very interesting is that we've been a very hospital-oriented culture for a long time. Gradually, insurance companies began to eclipse revenues of hospitals. In my experience, hospitals are typically very committed to the population and to their communities. How we use those facilities and the expertise that resides there is going to shift a bit. I can absolutely see that. I can see more outreach that's going to happen. I can see people going out into their communities far more than waiting for them to access a hospital.

"What I have seen consistently with the leaders that I work with . . . Is that when people aren't seeking solutions that help the greater good, they are not as creative."

There is creativity and a willingness to look at alternative methods and really embrace those—to bring those into the hospitals and the healthcare communities and join with many more alternative practices. This is a new movement. It isn't drawing back on the thought of, _How can we just stay afloat and take care of our own?_ It's becoming, _Embrace that, go forward, and come up with solutions for how we're going to make this work for the populations we serve._

The people who are servant leaders, which is a term used often, are going to have to know how to impact communities. They're thinking much broader than their hospital or their particular unit; they're thinking in terms of communities, which I'm very excited about.

LEADERSHIP OPPORTUNITY:

I coach leaders to think less, which sounds a bit counterintuitive. I want them to block out the noise and focus narrowly—to actually think fewer thoughts. The average person is bombarded with daily distractions that scatter their focus. That squanders enormous energy.

To think less means to narrow your focus to those few powerful elements that will take you where you want to go. Again, I have to have simple practices that people can install quickly, so they have to be short. "Think less" triggers people to realize, *I don't need to go down every path and follow every link of every e-mail that people send to me.* To think less means to focus only on the path that leads to your destination.

LEADERSHIP SUCCESS:

I was working with a leader who was very frustrated and felt that his team wasn't on the same page as him. He didn't understand why they couldn't see it the way he did.

I was new to working with this person, but during the first couple of sessions I had listened a lot and learned how inept he felt his team was. He was actually planning to quit and seek another position which he felt would better suit him and would help him achieve his goals. I started by coaching him to stop seeing his team members as the problem. Again, I used the question, "What is it like to work for you?" This caught him off guard.

We really started looking at some of his behaviors and the fact that he chose not to mentor anyone and pretty much chose to see people as the problem. Then I worked to help him see what it was like to work for someone who sees you as a problem. He really got that, and eventually he began to see his team differently—to see their talents.

As a result of his being willing to see their talents, they in turn began to trust him, and he stayed. The organization went on to have the highest revenues they had ever produced that year.

It still gives me goose bumps. It's one of my favorite success stories. It illustrates yet another reason why I love working with leaders. Sometimes a simple question can make such a huge difference, even for the ones who don't appear coachable in the beginning.

Kathryn McKinnon

Marblehead, Massachusetts, USA

Satisfied clients have been singing the praises of executive life coach, Kathryn McKinnon, since 1992. As a former Harvard Business School Executive and teacher of the HBS Career Management Seminar, Kathryn has thirty-two years of corporate and business experience helping hundreds of women executives, entrepreneurs, professionals, and open-minded men create order out of chaos in managing their life, career, and time.

The strategies and tactics she shares will help you create and save the time to do more of what you want and end each day with a sense of accomplishment. She can help you develop the inner tools and strategies to stay organized, focused, grateful, and engaged in your life.

I. What do you do to ensure your personal and professional leadership growth?

KM: As an executive life coach, I must lead by example, so I continually invest in and take care of myself to nurture my body, my mind, my intellect, my heart, and my soul.

I am also an online marketer, the owner and operator of two businesses, a professional singer, a wife, mother, and volunteer. My husband (of twenty-two years) travels a great deal, so I have to make the most of my time. I have to stay current with the latest trends. I regularly read new books, invest in self-development programs, and learn new tools and techniques to keep my coaching and businesses on the cutting edge so that my clients will experience faster transformation and success with their results.

Success rituals are incorporated into my personal and professional day. For example, I monitor my thoughts regularly. I focus on my goals and what I want to accomplish rather than all the things that could go wrong. Those simple activities eliminate most of the potential stress in my life and help to keep me on track.

I take time to renew my body with exercise and nourishing food. I spend time with those I love and who energize my spirit. I surround myself with people who are smarter than I am and who inspire me. In addition to having worked at Harvard Business School, I'm also a graduate of their MBA Program. I maintain ties to the school as a mentor to women MBAs and I keep up-to-date with evolving trends in business and leadership.

I spend some portion of each day in quiet thought, meditation, or prayer focusing on my intentions and what I want to create so that I can continue to live my purpose. I get plenty of rest, especially when my energy begins to feel depleted. I take time to have fun, to do things I enjoy, and to appreciate the gifts and abundance each day brings.

One of the ways I express creativity and innovation is by designing and marketing custom-made jewelry with a purpose. Singing professionally also helps me express my creativity and renews my spirit.

Over the years, I've learned systems and formulas to use my time effectively so I can accomplish my goals. I recently wrote and published my first book on Amazon in less than ninety days. It also made the best seller list for its category within sixty days.

Triple Your Time Today: 10 Proven Time Management Strategies to Help You Create and Save More Time! was written to share my best strategies and tactics with others who need help managing their time. The book discusses proven strategies, success stories, and tips to help you become more effective with how you think about your time, how you spend your time, and how you can save time each day.

All these activities ensure that I continue to grow personally and professionally each day so that I lead by example as I help executives quickly transform their own lives.

I. How does leadership impact your specific niche or area of specialization today?

KM: As an executive life coach, entrepreneur, singer, and Internet marketer, my business is about creating transformation for my clients' lives, careers, and time.

The style of leadership I teach helps executives, professionals, and entrepreneurs to change their mind-set, to change their perspective on their own ability to reach their goals, and successfully lead their own lives.

I help executives understand that what they think and say, how they feel and respond, and how they choose to spend their time are all aspects of life that we actually control. That's where I teach my clients to direct their focus. That's where the transformation takes place.

"Everyone is capable of transforming any personal or professional challenge as long as there is an awareness and a commitment to change."

Everyone is capable of transforming any personal or professional challenge as long as there is an awareness and a commitment to change. The issues and challenges that clients face manifest themselves as stress, chaos, disorder, guilt, indecision, confusion, fear, worry, self-sabotage, lack of confidence, denial, distraction, unwanted behaviors and habits, and physical symptoms. These all lead to being stuck and unable to move ahead. These issues result in an inability to reach your goals and dreams or to be an effective manager, executive, and leader. These issues can be transformed using the processes, strategies, and tools I share.

You may not believe you have control over your life, your career, or even your time because of the demands that others make of you; however, you do have control over how you think about any situation. You have control over what you think about as you spend your time. You have control over the priorities you choose. You have control over what you say, how you feel, and how you respond to a situation before you take action—before you take the time to do anything. When you create this kind of mind-set, you begin to live with a greater sense of awareness and freedom about the choices you make and what you choose to do with the time you have.

I: What are the greatest leadership challenges you see today?

KM: There are three primary leadership challenges facing us today:

Three Leadership Challenges

#1: Time—The first challenge is not having time to meet all the demands and needs that our job, business, colleagues, clients, customers, friends, and family place on us and still have enough time to meet our own personal needs, goals, and dreams.

#2: Efficiency—Another challenge is learning how to become more efficient with our time by eliminating distractions and interruptions

#3: Productivity—The third challenge involves learning and implementing ways we can leverage our time to increase our productivity and to improve our results.

I. What are some strategies we can use to create more time for ourselves and find extra time in our day?

KM: In *Triple Your Time Today!* I discuss ten strategies to help you create and save more time. Here are a few of those strategies:

Strategies to Help You Create and Save More Time

Develop the right mind-set. We all know we have twenty-four hours in every day. That means we have 1,440 minutes or 86,400 seconds in every day. Do you know how you spend those seconds each day? Were you focused on your goal and what you were doing, or was your mind somewhere else? If you're not getting the results you want with your time, maybe it's because you're not focusing on the right things.

You can become far more efficient with your time when you become consciously aware of what you're thinking about each moment. Developing the right mind-set helps you to focus on your goals.

Do the right things at the right times. Your time is a precious commodity. Once it's gone, you can never get it back. If you're doing one thing but your mind is somewhere else, then you're not doing the right things at the right times.

Know what you want to accomplish. You must know what you want to accomplish in order to do the right things at the right times. Set short– and long-term goals and take note of your accomplishments each day to achieve the results you want.

Systemize and take control over your time. It's not how much time we spend on something that matters. Rather, it's how we spend the time we have. When you put systems in place to organize your personal or professional life, and then you keep track of how you spend your time, you can repeat the process over again. That habit of systemizing processes can free up your time so you can accomplish more with the time you have.

Use your time and your learning style to your advantage. You learn best using one predominant learning style. That means you require time to process information in your own unique way to help you experience and function in the world. According to research by Dr. Howard Gardner from Harvard University, there are three predominant learning styles: visual, auditory and kinesthetic. If you know your individual learning style, you can use it to your advantage and accomplish more in less time.

Find extra time in your day. We all have the exact same amount of time in each day. If you don't learn how to make the most of your time, you'll always struggle to accomplish everything in your business, your career, and your personal life.

Here's a simple but effective activity: Take an hour of your day when you have a goal to complete and track your activities during that hour using a stopwatch. After the hour, record how you spent your time—the goal you set, what you did, what you thought about, etc. If you track your time for a day, you can save yourself five to fifteen minutes out of every hour. That's potentially seven to twenty-one days of free time a year. **What could you do with all that extra time?**

Let go of stress and overwhelming feelings. Living in a state of constant stress is the greatest waste of time. The problem with being stressed is that it's overwhelming; you may not even realize you're living in that state. Stress interferes with your ability to think clearly, to make decisions, and to take steps that can get you out of the confusion and allow you to take back control over your time.

Use sleep to save more time. Do you know you have approximately twenty thousand thoughts a day? Unfortunately, roughly 80% of those thoughts are negative. Negative thinking gets in the way of achieving the results you want because negative thoughts create doubt and fear which create hesitation, immobility, and inaction. If you go to sleep with the positive intention of solving or coming up with a workable solution to a problem, your mind will suspend its negative thinking and find a way to deliver a solution to you.

LEADERSHIP OPPORTUNITY:

Leverage means doing more with less. Leverage allows you to work smarter, not harder with your time. Do you know how to leverage your time so you can get the most value from it?

Doing the laundry, checking e-mail, cleaning the house, shopping for groceries, doing yard work, picking up the kids, doing the taxes, and bookkeeping are all activities many of us have to do. However, some of these activities just keep us busy, not productive. We could learn to leverage our time with some of these tasks.

The next time you're about to engage in an activity or job, ask yourself these questions: Is this activity worth my time? Is there something else I could be doing that would be a better value of my time?

If you're not leveraging your time—if you're not spending time on things that are equal to or greater than the value of your time—then you'll forever be wondering how to find more time.

LEADERSHIP SUCCESS:

Ali came to me as a forty-year-old professional woman recovering from breast cancer. She had recently undergone surgery. She was in a great deal of pain from the procedure and was experiencing limited mobility in her arms.

She had the kind of life everyone envies. She had a loving husband and children, she lived in an affluent community, she was well-educated, attractive, and she had a great job, but it was stressful. She had everything—except her health and a positive attitude.

During several meetings together, Ali learned how to focus on the more positive aspects of her life and even began to see the cancer as a blessing—as a gift to help her transform her attitude and her life. She let go of the things she couldn't control and began to focus on changing the things she could control, namely her attitude, her thoughts, her feelings, and her choices.

During our coaching sessions together, Ali's pain dissolved and she regained full mobility. She quit her stressful job and decided to focus on living a life of great health and gratitude. She developed a much more positive attitude. Ali now believes she deserves to be happy and is living a healthy, vibrant life. She works in a less stressful job and remains cancer free.

Duane Reed
Denver, Colorado, USA

Indiana born, raised, and educated, Duane Reed has been using his listening and leadership gifts since childhood. From setting the emotional tone in his kindergarten class to achieving the honor of being the youngest Eagle Scout in Indiana, and eventually managing over sixty employees, Duane's skills have resulted in drawing over 8,500 audiences to his training, coaching, and consulting company over the past twenty years.

In 1998, Duane founded Inside Success Training and Consulting, Inc., and has facilitated proprietary and customized assessments leading to leadership and management trainings for NASA, U.S. Army recruiters, and hundreds of companies ranging from Fortune 500 companies to small businesses. Duane conservatively estimates that he has consulted or trained in over seven thousand organizations and for hundreds of thousands of individuals, managers, executives, and business owners in some 120 different industries.

I: How do you define leadership?

DR: I use characteristics as the methodology for defining leadership. Characteristics define who is and who isn't a leader. It's not positional power. It is situational.

Leadership is driven by characteristics, which are a belief system that one has about one's self. It is also a lot about what leadership is not, obviously. Leadership is not about dictating to people; leadership is about involving people in the process of decision making and helping them to achieve their potential. I can't stress that enough. Leaders help other people achieve their potential in multiple areas, not just around a specific skill or function within the organization itself.

I: Can leadership be developed, or is this something that you feel we're either born with or not?

DR: Some people will argue and say, "He's a born leader," or "She's a born leader." I don't totally disagree with that, but I also know that it can be developed. How do I know that? I've been helping other people achieve their leadership potential since I was a Boy Scout several decades ago.

"Leadership is not about dictating to people; leadership is about involving people in the process of decision making and helping them to achieve their potential."

The development of leadership characteristics is not something that's necessarily taught in our school systems or in college. Some people automatically rise to the top and take leadership roles. They see a void and they fill it. And that's great, unless the void is filled with some form of "pushership" which I characterize as a continuum between dictatorship and abdication.

I: How can one enhance their own leadership skills?

DR: It is kind of a self-actualization process. It is consciousness. It is becoming aware of what is and isn't leadership, and we accomplish that by the use our own life experiences. Just ask anyone who's ever had a job, "Can you identify the best boss you've ever had? What were the characteristics of that boss? Identify the worst boss you've ever had. What were the characteristics of that boss?"

They will have long lists for you of the characteristics that they like and don't like. Invariably, those folks are identifying the positive characteristics of a strong leader and the negative characteristics of a weak leader. Then it becomes about how to integrate positive characteristics into one's own behavior and eliminate or let go of the characteristics that don't serve a leadership role. By the way, these same people will also tell you that they were more productive and viable employees when working for the strong leader.

I: What do you think are the biggest challenges facing companies and individuals in a leadership role, and what characteristics are the most important in order to be able to overcome those challenges?

DR: I'm really glad you asked me that. It would be really easy to sit here and say that in listening to the business owners I've been working with over the years this seemingly epidemic sense of entitlement that permeates the workplace is the biggest challenge today. Instead, I'm going to say that the greatest challenge today is people who can't differentiate between what leadership is and what it is not.

What that means is that for people in a leadership role—those who have position and power within an organization, a title, and responsibilities—it's how they go about fulfilling those responsibilities that determines whether they're a good leader or a bad leader. For instance, leadership that is dictatorial, transactional, or based on reward and punishment is not good leadership. Those leaders may get the job done—they may even get the right result—but it's short-term.

> *"Failing as a leader helped me to understand what I needed to change about myself in order to become a better leader."*

I know this through my own personal experience. Thirty years ago I managed sixty people but I was not a good leader. I got the job done, but I also had very high turnover. Some of the characteristics that I used were favoritism, a double-standard, and not walking the talk—the incongruence between, "Don't do as I do, do as I say." Those are not good leadership characteristics.

That's how I discovered the characteristics of good leaders. The tool I used was list making. Pain drove this. Failing as a leader helped me to understand what I needed to change about myself in order to become a better leader.

It involved creating a list of all my negative characteristics at play in the workplace, understanding what the exact opposite characteristic of that negative characteristic was, and then becoming conscious and aware of when I acted out negatively. Changing that consciousness little by little helped me behave more optimally as a leader.

I: You have coined or titled this work "MicroLeadership™: Evolving From Pushership to Leadership." Can you share a little bit more about those terms that you use to describe this discovery?

DR: Over the years I've conducted assessments within organizations including NASA, the United States Army, many of the recognizable

Fortune 500, and even small companies that I work with now. These assessments ask, "What do you like? What don't you like? What would you change about this process or that department?" The overwhelming majority of individual contributors have one thing in common: they do not want to be micromanaged. The term *micromanagement* is very recognizable. People know what it is. They've been micromanaged in some form or fashion in their lifetime.

MicroLeadership™ is the opposite of the negative style of micromanagement and pushership. Micromanagement is pushing people to do the right thing, in the right way, at the right time, for the right reason. Another negative management style is abdication. Employees who get abdicated to are not in touch with or connected to the organization very well. They think they're doing a good job until one day they get their annual review and they learn that eight months ago they did something wrong but no one told them. That's abdication.

My strategy is MicroLeadership™. My clients attain a higher level of connectivity to their employees by being proactive and paying attention to the "smaller" personal needs that make employees individuals.

Everyone wants to be heard. Everyone wants to be understood. Everyone wants to be trusted. Everyone wants to be actively involved in decisions that affect them. These needs are real, and a MicroLeader is someone who understands those needs and does the necessary things to help those personal needs be fulfilled proactively. The more proactive a MicroLeader is, the less reactive management is meted out.

Based on my own experience, when the personal needs of employees are fulfilled, they perform better. They can achieve a level of optimal productivity. I don't care what the industry is or what kind of work it is, for me that's almost an absolute.

I: You have been so predominant in the field of helping others discover how to enhance their leadership. How do you do this for yourself?

DR: My quest in life is to integrate MicroLeadership™ principles into the moment-to-moment thinking and day-to-day living. I do this by taking a conscious, personal inventory at the end of an interaction with another person. What could I have changed or done differently that would have been better for them? Not what would have been better for me, but what would have been better for the other person? Just taking the time and investing that effort on a regular basis—asking, "What could I have done better?" or, "What could I have done differently for that person?"—could make a world of difference in productivity in the long run.

Many people in leadership roles do not take time to reflect on how to improve day-to-day interactions or work on evolving from being self-centered to others-centered. To me, another part of being a MicroLeader involves being proactive in understanding the career goals are that each individual has. What do they want to learn? What's important to them? Knowing what employees want to learn, helping them learn it, and then finding the opportunities for them to use what was learned is the epitome of good leadership.

I: So it's a constant process of introspection and evaluation as to how you're interacting with others, and then prompting them to their best potential. Is this something that you feel is important on a regular basis?

DR: Having an introspective nature daily is very important. It's also okay to ask the other person, "What could I have changed or done differently that would have helped you better understand what I was asking you to do?"

An example of this could be in the delegation process. Leaders are constantly delegating to get things done, and that process of delegation needs to take into consideration the personal needs that people might have while communicating clearly what the expectation is or isn't. That's part of MicroLeadership™.

I spoke earlier of my characteristic list; I ended up with over sixty-six different items on that list. These were things I identified about myself that I knew I could improve upon. An example of this exercise is included in the Leadership Opportunity on the facing page.

I can fool myself. I can justify and rationalize almost anything, and as a result, sometimes that self-analysis isn't enough. Sometimes I need more input from other people about what their perception is, because their perception of me as a leader is more real than my perception of myself as a leader.

LEADERSHIP OPPORTUNITY:

Determine which characteristics best describe you. The terms in each column are opposites. This is not by any means a complete list; I encourage you to add to it. If you do, always add to each side. You may come up with opposites that are different than the ones listed below. Remember, growing in consciousness is the goal. As you go through your day and/or at the end of each day, assess when you could/should have used the more positive opposite behavior. Work each day on displaying more of the positive behaviors more of the time.

SUSPICIOUS	TRUSTING
PRONE TO GOSSIP	TRUSTWORTHY
POOR COMMUNICATOR	STRONG COMMUNICATOR
INDECISIVE	DECISIVE
DEPRESSED	CHEERFUL
FEARFUL	COURAGEOUS
UNKIND	COURTEOUS

LEADERSHIP SUCCESS:

I'm working with a company that has two owners who are quite young. This company is now achieving a revenue run rate each month of well over a million dollars. It is a very fast-growing company. They have never had any kind of management training, leadership development training, or communication training. I'm working closely with this company right now and helping them to develop the skills internally to be able to help their people fulfill their potential.

I will tell you that in the period of time I've been working with them, revenues have gone up, sales have gone up, and the culture within the organization is healthier than it has ever been. People are happier. They're showing up on time without having to be prodded. There's more of a sense of team there than there ever has been. There is a waiting list of people who want to work there. It's fascinating to see what happens to a company when the culture improves.

That managed growth is a very difficult balance to attain within an organization.

Anastasia Montejano
Yuba City, California, USA

Anastasia Montejano, ACC, CPIC, PMP, is creator of the Visionary Leaders BreakThrough program, an experienced multinational leadership consultant, a conscious reinvention coach, intuitive, and best-selling coauthor. As founder of the Conscious Reinvention Movement, she stands at the forefront of a groundbreaking vision to see one million people move from career to mission by aligning with their destiny's path.

The Visionary Leaders BreakThrough is where this vision meets reality. Through a unique gift of powerful intuition, practical leadership experience, conscious reinvention coaching, and the ancient wisdom of numerology, Anastasia helps leaders break through the obstacles that are keeping them from their full leadership, income, and career potential in order to discover the great work they were meant to do.

I: Can you share about the term *conscious reinvention*?

AM: Conscious reinvention is a call to remembrance for individuals across every level and industry to remember how powerful you truly are, to reconnect you with your soul purpose, and to help you see that your dreams and talents are there to be used to fulfill the destiny work that you came here to do.

The number of people who are unfilled in their professional lives is epidemic. Gallup polls show that 73% of people in the United States are completely disengaged at work. Globally, in places such as Japan, it is as high as 93%. In addition, a recent Parade poll showed that 61% of people would not choose the same career if they could do it all over again.

The Harvard Business Review recently reported these startling statistics:

- One in three high-potential employees admit to not putting all of his/her effort into their job.
- One in four believes they will be working for another employer in a year.
- One in five believes that their personal aspirations are different from what the organization has planned for them.

If you've ever felt a longing for more meaning and purpose through the work that you do, then know you are being beckoned into a higher truth of who you are, why you are here, and what you came here to do. Your greatest work uses your pain, gifts, and dreams to serve others, and in turn brings you true abundance. It's time to remember who you are—to unleash your full potential and become the solution to make a difference in the world around you. You've been given your dreams, talents, passion, and abilities for a unique purpose—a purpose no one but you can fulfill. If you're not using your talents where you are, then why not?

What would your life look like if you stepped solidly into that knowing? What's holding you back from living your highest expression in the world? What stories are you telling yourself about what you can and can't do?

Your dream job is waiting. You don't have to trade a life of purpose for a paycheck. You *can* have both meaningful work and success. If you're hiding, ignoring, or stifling any part of yourself, then it's time to come clean about what's really important to you and how you want to use the talents you came into this life with. Every situation you're navigating is there to serve you—to either nudge you forward to your next chapter of greatness or to get you back on the path you are meant to be following. It's time to remember who you are, to explore what's defined you up to this point, and to rediscover what is being awakened in you to make a difference in the world around you.

I: Have we all come here with a purpose or mission?

AM: Yes! Many of us don't consciously recognize or acknowledge that we have a specific life purpose, yet our soul knows what we are here to do and constantly tries to reach us through our dreams, intuition, and desires. Money can scare us into playing dumb. But our soul knows what we are here to do, and it will create all kinds of scenarios to ensure we awaken to our potential.

Before we came to this earth, we created a soul contract, agreed upon a specific mission, and chose the events, circumstances, and details for this lifetime. We encoded the mission of our great work into the date of our birth and the vibration of our name. We drop in to this life, intending to live up to that great and lofty potential.

Then we hit this dense realm and we completely forget who we are and what we're doing here. We have many moments of reinvention pre-programmed into our lives that occur every nine years that help us to remember. Often those moments are painful because that seems to be what gets our attention best. It's during those times we're hurting that we ask the questions, "What am I doing here? Who am I? Why am I in this career?"

The pain you've experienced is on purpose. Pain becomes the motivation to either nudge you back onto the path you came to fulfill or to step up to the next level of your great work. In each case, the pain is there to prompt you to remember the very mission you came to this lifetime to fulfill. Nothing and no one is an accident. You chose the players in your drama (family, friends, and acquaintances) because they would push you past your limitations and help you rise to your potential. Until you recognize and align your life with your destiny path, you may feel like there's something that you're here to do but can't quite grasp. You may feel that what you're doing now doesn't bring you any satisfaction or you have everything but feel empty inside. As you look back on your life, realize it was all on purpose to get you to this moment.

Your greatest work always offers to others what you wished had been offered to you in your moments of deepest pain. In my case, I was at the peak of my career making incredible money with a multinational company, traveling internationally, managing a team responsible for organizational change and a fifty-three million dollar project portfolio. I was very surprised when I realized it wasn't enough. My ego was fed but, inside I felt like I was dying. Ultimately, after much pain and confusion, I made my own conscious reinvention and allowed my gifts as an intuitive— something I had long stifled—to be expressed in the work that I do alongside with my leadership experience. Now my greatest joy is to work with leaders across all levels to remind them of who they are, why they are here, and what they came here to do. My mission is to guide leaders of all levels to discover and achieve leadership excellence through conscious leadership and reinvention coaching, consulting, and speaking services.

The same is true for you. Tapping into your mission can transform your life if you allow it; but you must understand that what that looks like is different for each one of us. You can't look at someone else and follow their path. You chose a specific mission when you came to this life and you can only find answers by looking within to find what's right for you.

I: Can anyone know their destiny path?

AM: Yes! You can receive information and insights specific to your life which allow you to gain the clarity for which you've been yearning. Many clients tell me that they have gotten hints and stirrings about their purpose but couldn't put it together in a way that makes sense for them. Fortunately, you don't have to stumble along trying to figure it out by yourself like I did for many years. Your birth date and name provides clues to the life path you chose for this lifetime. You will be amazed at how the destiny numbers reflect the choices you've made or long to make in your career and reveal how to connect with your purpose to bring the abundance, meaning, and fulfillment that you want. Numerology reveals how you outlined your direction for this lifetime.

Numerology—an ancient science based on the mathematics of the universe—was developed by Pythagoras, a Greek philosopher and mystic who taught that the numbers in our birth date and the letters in our name reveal our lifetime mission. Your destiny number contains the vibrations of the greatness you came to achieve along with the potential pitfalls of your path. The power and truth that the numbers reveal can help you identify the work you came here to do and understand whether it's time to start something new, stay the course, or let go and allow a new work to begin.

The strong messages I receive from my intuitive gifts and the powerful insight that numerology provides allow me to share specific guidance with my clients about their true work and how to navigate the turning points of their life, career, and leadership. I help clients to do each of the following:

- Find clarity about what they came here to achieve
- Reveal destiny clues
- Identify their unique mission, path, talents, and values
- Understand the role that pain plays in their life to help them fulfill their great work
- Explore new opportunities that align with their life's mission
- Formulate a plan to align with their life purpose
- Recognize the significant transitions, turning points, and wake-

up calls on their path

I now guide all clients with insight from the numbers because they provide an intuitive gateway that helps connect me to the person's mission. The Conscious Reinvention process was subsequently born out of my work with many clients seeking to understand how to move through the process in their own lives. Not only can this information be used for individuals but also within companies as a tool during the recruitment process or for employee development planning. Can you imagine the impact an engaged and motivated workforce could make in *your* company?

We are deluged with information but starved for wisdom. We lead lives of quiet desperation, wondering why we can't shake the restless feeling that comes from being off path, not realizing that our hidden dreams and desires are the pathway to the meaning and sense of purpose we seek. We can get so caught up getting through the day-to-day grind that we can forget that our dreams, desires, and talents were gifts we brought with us to **use** and are to be embraced, not denied. Consider the possibility that you chose every important job you've had in this lifetime because it was healing you. What pain needs healing now? Let that answer guide you to align with your mission.

Get real about what is important to you. Not just your priorities, which are where a lot of leadership books and courses stop. I'm talking about your long-forgotten dreams, desires, and talents. Connecting with those is where the magic happens. What matters to you is important and by divine design.

I: What you do to grow your leadership skills?

AM: There are all kinds of strategies and thousands of leadership books all touting the latest techniques. Fundamentally, I have found that I need to know myself and what's right for me. I'm here on a unique mission that has nothing to do with how someone else succeeds. My greatest opportunity is to understand what's important to me and to align my life with my dreams—not the other way around. Only then can I focus on developing the skills. Skills can always be taught, but passion can't. Passion aligned with vision and purpose can drive unparalleled innovation for the leader and the organizations in which they serve.

LEADERSHIP OPPORTUNITY:

Get in a quiet place where you can sit for ten to fifteen minutes.

1. Now ask yourself, "What isn't working in my life and career today?" This is a great place to start because it's usually easier for us to identify what's *not* working that what it is we want.

2. Next ask, "Who am I if I strip away my titles and achievements?"

3. Finally, ask, "What mattered to me when I was young?"

These questions hold the key to YOUR leadership breakthrough.

LEADERSHIP SUCCESS:

Andre was a professional in a large multinational firm. Having achieved a successful career, he came to me searching. He wasn't quite sure what was missing, but he felt dissatisfied. He worked at great firm, made excellent money, and was recognized for his contributions. Yet, in his words, he was "bored to death" at work. Full of energy and ambition, he had everything going for him, but something was missing where he was.

During the course of our coaching engagement, he identified and addressed a limiting belief that was holding him back. He had been told by his manager that he was too ambitious and he was starting to believe it. As a result of some coaching, he went on to share that he loved pursuing new opportunities because he loved seeing his team's "aha" moments as they developed. He also thrived when he was able to provide management a perspective they hadn't considered.

This awareness caused a significant shift in Andre's perspective. Within days of that session, he saw a job posting in his current company for a new position that he was qualified for and was promoted to.

Today Andre is excelling in his position and has been added to an elite leadership development program designed to groom the next generation of leaders. His success is a result of remembering who he really is, why he came to this life, and what he came here to do.

Theresa Garwood
Lake Villa, Illinois, USA

Theresa Garwood specializes in efficiency improvement projects in a major pharmaceutical corporation including Lean Kaizen, change management initiatives, team building, and frontline leader training.

She is an experienced facilitator working with cross-functional teams to change critical business processes to reduce cost, eliminate waste, and create efficient business processes—ideas that are probably more important than any other time in our economy.

Theresa is a certified coach and has over fifteen years of experience in her field. She is a lifelong learner and has pursued helping others through coaching. Her coaching specialties include career coaching, personal development, and personal budgeting. She is also the co-owner of Kelsa Coaching.

I: You've done some amazing work helping people identify their aspirations and attain the personal and professional leadership skills they need. My understanding is that there is a basic, three-step process that is very effective. Can you tell us a little bit about that process?

TG: I'd be happy to! It really resonates personally with me and my cofounder of Kelsa Coaching, Kelly VanReeth.

Three-Phase Process for Identifying and Attaining Your Aspirations

Phase 1: Discovery—The Discovery phase is about understanding who you are, where you're going, and what you want to do.

Phase 2: Resolution—The Resolution phase comes when things start to get hard. This is the point when you grab yourself and say,

"This is my goal. This is where I really want to go." Be resolute in what you're doing. Understand yourself and where you're going with it. Then continue to take those steps and make it happen for yourself.

Phase 3: Endeavor—In the Endeavor phase, you have taken steps that to go forward, so you then persevere in those steps.

I: It can seem complex but you've broken it down to a really great, simple formula.

TG: That's what we were shooting for—to make it simple enough to go back and revisit the phases. After you get through the Resolution phase, you go back to Discover, because it's evolutionary. You go back and ask, "Now where do I want to go next? What new steps do I need to take?" Then you go through that whole process again, beginning with the Discover phase.

I: How does this process work from the standpoint of true empowerment and discovering your hidden leadership skills?

TG: It basically comes down to the Discovery phase. This is where you get to understand yourself at a deeper level—to know what drives you and what brings you to the next stage in your life that you desire. What really drives it is to fully understand yourself at a deeper level to know what's really going on in that Discovery phase.

I: Can you share with us a little bit about what you do personally to ensure your leadership growth?

TG: Actually, it's a curiosity in the world and curiosity in learning new things. I am continually changing and moving forward with understanding the world at a deeper level and what's really going on today.

Many of my clients and friends feel they're too old for this or that, but I refute that idea. We need to know what's going on, not only with our young children and teenagers, but also with twenty and thirty year olds. If we don't know what's really going on in their world, then we can't speak to them. We need to be inter-generationally connected.

Especially in the workplace, you are touching people inter-generationally and culturally. Different cultures are fascinating. That's what drives me personally to continue to seek and find new

things and to continue to learn.

I: That's a really good point considering all of the changes out there now. You really see it throughout so many different generations that are participating in what is happening with things like change initiatives and teamwork.

TG: Culture is such a big factor. People want to work internationally, and I say, "That's really a good point, but you have to realize that in a large corporation, the majority of us already work internationally." Consider the faces in the cubicle next to you; there's a myriad of nationalities represented in today's businesses, so even in the U.S. you are usually working internationally and may not realize it.

I: I've never heard it put that way, and that's such a beautiful and eloquent thought. We really do touch the whole world in whatever environment we're in because we're so culturally rich.

With that being said, what do you find really impacts your niche? You work with large corporations and smaller business as well as individuals. What are you finding is impacting your niche or the areas that you specialize in as far as leadership today?

TG: The biggest thing that impacts me in this field as it relates to leadership is that it's ingrained in me. It's what I do. It's something that I've developed within myself when I discovered true self and understood who I was; I understood that being a leader was who I am.

Then, with leadership, it is what you do to get to the next level to keep the project going forward, making sure that it is on time. I use leadership as my model, and they respect that. They see that in me, and they're drawn to me to ask, "What's different? What makes you different than the rest of the leaders?" I've had that particular question on several occasions.

It's very interesting to see that it's through the leadership style, a very participatory management model, that people feel free to approach me.

How does it relate to my specialization? It's career coaching, and without that leadership, people are not drawn to you to ask questions or feel free ask.

If I didn't have that leadership, it would not have allowed me to transform my career from being an administrative assistant to being a mid-level manager in a Fortune 500 company. It's taken me every step of the way. The leadership-driven piece within me has taken charge, and that leader within me knows fully who I am.

So with my niche, I'm able to impart that concept to my clients and ask them, "What do you want to do?" and get them to understand who they are and what drives them. This helps to project them forward. They also see the changes I've made in my career and they know they can make those changes too.

I: What I'm hearing is that authenticity—being available and approachable—has been really important in your leadership style.

TG: Yes, it is.

I: That hasn't always been a popular leadership style. Are you finding that this is more predominant now from the standpoint of being an effective leader? Are older leadership styles that were maybe a little more commanding and not as approachable losing their ability to be effective?

TG: They're not as effective in a cross-functional team world, but there are times when you have to have that top-down leadership approach. Sometimes that is the only way to explain something.

The Kaizen process is getting cross-functional teams together. I work in a company that has an extremely old process. For over fifty years this process has been in place. My job is to get cross-functional teams together to change the process. At times, this can be difficult simply because it's so ingrained into the culture. I hear things like, "This is the way we do it." Not only that, people aren't used to being asked, "How would you change it? What would make it easier for you to do your job?"

To be able to get those processes to change, I have to partner with them and use that participatory management to draw that out of them, to coach it out of them, and to make the process more efficient. That's where I use my leadership abilities.

I: You're probably very effective at getting consensus on what the future should look like.

TG: Yes, and a lot of time it's not only the person on the floor that needs to make that change and understand it, but it's also about getting the leadership to buy-in that these are the changes that need to be made. It goes both ways. I'm the bridge between the two.

I: That certainly describes one of the challenges that you face every day in your work with major corporations. Can you share any other challenges, either specific or general, that you're seeing today in leadership?

"Attitudes and morale have grown increasingly worse over the last couple of years, and it's up to me as a leader to coach and mentor individuals to come to a better conclusion for themselves."

TG: Today, every industry is facing cutbacks and budget constraints. Personally, I find the greatest leadership challenge is motivating and encouraging others. Attitudes and morale have grown increasingly worse over the last couple of years, and it's up to me as a leader to coach and mentor individuals to come to a better conclusion for themselves and the workplace. They need to be reassured that we are taking the right steps. In today's world, it's very hard to keep that morale going, but it's something that we all need to do.

I: I would think that when a company or a large corporation invests in bringing in a true expert like yourself to coach teams to success with future processes, that would reinforce the idea that the company truly has an investment in their people.

TG: Definitely. It's taken a while for that to come across to the worker on the floor; it's taken a couple of years along with a couple of really good Kaizen projects to see changes and that we have made successful progress. But once the success is there, they are all gung-ho to help.

LEADERSHIP OPPORTUNITY:

A lot revolves around making decisions. A lot of people—myself included—get stuck when it comes to making a decision. Which way do I go? I've learned that there's really no wrong decision; each decision just takes us down a different path. If we find it doesn't work well when we go one way, we can change it and do it the other way.

Prior to making a decision, a little tip that has helped me has been to write down on a piece of paper all the things I will gain if I take the action, how much it will mean to me, and what will change because of that. Then I also write down right next to it what I'll lose if I don't take that action. Then I see that I have more pain in not taking the action, and I have more to gain by taking the action. That has prompted me to make several big changes in my life.

LEADERSHIP SUCCESS:

I was raised in a 1950s world in a "father knows best" type of atmosphere. I went through a divorce and raised two children. When they were in high school, I decided it was time to go back to school. It was in 1999. I did it one step at a time. I took one class and thought, *How can I do this?*

It was very intimidating being in college. Everyone in the classroom was definitely much younger than me, but I learned that I loved to learn. I earned my associates degree, I earned my bachelors degree, and from there I said, "I'm not done." I wanted more. I went on to earn my MBA in two years and I worked full time throughout all of this.

It was an exciting journey for me, and the one thing that kept me going was something a friend said to me one particular day when I was pretty discouraged. I mentioned to her that it was going to take me five years just to get my bachelors degree.

She said, "Are you going to be alive in five years?" I said, "I certainly hope so!"

She said, "You can be there with it, or you can be there without it."

That sustained me every step of the way. My drive came from wanting to be there *with* it. That kept me going.

Zeina Ghossoub
Spring, Texas, USA

Zeina Ghossoub is the founder, owner, head clinical dietician, and wellness coach at Vie Saine. In French, Vie Saine means "healthy life." It's a health center like none other. It was developed in March of 2000, and since then it has continually grown and diversified to offer the most incredible services possible.

The basic philosophy is, "Together we can make a difference." No other center stresses this point as Zeina's does. She believes that the approach to any problem, medical condition, or issue is a team effort. It's a combination of your input, her experience and that of her team. It takes your effort, and her guidance to help you to achieve your goals and objectives.

I: Because health and wellness are central in your life and this is an area of tremendous expertise for you, what do you do to ensure your own professional and personal leadership growth as it applies to those areas?

ZG: First of all, I work a lot on studying myself. I attend many conferences each year for my CE credits, and I also get coached myself. At least half of the year I have one mentor coach and other coaches with different niches that help with my growth. I also have the honor of working with Dr. Cathy Greenberg and Dr. Relly Nadler with the XCEL Institute.

I am currently pursuing my Ph.D. in Counseling and Human Behavior and working toward completing my dissertation next year.

I: That's wonderful to hear. Education is important for all of us.

ZG: It is very important. Part of being able to give to other people is for you to grow yourself daily. The small things that you do—the small things that you accumulate—those are the bigger part of the coaching world and the science behind it that is amazing and exciting. Just keeping up with what's new in coaching helps you to give back to the people you're working with, and they will feel your excitement. What you are doing may become an inspiration to them to take their own path in life.

I: That's so beautifully put. We don't always think of ourselves as having leadership roles, though we all do, not only in our personal life, but also in our professional life. How does leadership impact your specific niche of health and wellness?

ZG: It does so at many levels, actually. On a personal level, when I am working with leaders themselves, it has a huge impact. I'd like to also emphasize that I come from the Middle East, and having woman leaders over there is a totally different niche altogether that we need to work on.

Women working on their health and wellness is somewhat forgotten about because they put everyone ahead of themselves, even if they are leaders in their field of work. They are the CEOs of their homes, but they are also CEOs and leaders in other aspects of their lives.

From a personal perspective, just being able to let these people understand what an impact their well-being is on what they do on a daily basis is really a challenge for me. When they are in leadership positions they can impact the community. They can inspire other people if they are practicing what are called the levels of well-being strategies of body, mind, and soul. That leaves the greatest mark on people because it's walking the walk and talking the talk.

I: It is a powerful concept of leading by doing.

ZG: Definitely. There's a sect that needs a lot of work, and it's that women's section. I am the first Lebanese PCC with ICF. I don't think there are any PCCs in Lebanon at this level who are working in wellness. There are a few ACCs who just started the Lebanese Coaching Association.

With the affiliations that I have at an international level I am able to perhaps influence women in Lebanon and the Middle East. I hope that I can affect the women in a positive way. It is something that I have wanted to achieve. I have to be doing this in my own health and my own well-being so that people really believe it can happen, even if I'm a career woman, a mother, and a wife. I must lead by example.

Leading by doing is what I find to be really powerful in that part of the world and with the people I work with here in the U.S. It has a lot of impact. With everything that is going on in the U.S., I can see women here are more empowered than women in the Middle East.

"Sometimes people want to change but they're just not ready to do so. Acknowledging that they can do it in this time frame and in this place, and understanding that the answer lies within them and their strengths, can make an enormous difference."

I: It's kind of a ground root movement in the Middle East whereas here in our culture women in leadership is a more predominant idea. What are the greatest challenges that you see in leadership today with your clients?

ZG: The greatest challenge would be to help others understand what coaching is at its core. Not many people—even in the U.S.—really grasp what coaching can do for them. I can see that when I'm working with leaders on the concept of leadership. I believe that we need to break the barrier of understanding what coaching is and what it can do.

I: Can you share with us about what coaching does and how to achieve the best results?

ZG: Coaching is about identifying where the clients are, what their strengths are, and what their goals are—whether they're health goals, wellness goals, etc. Then, it involves looking at the deficiencies—or what the clients see as a deficiency in themselves—and what the clients really want. What do they want at a wellness level? At a health level?

Just looking at that and understanding what they are able to do now—in this time frame, in this place—and what obstacles they may have is a big step. Who are the people that can help them achieve their goals? These are the questions we need to ask.

It's about understanding that the solution comes from them; it doesn't come from anyone else. They are the ones who are the decision-makers in the end, and the answers have to come from them.

I do both counseling and coaching. I don't know if you're familiar with Prochaska and DiClemente's Stages of Change Model. The stages are pre-contemplation, contemplation, preparation, and action. Sometimes people want to change but they're just not ready to do so. Acknowledging that they can do it in this time frame and in this place, and understanding that the answer lies within them and their strengths, can make an enormous difference.

I: What are some of the parameters necessary to make this relationship between the coach and the client successful?

ZG: Once the clients understand coaching and learns how to focus on themselves, the greatest parameter for success is the rapport and trust between them and their coach. This level of trust moves the clients from a lack of focus to a level of being very relaxed in the coaching session to an extent that they can go within themselves and experience those "aha" moments.

Many clients do not trust in what they're going to come and do. Once this rapport is strong and they have built trust and faith in the coach, then successful outcomes of the coaching can occur.

I: What do you think is the single most important factor necessary in order to achieve success in coaching?

ZG: Understanding and clarifying the client's goals and expectations is crucial. What is it they want by the end of the three months or six months or a year? It's necessary to clarify what they have come to do. Sometimes they come with many goals and the coach must have the ability to whittle them down to those that are most important goals or have the highest priority at that time and place. Clarifying expectations and priority of goals is most important.

I: Do you think coaching is necessary for everyone in order to realize our real leadership greatness, whether it be professional or personal?

ZG: Yes, I definitely think so—that is, if you want to move forward and you want to change. If you acknowledge all of this, then that is what really makes the difference between people who have the clarity to receive coaching and those who are still in denial of a few things that will set limitations for them.

I believe everyone is coachable. However, there is a certain mind-set and a certain acceptance you must have in order to be coached. That is the key to being able to do so successfully.

LEADERSHIP OPPORTUNITY:

I use the acronym GREAT for striving to reach a great goal:

Goal—Specify the goal.

Realistic—Make sure the goal is realistic and doable.

Exciting—The goal must also be exciting and enjoyable. You must enjoy what you're doing so that you can reach what you are attempting to reach.

Achievable—The goal must be achievable. This involves setting meaningful expectations and not going overboard. Unrealistic goals are those above our abilities. They will often lead to frustration and sometimes may even cause failure. I never refer to this as "failure" actually; I call it an experience because it's about wanting to learn.

Tangible—This is where you can actually hold on to or feel the success between your hands, via an outcome, or via whatever you have as a performance appraisal.

I use this with all of my clients, and we drive action steps around all of these.

LEADERSHIP SUCCESS:

I went on a hiking trip not long ago. We went to Europe and there were 150 people on the trip. It was a seven-day experience in the mountains and it was great.

On the fourth day, a woman around the age of fifty fell down on a very steep mountain. We were on top of the mountain and she was experiencing shortness of breath and showing symptoms similar to those of a heart attack. She was really scared. I happened to be next to her, and I helped her on the mountain to breathe through it until the ambulance came and she was able to go and have some tests run.

After a week, she came by my clinic and we started talking. I did some assessments, and I told her that she might have a disease called fibromyalgia. It is not a very well-known disease, but it causes a lot of aching in your whole body and it causes fatigue. Sometimes it causes migraines and mood swings.

She'd been experiencing this for more than fifteen years. She had been going to doctors and she had been diagnosed with everything except fibromyalgia.

After several tests, we decided to start helping her to at least alleviate her symptoms. This woman was overweight. She didn't have any problems with her blood tests, but she did have inflamed muscles. She had learned to live with the pain for fifteen years.

I started working with her, and as I usually do in coaching, I started asking her what she could do and what her strengths were at the time. She started slowly. She started exercising, she started doing heat therapy, and she started a weight-loss program. We started talking a lot and coaching.

After a few weeks of intensive one-on-one coaching, she started to understand who she was, what her body was doing, and what her goals were. She realized she was being unrealistic by overworking, because with fibromyalgia, she needed to rest when she was having an attack. It took one and a half months for her to realize who she was, to identify her problems, and to set her goals.

I can say that at this time she is not fibromyalgia-free, but she is 95% symptom free. She has become more fulfilled and happier. Her pain has decreased so much. She does receive a bit of medical treatment from time to time when an attack comes, but the turning point for her was to be able to understand who she is and what her abilities are and accepting them. This allowed her to feel comfortable in her own skin and gave her the power of knowing that this will pass so that she now knows what to do with it.

Hers is a great success story. Anyone who knows what fibromyalgia is knows that it's a debilitating disease. She is doing a great job, and I applaud her. I'm really happy with her achievements.

Ken Blanchard, Ph.D.
San Diego, California, USA

Dr. Ken Blanchard is the cofounder and Chief Spiritual Officer of Ken Blanchard Companies, an international management training and consulting firm that he and his wife, Margie, began in 1979 in San Diego, California. In addition to being a renowned speaker and outstanding consultant, Ken spends time as a visiting lecturer at his alma mater, Cornell University. He is also a trustee emeritus on their board.

Ken's phenomenal best-selling book, *The One Minute Manager,* which he coauthored with Spencer Johnson, has sold more than thirteen million copies and still remains a best seller. Since then, he's added many additional books to that list and all are receiving critical acclaim.

Ken has received numerous awards and honors for his outstanding contributions in the fields of management, leadership, and speaking. Ken has been inducted into Amazon's Hall of Fame as one of the top twenty-five best-selling authors of all time. The business school at Grand Canyon University bears his name, and Ken teaches students in the Masters of Science in Executive Leadership Program at the University of San Diego.

I: Can you share your philosophy and some of the key people who influenced you so that we can get to know some of the foundations that made you who you are?

KB: When I think about who really got me into this field, I first think of my mother and father. My father was a wonderful character. He retired as an Admiral in the Navy, but he was kind of a Mister Roberts character. I'll never forget, in seventh grade I was elected president of the class, and I came home all pumped up. My dad responded by saying, "Congratulations Ken, but now that you have a leadership position, don't ever use it. Great leaders are great because people respect and trust them, not because they have power." So here I am, a young kid with a father starting to teach him lessons like that.

My mother believed in positive thinking. I think before Norman Vincent Peale started talking about it, my mom told everyone, "I laughed before I cried. I danced before I walked. I smiled before I frowned." So it's pretty hard for me not to come out as a positive person who thought that leadership was not all about power and control and all those kinds of things.

You know, in my recent book, *The One Minute Entrepreneur,* there are excerpts at the end of each section called One Minute Insights. The heart of the leader is really like a one minute insight because, as I look back, I realize that the people who have impacted my life the most didn't go on with long diatribes. It was just short, pithy advice that made a difference, like my father saying, "Now that you have a position, don't use it."

My mother used to say, "Choose your friends carefully because people are going to be looking at who you associate with, and through that they're going to get an impression of who you are and who you gather around you. That's kind of a key. I wish the presidential candidates would tell everyone in advance who their cabinet is going to be. I want to know who's going to be gathering around them.

I: When you look back on your years of experience, from your perspective, why are management strategies so difficult to understand? You've made it your life's work to help make these strategies simple and easy for anyone to achieve. What have you done differently that has been so successful?

KB: What happens with most people when they want to teach someone is that they want to teach them everything. We have a belief that you ought to give people only a 20% or they'll give you 80%—it's old Pareto's Law. So every time I work on a book, I think about what the key things are that I want people to understand in terms of this topic that can make a difference. Then I consider how to focus on that rather than on everything else. We paralyze people with overkill instead of giving them some simple, key things.

The One Minute Manager is still a best seller today—twenty-eight years later—and people come up to me and say, "That changed my life." I realized I just needed to be clear on goals and then wander around and catch people doing things right. If they made a mistake, I would redirect them and reprimand. Those are three things, and if people remember those, they're going to be effective.

I wrote a book with Paul J. Meyer called *Know Can Do!* which is about why people don't just take what they know and do it. The first reason is that they learn too much. They've got to focus on a few things and then you've got to get rid of their thinking. The biggest problem is how to get what's in their head into their behavior. That's why I'm such a big fan of the whole coaching movement. I tell you, there's a much better probability that people are going to be able to use and be successful with what they learned if they have follow-up coaching and follow-up structure that could make a difference in their lives.

I: Let me pass on a couple of these quips that you have published so beautifully, and if you could, tell us a little bit about what you were thinking when you designed them. Here's one I love: "People with humility don't think less of themselves, they just think of themselves less."

KB: My big thought there was that a lot of times we think that if someone is humble, that means that they don't have a very good image of themselves. In his book *Good to Great,* Jim Collins found that humility is one of the greatest characteristics of great leaders. He had never anticipated humility.

To me, people who are humble feel good about themselves, and as a result, they don't have to spend a lot of time stroking themselves and having other people stroke their ego. This allows them to be able to spend more time helping other people develop their skills. That's why humility is so important. Egocentric leaders who think leadership's all about them are nothing but problems.

I: Excellent. Here's another one that touches my heart: "Don't wait until people do things exactly right before you praise them."

KB: Some people say, "Well, you're going to have to praise people all along, and it takes a lot of time." I say, "Absolutely, because if you wait until they finish something, the praise might be too late." I use the example of Shamu the whale. How did they get a killer whale to jump out of the water over a rope? Well, they start the rope down under the water. Every time the whale swims over it, they feed him. Every time he swims under it, they don't do anything. After a while he thinks, *Hm . . . this is interesting.*

You want to praise progress; it's a moving target toward where you're trying to go. I ask people all the time, "Are you sick and tired of all the praise you're receiving at work? Do you wish they would lay-off?" Everyone laughs because most people get caught doing things wrong in their organizations, not doing things right. They have managers running around until they make a mistake and then those managers fly in and dump on everyone. That is not helpful.

"You want to praise progress; it's a moving target toward where you're trying to go."

People need recognition. Your job is to help people win and to accomplish their goals, not to sit back, evaluate, judge them, and put them into some kind of normal distribution curve. Managers and leaders need to get out of their office and start wandering around, seeing if they can catch anyone doing anything right. And you know what? If they start doing that, they will be amazed at how much people will be willing to share with them. If that happened, managers would know where all the trouble spots are or where money could be saved. They'd know where everything is. But if you don't reach out to them, they're certainly not going to reach back to you.

I: How do you think your leadership style today differs from other practitioners in your field?

KB: I think there are a lot of people doing good work. I think there's one big difference in this field. Some other people do good here, but I really push the idea of servant leadership. When you talk about servant leadership, a lot of people think you're talking about some kind of religious movement. I say they don't understand leadership because there are two parts of leadership I support: one is vision and direction, and the other is implementation, and they're both leadership positions.

Vision and direction is about where we're going, what we stand for, and what our values and our goals are. People look to the leader and the organization as a whole to take the lead in that. It doesn't mean you don't involve other people, but you're responsible for setting the tone. I was with Herb Kelleher and Colleen Barrett and all their top people at Southwest Airlines in Dallas. You know, Herb and Colleen and Gary Kelly kept saying, "Here's where we're going, here is what we stand for, and here are our values." They involve a lot of people,

"You finally become an adult when you realize that you're here to serve rather than be served— to give rather than to get."

but the part of leadership that is so critical is servant leadership.

Implementation is about understanding how we make it happen. That's when the really great leaders turn the traditional hierarchy upside down and place themselves at the bottom, cheerleading, supporting, and encouraging people to do their thing and giving them the power to do it. That's the servant part of servant leadership.

Colleen Barrett is a great president. Her office sent out 45,000 notes, birthday cards, and anniversary cards to people in their organization. She handwrites about three thousand of them each year and all because as president, she saw herself as the cheerleader.

The vision and direction is already set, and our job as leaders is to keep people doing it. Servant leaders are people who know where they're going, and they're going to shout that up, but also, they're going to build the power in the people to make it happen.

I: You have been quoted as saying, "We are not human beings having a spiritual experience; we are spiritual beings having a human experience."

KB: My belief is that you finally become an adult when you realize that you're here to serve rather than be served—to give rather than to get. It's a journey because I think we come into this world self-serving. Along the journey, you realize that it's not about you, and you know you're here to serve and to be a servant. You're a spiritual being having a human experience, and how you bring about those wonderful values and the Golden Rule that we're here to help each other is what makes the difference. When you start asking, "How do I make that happen in my lifetime and in my work?" then you become the human being who realizes that they are a spiritual being having a human experience.

LEADERSHIP OPPORTUNITY:

There's no better way to help and influence people than these four different leadership styles; directing, coaching, supporting, and delegating. As people increase their own competency to be able to lead, they commit to do things on their own. What we are trying to do is get people to match leadership style to where people are. So if you delegate to someone who is an enthusiastic beginner and who has never done what you're asking him to do, he is going to fail with vigor.

Again, if you get a highly competent, motivated person in an area that they know something about and you're in there telling them what to do, how to do it, and where to do it, you're going to have the same problem. You are over-supervising in this example and under-supervising in the previous example. What you want to do is get a match for people.

The reason we think coaching is so important is very often in training, there's a lot of directing, coaching, and training, and then all we say is, "Good luck! Apply what you've learned!" The problem is that a lot of people aren't ready or confident enough to run with the ball, so we use this model to help people understand where they are.

LEADERSHIP SUCCESS:

I think about all the things that I've taught and what I'd hold on to. I think that the key to developing people—the key to creating great organizations—is to catch people doing things right and to accent the positive. We don't do that enough in our society.

I listen to the radio and the news, and all of them focus on the bad news. I never figured it out. I asked Norman Vincent Peale one time, "Why doesn't the news say much more about positive things?" He said, "I'm so glad they don't. If good news was news, there wouldn't be much to it because it is happening all the time. The only reason bad news is news is because not as much of it is happening."

We need to accent the positive. We need to cheer people on when they do good things so they don't get to thinking that it doesn't mean anything because no one pays any attention to it. Look at your kids—catch them doing something right. Look at your spouse, your friends, your colleagues, and everyone around you and accent the positive.

Candice Smithyman, D.D.
Orange Park, Florida, USA

Dr. Candice Smithyman is the Founder and Vice President of Dream Mentors Transformational Life Coaching Institute, a biblical life coaching educational organization that teaches and trains educators and coaches in the specialty of life coaching. She received her Doctorate of Divinity from Truth Bible College in Jacksonville, Florida and received her Masters in Counseling/Human Relations from Liberty University. She has also served as an adjunct professor for Liberty University and many other universities and colleges.

Candice has appeared on international and local TV and radio programs including her own radio shows, *The Get Real Connection* and *Coffee Break With Candice*, which have aired in various states across the country. She is a published author of *His Sufficiency For My Authenticity: Eight Keys to Authentic Relationship With God and Others* as well as *Biblical Life Coaching Curriculum for Secular and Christian Organizations*. Candice is a board-certified Christian counselor, an ordained minister, and co-pastor of Freedom Destiny Christian Fellowship in Orange Park, Florida.

I: I want to start out by asking why you think it is important to integrate leadership skills with a person's personal faith system, and how do we do that effectively?

CS: It's important because, depending upon your belief system, it can determine how you lead your group or your organization. All of our leadership skills—everything about who we are—is dependent upon our belief system. We can't exclude our leadership skills from who we are, and since our beliefs make up who we are, everything flows out of that in how we operate in this world and do what it is that we're called to do.

Leadership skills are essential in being integrated with our faith system. We want to make sure that we are positioning ourselves to constantly be training and facilitating ourselves so that our leadership skills can expand. As you grow personally and professionally, you will then grow in your own belief system or your faith in God. As you grow in that area, your leadership skills are going to grow and advance as well.

I: You work in a Christian environment and you're a real leader in this field. Many Christians want to know how God's plan and purpose for their life works. How does leadership play into the definition and them discovering that role for themselves?

CS: God gives you a plan and a purpose for where He wants you to meet His people at some level as soon as you first begin to seek the Lord and this plan and purpose. Whether you're leading your children in your home, whether you're leading people at your job, whether you're leading people in your church, or whatever it is, we're all called into various leadership roles. As we develop in our personal relationship with God, He is going to share with us His plan and purpose for us, and it's always going to mean that He's asking us to lead others and to build others up effectively.

The work of the body of Christ that God has established is such that leadership is to equip the body of Christ to help the members around you—to help the people around you in your community, your church, and your home. We are to help them to grow, develop, and to become spiritually mature, not only in their relationship with God, but in their relationships with others.

Once again, you cannot segregate God's plan and purpose for your life and the ability to step out in leadership roles; they are one in the same in many instances because we're always leading someone. It's always God's plan and purpose that we're to be equipping the body of Christ, and that requires an element of leadership.

I: In your coaching programs at Dream Mentors you have many great strategies to help Christian clients understand why they do what they do. Can you share how this helps to hone their personal and professional leadership roles?

CS: One of the primary things we do at Dream Mentors is help people understand why they do what they do. When you can come to a place where you can begin to understand why you do what you do, then you'll learn more about who you are. That is when this will strengthen your leadership skills in the environment that you've been called to lead.

One of the core focuses of Dream Mentors is our motto, "Be a coach—don't just do coaching." There's a whole focus on the "being" component. In the "being" state, we learn and grow in who we are. The more we develop and have an understanding of who we are in Christ, what our relationship with God is, and what His relationship is with us, the more our leadership skills will grow and strengthen.

There's one component that we stress in Dream Mentors, and that is our understanding of provision, protection, and acceptance. They are motivational keys that we teach in our courses. They help you to understand how we function as human beings around our needs for provision, protection, and acceptance, and how God has met those needs through Jesus Christ in our lives.

When we can understand how provision, protection, and acceptance cause us to make certain decisions and move in certain areas, then we become more effective leaders, because it is then that we know what to avoid. We learn some of the snares and traps in our life and how we can best help people when we understand who we are and what we need.

I: That is so powerful. We've spoken before about some of the challenges that leaders face on every level today. You feel that there is a real authority problem. Could you share more about that?

CS: There certainly is an authority problem. People are rebellious to those in positions of authority, generally because of pride. For anyone who is in any leadership position—whether you're a mom or a dad to children or a boss in your work environment, church environment, etc.—there are always going to be people you're leading who do not want to go in the direction that you're asking them to go. This is what we call the authority problem, because those people are not submitting to your authority in the role to which God has called you.

"Submission is not a dirty word. It's not something that people need to feel uncomfortable with."

Submission is not a dirty word. It's not something that people need to feel uncomfortable with. It simply means that in order for systems to flow properly, there will always need to be a head of something as well as subordinates. When those in your organization or your church are not subordinate to the leadership, it stops the growth of the organization, it stops the vision, and it stops the mission. This idea of rebellion can also create conflict and problems within the leadership and the people in the organization.

In order for things to flow effectively, subordinates need to respect authority and follow after it. You don't necessarily have to respect a person in order to be able to follow them. You should simply be respecting the authority that God has given that person in that position.

A lot of times people won't follow others because they'll look at the person in leadership and say, "I don't respect them; therefore, I'm not going to follow them, even though we're in this organization together." Really, what they need to be doing—because of their love for God, their belief system, and their understanding of the fact that God has placed that person in an authoritative role—is to simply follow. In doing so, they're following after the person that God has put in that place, and it is respectful to their relationship with God.

It is a very difficult concept, and most people have difficulty grasping it, but God doesn't want there to be conflict in your organization. He wants things to flow effectively because He set aside the mission and the vision. He also knows that quite often people will make excuses and/or create issues rather than being able to follow after the leader that He put in place.

We have what we call the authority problem and it is a difficult issue. It takes place all the time, anywhere. Whether it be in your home or in your community or in your work environment, it's there. We have to learn creative skills, techniques, and ways of reaching out to people so that the authority problem can be diminished and we can move forward in the vision, the plan, and the purpose that God has for this organization.

I: That is very powerful. Since you have done so much to help people get in touch with their life purpose and higher authority, exactly what do you do to ensure your own continual personal and professional leadership growth? Is there anything you do on a regular basis?

CS: There is. I pray constantly. I fast a few times a week. I am always positioning myself to listen to the Lord and to learn to submit to Him and His leadership in my life. The more I submit to Him and His leadership, the better leader I am to those people that He has connected to me.

If I am constantly positioning myself for the Lord and my relationship with Him and allowing Him to get in my stuff and tell me how I can be better at this or better at that or better for His people in this way or the other. Then I open myself up to the Word of God and to criticism and critiques from Him on my heart and even critiques through other people, like my husband who is head over many of our ministries, and God deals with me about the things I need to change. Then I can become more respectful and I can build my character properly so that I can become someone that people can follow.

I always hold myself to Him as my highest authority and then people will follow me as a leader because they know that I have positioned myself to be accountable to Him and Him first. This then leads to peace in an organization because those members of the organization are aware, "She holds herself to the highest authority; therefore, whether I personally think I can respect her or not about this decision she might have made, I know that she is holding herself accountable to God, so I can listen to what she says. I need to get over myself and just follow after her and move forward."

I'm continually putting myself in a position of being disciplined and accountable to God so that I can constantly be a better leader.

LEADERSHIP OPPORTUNITY:

I have an exercise that I call the Discipline of Solitude. It's an exercise where I sit with the Lord anywhere from two to three times per day for about ten minutes. During that time, I simply say a praise word of some sort; I praise Him. I might say the name of Jesus, I might say thank you. I say a praise word, and I sit quietly.

I allow thoughts that are destructive to me and emotions that are negative to just kind of pass by. I sit in solitude with God, not focusing on anything except for Him and his presence, and I let anything that is condemning or associated with guilt, worry, or anxiety—anything like that—just pass right over me. I don't attach to it; I let it be its own thing where it is not a part of me.

This keeps me healthy. It keeps me strong. Many times I'll read the

Word of God beforehand. It may just be a few Scriptures to get my heart right, but this exercise—this Discipline of Solitude—done on a continual basis helps keep me in a place of submission to God's authority in my life and helps me feel His presence and realize the depth of our relationship.

This makes me a much better leader because I'm taking this time out during the day to meet with Him and to be ministered to by Him. God ministers to me and ministers peace to me so that I'm able to carry forward in what He has called me to do.

I would recommend that exercise for anyone at anytime. I have written a book called *The Discipline of Solitude* which can be found on my Dream Mentors Web site. It's a manual, and in that manual I teach you in a twenty-one-day period of time how to enter into this place of solitude with the Lord. We've had a great response from it and have received a lot of encouragement. Many people realize a deeper connection with the Lord and they realize the essence of being able to step into greater leadership because they're holding themselves accountable to Him with these ten-minute moments throughout the day.

That's what I do personally, and it's very effective. It's the practice of the spiritual discipline that helps me be who I am and carry on with the life that He's called me to lead.

LEADERSHIP SUCCESS:

About the Discipline of Solitude: When people are practicing that level of accountability and leadership and they're practicing the Discipline of Solitude, almost always they come out with an understanding that they are empowered to lead people. They're empowered to step into what God has called them to because they feel so much of His presence and so much connection with Him. That's the extra confidence they need to be able to do what God has called them to do.

I would just like to say generally, as a success story, that when you're practicing the Discipline of Solitude, you come to a place of knowing who you are and what God has called you to do, and you have a sense of peace and confidence in leadership to be able to step out and lead people. Even if an authority problem or something else comes along, you know that you have submitted yourself to His authority so many times a day, and that helps to carry you through whatever situation you're in.

JoAnne Ward
Vancouver, BC, Canada

JoAnne Ward is the founder of Grow Forward Youth Success. For more than twenty years Joanne has inspired thousands of teens—future leaders—to achieve higher grades than they ever thought possible and to progress further than they ever imagined.

She has assisted hundreds of high school students who are frustrated with their school marks and lack of support from teachers. Those kids who have fallen through the cracks and missed out on opportunities for a better education, career, financial security, positive relationships, and the ability to become the true leaders of our future, she has made successful.

I: What are your views on today's leadership and the place that our youth have in that leadership?

JW: Probably one the most challenging things that kids have to deal with today is that they have these wonderful dreams for their futures and in many cases, parents have told them that they can be anyone or anything they want to be. They create this life for their children saying, "The canvas is yours—paint your story," but they're not preparing their children for the obstacles they are going to face; teachers and counselors do not necessarily prepare the kids for these obstacles either.

We have teens and young adults who have fabulous dreams of being leaders in our countries and taking on big challenges. The problem is that they've gotten stuck on how to actually progress—how to do it step by step, how to improve themselves, and how to prepare for the obstacles they are going to meet along the way. There are inevitably going to be lots of obstacles.

From the research I have done, there is just no time to properly mentor kids today. There is not enough staff or parents who are around their children to actually have long conversations about how to cope, so these wannabe incredible leaders are stumbling rather than feeling empowered.

I: So they have the vision piece in place, but they do not have the concept of the reality they are going to face?

JW: Yes, that is exactly it. In many cases, they are not outfitted with the coping skills or the problem-solving skills that they will need later. They want to be leaders—they want to be great at what they do—but they have not received the encouragement and they do not necessarily have the support. They are bombarded with so much technical information, social media, and little snippets of advice here and there, that I have found a lot of students and young people would rather give up on their dreams than actually plow through them, warts and all.

I: How do you help them wade through all of this?

JW: We all—whether we are running a business or running our life—have to be very clear on what it is that is going to make us happy, so I usually start there. We start out by taking a look at what is important to the youth, what values they have, what some of their dreams are, and what their strengths are.

Once they start to realize that they have these fabulous intentions, we put them down on paper, and we develop them into a plan of their vision. We also get a fabulous resume out of all this, too. It multiplies or duplicates itself in many areas. Not only do they find that they may not have a clear and definite purpose, but this is an indication that says, "Here is the map of the direction I want to go."

A lot of young people say, "My parents want me to be a doctor, but I would just like to be an actor." Parents have one particular roadmap and youth may have a different one. We try to get them on the right roadmap so they are not going off wasting time, money, and effort heading in the wrong direction.

I also teach them how to have those communication skills with their parents to so they can say, "I really don't want to be a doctor," and maybe they can come up with something more suitable to the youth's strengths and interests.

I want to empower them by helping them take a good look at who they are, what they want to be, and what their strengths are. In doing this, they see the value they have in themselves and how that can be put to good use in their own personal purpose.

I: What are some of the most important skills for youth to possess today in order to be our future leaders?

JW: What I see—after teaching high school and college students—is that youth aren't necessarily curious. They are not asking, "Why?" enough. They are not asking, "What if?"

"Youth aren't necessarily curious. They are not asking, 'Why?' enough. They are not asking, 'What if?'"

Their creativity skills are squashed because they are being fed so much information through games, television, technology, teachers, and parents. They are being bombarded with so much information that kids just say, "Well, someone is going to do it for me or someone is going to figure it out," but they are not really using their own creative skills to say, "What if I did it differently?" or "What if I did it for this purpose instead of that one?" or "What are several other ways that I could solve this problem?"

One of the biggest things I find is that they are just accepting and saying, "Okay, the textbook says this, so it must be true," or "Google says that, so it must be true." Not necessarily! They are not questioning themselves enough.

Another important skill area is communication since everything is driven by a screen, a keyboard, or a phone these days. I am finding that a lot of youth are not able to properly communicate what they are feeling or sensing. They don't have an opinion because they don't have the confidence to actually state what their opinion is, and they feel comfortable about that. If they have problems, they don't know how to problem solve through proper communication. Problem solving and communication are absolutely key in moving forward and growing.

I: How do you help them develop a curiosity for problem solving and the confidence to move forward that they will later need as leaders?

JW: I used to teach entrepreneurship, and the kids would have to come up with a product or a service. One of the exercises I would have them do was to come up with ten extremely useful purposes for their service or product.

A lot of them found it was easy to come up with the first four, but the last five or six were really difficult. Those last few ideas, however, were usually the ones that ended up being the most marketable. Students started thinking out of the box, and all of a sudden, we had some students saying, "Wow, I never realized I could have two or three different markets if I just changed this a little bit."

That's one exercise that people can use on almost anything. By asking, "What other ways can I think of that will help solve this problem?" they can think of alternative solutions rather than just the best or most obvious solution.

This next exercise is a formula I use in business and in problem solving with students. It has four key points.

Four Step Problem-Solving Formula

Step 1: Define the Problem—This is probably the hardest step. For example, a student could be getting poor marks and just say, "I'm not smart enough," but the actual problem could be, "I don't have the confidence to be perfect, and if I am not perfect, I might as well not tackle the job at all."

I see that a lot. The problem is not that they're unintelligent; the problem is that their expectations are unrealistic or they are trying to be perfect and that simply does not exist. They may be lacking confidence in doing well in anything. Defining the problem, not the symptom, is key here.

Step 2: Gather All the Facts—List the facts, or what I call an analysis. Here is a sample listing of facts:

- I don't hand in my homework on time.
- I'm afraid I'm going to appear stupid to my friends.
- I feel criticized by my teachers when I don't do well.
- I know I can do better, but I don't know how.

These are all facts. They're not opinions, they're facts. A couple of my clients have had a situation where they are barely passing two courses out of five. The other marks are anywhere from 5% to 45%. Within three months, through a very simple process, all of their marks rose into the 60s and 70s. By the following year, some of my clients have been on the President's Role, which means they are achieving 80% or better. It is a matter of taking things step by step.

235

Step 3: List Alternative Solutions—These are usually from the ridiculous to the sublime. Examples of ridiculous solutions would include the following:

- Quit school.
- Don't hand in any work.
- Settle for being a loser.

Better solutions might include these options:

- Get a tutor.
- Get some help to build my confidence.
- Hire a coach.
- Learn how to do _____(whatever is lacking).
- Set up a schedule to manage my projects and time.
- Focus on getting better marks.

Step 4: Make a Recommended Solution—They could combine the better solutions listed in Step 3, or they could say, "I think getting a tutor or a coach might be the best result for me," and then act on it. It's so easy, but it helps the person focus on the real problem and on getting a real solution.

I: Since you are so actively involved in honing the skills of our future leaders, what do you do yourself to make sure you are growing in your leadership skills?

JW: As a lifetime learner, I'm always involved in courses—always. I have a masters degree in leadership as well as a variety of degrees and skills in business, marketing, and education. I have always been very creative in taking all of those skills and putting them into various opportunities, whether they are working for someone else or for myself.

I read at least three educational or human development books each month. Besides belonging to a lot of networking groups that keep me informed, I spend a lot of time with my own children—who are adults now—and they tell me what is cool and what is not. I hold mentorship/mastermind groups for young people each month and am blessed to be both their mentor and a student!

LEADERSHIP OPPORTUNITY:

Talk to your child. Really communicate. This is not simply asking, "How was school today? Oh yeah? That's good. Good work."

There are so many parents who say, "Gee, 94%? What did you get wrong?" Celebrate *everything* your child does. Catch them doing something right and acknowledge them. Give them value to show them that you care and make everything relevant.

Children are afraid of disappointing their parents more than anything, but if parents keep doing things for their children, those kids are going to grow up not feeling they have the skills to do anything for themselves. They are going to be dependent on their families for years. Without a doubt, parents are terrified that their children might still be living at home when they are thirty.

LEADERSHIP SUCCESS:

I started teaching one particular young man when he was in tenth grade, and I taught him until he graduated from high school. This young man had a health issue which made him sort of weak in his stature. He was bullied and teased at home and by other students.

He came in to some of my courses in business. He came to me with not a whole lot of confidence, but he just seemed to sparkle when we were talking about possibilities and building business. This young man was very shy, introverted, and very quiet.

He is now twenty-four years old, but when he was in twelfth grade, under my expertise, he was the president of a youth business organization that I ran outside of school as a school activity. We ran a school store. We made huge profits, and I gave back scholarships to our members for them to carry on to college. He also learned so many leadership skills.

In his entrepreneurship class, he wanted to be an interior designer, This young man—at the ripe old age of nineteen—started his own company, accelerated through University, paid for all of his training, and was top in his class. He graduated from the University of Chicago with a degree in design, and he is looking at earning his Masters degree. He is probably earning a six-figure income.

He is just remarkable in what he has accomplished and in such a short period of time.

Agnès van Rhijn
Paris, France

Agnès van Rhijn is an international coach, trainer, motivational speaker, and Personal Leadership expert.

The world is her playground and she believes that shifting our mind-set to take charge of our destiny is key to facing the challenges of an increasingly demanding world.

She has created The Conscious Life Academy® to help highly motivated people step into the power of their personal leadership. My Fulfilling Life®, My Unlimited Business®, and My Successful Career® are three signature programs delivered by TCLA. They help every person who is willing to make a difference to design a consciously successful personal and professional life.

I: Would you share your definition of this topic you care so much about—personal leadership? What does it mean to you?

AvR: Leadership is about showing the path, and in a personal setting, it's about giving yourself the ability to find the direction you want to give to your life.

I often refer to *Alice in Wonderland*: When Alice asks the Cheshire Cat what road she should take, she asks, "Which way ought I to go from here?" the cat responds, "That depends a good deal on where you want to get to." Alice says she doesn't care and the cat responds, "Then it doesn't matter which way you go." I think it's really the same in life. Personal leadership is life transforming. When we consciously decide which direction we want to give to our life, it opens perspectives that are completely new. It is what makes the difference between someone who is successful in life and someone who is not.

I live in France where, generally speaking, people tend to focus on what is not working instead of looking at the possibilities. I don't work only with French people because my market is international, but let's look at them. They tend to let people and circumstances decide for them; it's almost cultural. It is amazing to see the results I reach with them when they tap into that power by developing a positive and can-do attitude. They really have a complete mind-set shift. When I say "complete" I mean really complete; there is a before and an after.

"When we consciously decide which direction we want to give to our life, it opens perspectives that are completely new."

I use four clearly identified steps and I'd like to share some of their aspects to help you reach that result.

Steps to Personal Transformation

Step 1: Awareness—It may seem obvious, but it does help to state that you can only change the things you are aware of. So the first step is to reach a state of awareness and there are certain things that help in reaching it:

- **Our thoughts and words create our reality.** Everything and its opposite can be found in the universe, but what we focus on is what we get as a result. If you focus only on things that aren't working, then of course things will continue not to work. Focus on what works and you will be surprised by the outcome!

- **We learn more from our failures than from our successes.** Of course we can learn a lot from our successes, but if we step back to reflect on what didn't work and why, there is so much more to learn that will help us grow!

- **Life is made up of continuous choices.** Every single moment in life we are making choices, but most people spend their lives without ever realizing that they can do so consciously. They let other people or circumstances decide for them. Give it a try. Once you start deciding consciously for yourself, your life becomes incredibly powerful!

- **Happiness is a journey, not a destination.** Seeing beauty in everything and everyone one day at a time is what transforms your journey into a happy one. This is not something that you find at the end destination only.

- **Time is only a structure invented by man.** In reality, there are no such things as past or future. The only place we can live in is the present. If we focus only on what we call "past" or what we call "future," we consequently forget to live our life.

Step 2: Acceptance

- **Certain aspects in life just happen.** Putting energy into complaining or fighting against things which are—and whether we like it or not, will be—is a complete waste of energy. Life is made of cycles, and that is just the way it is. I like to refer to happiness as a period between two periods of unhappiness and vice versa. These opposites are needed. In reality, they are not opposites—they are extensions of themselves.

- **Transitions are needed.** Transition periods are needed to rebuild ourselves and to learn from them. We live in a world where we tend to want everything immediately. We also only want the nice things. Unfortunately, that's not how life is. When we face difficult times, let's accept them as an opportunity to grow!

"Things happen, but the level to which we are capable of facing them demonstrates our level of security or insecurity."

- **Our vision of the world is only our own vision of it.** The way we have been constructed—our family's heritage, our parents, our siblings, our friends, our school system—has a profound influence on how our assumptions are made. If we start realizing that those stimuli are the primary conditions for our assumptions, then we can start realizing that our vision of the world is not necessarily the only one. That is how we can start realizing that the fact that I am right doesn't mean you are wrong. It opens a whole new range of perspectives!

- **Focus on what can be changed.** Don't waste energy trying to change things that can't be changed (as I already said, certain things just *are*). That is the uncertainty of life. What you are trying to do when you try to change it is addressing your feeling of insecurity, and that is only a feeling, that is to say that you are the one who creates it. Things happen, but the level to which we are capable of facing them demonstrates our level of security or insecurity. The better equipped we are to deal with our own levels of insecurity, the better equipped we will be to face those uncertainties in life which will happen anyway. The energy that we're putting into fighting against things that will be is energy that is not available to put into working on things that we can do something about.

Step 3: Clearance

- **Forgive and let go of the past.** I am convinced that this is a vital component of our transformation. Have you ever tried to build a new house on the ruins of an old one? If you do, the house cannot be stable and you set yourself at risk to see it collapse. You need to clear the space first in order to build strong foundations. Life is an evolution. What happened in the past is not necessarily true today, but our perception of it gives life to negative energy that, once again, is energy that is no longer available to focus on positive things.

Step 4: Dreaming Big

- **Be the change you want to see in the world.** I did not say it, Gandhi did! But it is so eloquent! What is your ideal world? How do you want to contribute to it? Dream big, you will be surprised how energizing that is!

- **Step out of your comfort zone.** I see it almost every day in the work I do with my clients. Because of all the limitations we have, we tend to think small. We do so because it is so scary to think big. Good news if you are scared: it means that you are stepping out of your comfort zone! If you do more of the same, you will get more of the same results, anyone can grasp that. So guess what? If you want a different result, you will have to do things differently, and that is scary because you are tapping into the unknown!

I: What is your personal view of leadership?

AvR: I truly believe that it is possible for people to be fulfilled and successful creating one's own business or working in a sustainable and ethical workplace. That is why I have chosen to work with both ends of the spectrum: the people and the system they belong to— the workplace.

I am very passionate about strengths-based approaches, and in order to contribute to my vision, I have developed a four-step coaching model that is the structure of the three signature programs that I offer at The Conscious Life Academy® to help people consciously enjoy their life and their business or career. It is inspired of a combination of the 4D model of Appreciative Inquiry, Personal Branding, the Seven Laws of the Universe, and Conscious Language.

This model has four cornerstones that are essential components of it:

Coaching Model—Four Cornerstones

1. Intention—What is the intention you are setting for yourself on a long-, mid-, and short-term basis?

2. Clarity—How clear are the steps that will bring you closer to realizing your dream, and how do you keep them clear?

3. Focus—What structure do you set in place to continue focusing on achieving your objective?

4. Discipline—This one is quite often forgotten, but I think it is key: how disciplined are you to ensure you remain focused?

My next move is to create The Conscious Workplace to help corporations implement an ethical and sustainable workplace for their employees.

That's where personal leadership has led me, and somehow I have a feeling that this is only a beginning!

LEADERSHIP OPPORTUNITY:

This daily routine is derived from the four cornerstones. The goal is to stay connected to your dream every single day.

When you wake up, stand up with your two feet solidly grounded on the floor and consciously connect to your dream.

Then ask yourself, "What overall intention am I setting for today?"

Then, in order to stay focused ask, "What concrete actions will I undertake today that will bring me closer to achieving my objectives?"

Finally ask, "What element of discipline am I missing that could get me sidetracked?"This is meant so that you can start considering what you need to do to put that discipline back into place.

Don't forget that you are—as everyone is—just human. It's okay to get off track as long as you know how to get back on track again.

LEADERSHIP SUCCESS:

As I mentioned earlier, letting go of the past and forgiveness are foundational elements of your transformation. And I know, because I experienced it myself. I grew up in an environment where, for generations, women were considered as barely more than a piece of furniture. As an adult, I have spent many years being angry at my father because of the way he treated my mother. Last year I spent his last six months with him. Our discussions have allowed me to realize that all he had done was replicate a model that he had witnessed himself. He just didn't know any better. Understanding that in his own way he had cared for her and that he never really had any intention to hurt her allowed me to forgive him. It also helped me understand that my perceptions were at the origin of my anger, not him.

I came to me that we tend to grant negative intentions to people, but when you give it a closer look, you start grasping that there are many more people in the world who hurt you without the intention of doing so than people who consciously want to.

Anger is a negative emotion and therefore energy that I don't experience anymore. It no longer stands in my way of achieving things. It feels like magic. It's incredible how much lighter I feel now.

Susan Guiher
Ivyland, Pennsylvania, USA

Sue Guiher is a certified personal and business coach and expert in thriving. She was a leader in corporate America for many years and was a self-proclaimed "corporate -aholic." She is passionate about supporting leaders to work less and play more so that they can thrive in business while also living the life they desire.

Sue is the author of several books, including *Stop Spinning Plates: How to Lose Your Balance and Become a Thriving Mother*, as well as a sought-after international speaker. Sue is also on the staff at The Wharton School at the University of Pennsylvania where she teaches current and future business leaders to communicate effectively. She is very active in the coaching community and has held several leadership positions for a variety of nonprofit organizations.

I: There's so much talk about on the subject of work/life balance and it relates to everyone, including leaders. What is your view on the best way to achieve this balance so that leaders can truly excel?

SG: My passion is helping leaders to *not* do work/life balance as everyone else does it. As a reformed workaholic in corporate America, I know about working long hours and then to figure out how to have a life. If you pick up any magazine these days, all you see is "The 7 Tips to Work/Life Balance," etc. Everyone is talking about balancing it all.

The problem is, when we work so hard at trying to do something, it becomes just another to-do item. We are trying to figure out a way to balance our work and then our life, as if they are two separate pieces of ourselves. There's a struggle and people say, "I must be doing something wrong. If everyone else is able to balance it all, there must be something wrong with me."

I want everyone to take a breath and come to a different place—a place of balance and harmony, and even going beyond balance. When you think about balance, think of a seesaw; you finally get it into balance and then something in life comes along and you're thrown off balance. It's a precarious place to be when you're just balancing it all.

Instead, I actually want to take leaders from within a business, an organization, or a family—leaders at all levels—to a place of thriving. Thriving is different for everyone. I like to start with the Merriam-Webster dictionary definition of thrive so we all are starting at the same place. That definition states that to thrive is, "to progress toward or realize a goal despite or because of circumstances."

To thrive is to grow toward something, despite of or because of circumstance. What I've added to this in my work with my clients, and how I bring it alive in daily practice, is that when you thrive—instead of just balancing—it allows you to continue to develop. You get to continue to learn. You make mistakes, you take risks, and you have do-overs.

You continue to move forward while always keeping in sight the goal of having that thriving business and living a thriving life. There isn't that pressure to know it all, to be perfect, or to have everything in this place of balance that is so hard to achieve.

I: How can someone achieve that sense of thriving?

SG: You first have to stop trying to balance it all and know that you can grow and change. There are five pillars that are the foundations to being able to thrive.

Five Pillars of a Thriving Mind-Set

#1: Vision—Thriving leaders have clarity of vision. They see the big picture of what they want in their life and it's very clear. They are not afraid to share this with those around them, and they support others to have a clear vision as well.

By having that vision, leaders who thrive are able to define very clear intentions for what they want. If you have a clear vision of the big picture and how you want to feel when you get there, you're able to obtain the necessary resources. These leaders create what they want. They have the tools and they know how to best utilize their resources.

When you feel overwhelmed and disconnected, you go off track and definitely are not thriving. Most of the time this is because you've lost that connection to your vision. A thriving leader will continually evaluate how connected they are to their vision so they stay on track, and they encourage those around them to stay connected as well.

#2: Focus—This is the one that I see thriving leaders demonstrate most often. Why is focus so important? Here is a research example: One group of plants was given all the water and sunlight they needed, but no attention at all. They had all the resources, but no attention was paid to them. A second group was given the same amount of water, the same amount of sunlight, and they receive a lot of attention or focus.

The only difference between the two groups was positive focus. That positive focus allowed those plants to grow, thrive, and to move forward vigorously, whereas the group with no attention withered and died.

It's the same with leaders. So many leaders feel like they're spinning plates, and that is why I wrote my book. Even early in his presidency it was written about President Obama that he had a lot of plates to spin. There are obviously a lot of activities that you do during your daily life and in business—even when you aren't the president of a nation. Sometimes there is a feeling of being overwhelmed and not being sure what to do first or where to put your focus. It is a sense of not feeling in control—almost like all the aspects of your business are pushing in against you. You may feel that your business or your work is running you instead of the other way around.

If you're busy all day long with this task and that task, this meeting and that meeting, and everything else that you need to accomplish, you will soon become overwhelmed and drained by your work instead of excited and energized. However, thriving leaders take back control; they focus on themselves first.

I created a tool called a Personal Thriving Sphere. Use of this tool involves first putting yourself in the center of the sphere and looking at where you are spending your time and energy for your business. You can also do one for your life and then overlap them. Doing this often is very enlightening and helps you make changes that support thriving.

When you can focus on yourself first and take control of your being, you can put that energy out into the right places. When you're focusing on work that you love and you're working and using your greatness, you take back control. Then you can do that with everyone around you.

Leaders also know where to put their focus. They focus on strengths. They focus on work at which they excel. They focus on their greatness. They get into a flow and focus on the right activities. They're not distracted by doing tasks that they really should not get involved in—it's not their greatness. They know how to delegate those tasks effectively.

Leaders know how to spend their time so they work fewer hours. I'm all about working fewer hours and playing more. It's not that a thriving leader doesn't work hard, but when you're in control and focused, you enjoy your work more, and ultimately you end up being able to spend fewer hours on work and more on play.

#3: Values—Thriving leaders know their values and they focus on fulfilling their values when making decisions for their business and in life. Values are something I am passionate about. It's my firm belief—based on the work I've done around values and the Thriving Values Profile I have created—that your values are your core essence. They are who you are deep down, and I like to equate them to oxygen. When you are not living and doing work in accordance with your values, it's almost like you're suffocating. I've had clients describe it as feeling like living in someone else's skin.

"Although your values may differ from those held by members of your team, you can still create harmony and be effective by honoring each other's values."

I've seen this play out over and over again. When a leader finally stops and takes stock of what their values are as well as the values of the people who are key members of their team, it makes all the difference. Although your values may differ from those held by members of your team, you can create teamwork and be effective by honoring each other's values.

#4: Transformation—Thriving leaders notice when they're off track or when they fear something. They feel fear just like everyone else. I hear from many people, "Oh, those super successful people don't fear anything." And that simply is not true.

All thriving leaders feel fear and have doubts. The difference is that they take risks despite their fear. They make necessary changes. They step out of their comfort zone and do it anyway. They go for it. They have a belief and confidence in themselves. If they notice there's a belief that doesn't fit with where they want to go or with what their vision is, they work with a mentor to make change. They bring the necessary resources in around them. They understand that they need to embrace change. They're not afraid of making changes for themselves and supporting change in those around them.

Being able to transform is essential for a thriving leader because you can't stay stuck in one place. If you do, you won't be able to move forward for yourself, you certainly won't be able to lead others to move forward, and you certainly won't be thriving.

#5: Results—You can't thrive without results. Thriving leaders know they're going to get results. They expect positive results. They expect to succeed. In order to do that, they set goals that are effective and they consistently measure the milestones. They move forward and check in at all the milestones. They reach out to mentors to help them achieve results. They bring in a team around them.

They also celebrate success, both their own and the success of others around them. They don't just say, "Reached this goal. Check. Go to the next one." They embrace success with those around them. They know what success means and they appreciate abundance. They appreciate what they've achieved.

Celebrating and acknowledging results are two crucial components to thriving because otherwise you have tunnel vision. You're just going along saying, "Did this, did that." There's no passion in that, and that's how you get burned out. There's no connection to what you've achieved and no excitement to moving forward to the next goal.

Appreciation is huge. By noticing, appreciating, and celebrating your own results, and being able to reach out and celebrate with those around you, you thrive as a leader.

LEADERSHIP OPPORTUNITY:

I hear from so many people who are spinning plates, "I don't have time. I don't have time to spend on myself." I use the phrase *Take Five to Thrive*. You can take five minutes to thrive. It can be just asking that question, "What can I do in this moment to thrive?" or it can be sitting still for five minutes and just breathing. It's just about taking five minutes to focus on you and asking, "Am I honoring my values today?"

Anyone can Take Five to Thrive every day. Carve out five minutes, sit down, and ask yourself, "What am I doing today to support myself in thriving?"

LEADERSHIP SUCCESS:

I was doing a workshop and leading a values exercise for a company, and the president, owner, and founder of the company called Athena's—Jennifer Jolicoeur—was part of the group. She was sitting down, but when we did the values exercise, all of a sudden she got up and left. So did several other people in the audience, which sometimes happens.

She came back afterward and shared with me and everyone else in the group that she had been struggling with the vision of her company and where the company was going. When she got to her top three core essences or values and she was looking at her paper, she knew that those values were not what the company was connected to anymore.

Somehow she and the company had gone off track. She shared with the group that she had a breakdown and then she had a breakthrough; she needed to make changes. As a great leader, she took that and decided to do something with it. She didn't just sit there and say, "Oh no, we're off track, we're having problems." She gathered all of her leaders in the company the next morning and said, "Here are the values that this company was founded on and we need to do something to get back in line."

She actually created this amazing initiative called The Athena's Cup and as a company they are supporting the Susan G. Komen breast cancer organization by collecting bras and making donations. Her goal is to raise half a million dollars. It's huge, and it came from her having that breakthrough around her values and then taking action.

Lee Strauss
Sutton, NSW, Australia

Lee Strauss has worked with and coached some of the world's most influential people on dealing with disasters and crisis. From his work behind the scenes providing guidance to government officials, to advisory roles with captains of industry and ministering in both crisis management and crisis leadership, his focus hasn't wavered.

By paying attention to three key elements—communication, clarity of values/vision, and caring for others—leaders can develop and manage the human dimensions of a crisis.

Lee has observed that in the calamites of the world today, we are suffering as a result of failed leadership from leaders who didn't follow their true north.

I: You say that crisis is a defining moment for a leader. You've acted as a powerful guide to leaders to ensure that they can meet the challenges that occur when this comes up. Can you share with us what you perceive are some of the greatest challenges now and how you're helping leaders through them, particularly in a crisis?

LS: When a crisis strikes, it's a very emotional event, and not just for the people it affects within the organization. It is probably one of the most challenging events that a leader will face. As you can imagine, they're being bombarded with all sorts of information and are not sure what's correct and what isn't. It's a solemn event. It sometimes leaves a leader doubting their ability to get to the bottom of what happened.

Absolutely normal people behave in some strange ways during times of crisis because their security has been threatened. They're not sure what's happening around them or how it's going to affect them and their family. It's a leader's job to calm the situation down by being level-headed and very clear about sifting through the information that's coming in, verifying that information, and making sure they're telling the people within the organization what the true extent of the crisis is. A leader must reassure them that they have a plan to get on top of the crisis.

I: I would think that many times you must be consulting and coaching these leaders on situations that they have never had to deal with before. How do you bring forward the skills that they need in order to handle the situation, particularly if it's something that they've never experienced?

LS: You're right. I usually find myself in a situation where the crisis or the disaster has just happened. The majority of my strengths are with natural disasters, although in the last year I have been dealing with companies that have had organizational disasters caused by various things. Again, it's about knowing how the people within your organization are faring and getting the leaders to lead through that crisis.

I start by reassuring the leaders that they have everything within them to be able to lead their organization, and then we focus on three simple but very effective principles: communication, clarity of vision, and caring for others.

Three Key Principles for Crisis Leadership

1. Communication: We start by making sure the communication is clear. In the world we live in, quite often the media is all over a story before the leader is approached about what's really happened. If they don't get on top of the media and start releasing accurate information about what's happening, the media will run with the information they have. The media's information is usually an inaccurate portrayal of events, and that can lead to people inside and outside of that organization being emotionally affected by that misinformation. It's important to get a really good communication plan together.

2. Clarity of Values/Vision: Get really clear about the visions—the values—that are important to the organization.

3. Caring for Others: Begin showing a lot of care and sincerity to the people within the organization through the relationships you've built. Generally, this is where I find a lot of leaders lead from behind. They don't have the relationships that are required before the crisis. I find that there's a lack of trust from the direct reports that their leader is really on top of the situation. It's very important to get this under control and start building relationships and reassuring people during the crisis.

I: It seems that would be very challenging, particularly during a crisis, because it can be challenging to build those relationships even when there is no crisis.

LS: Yes, that's absolutely right.

I: How do you help the leaders at the very top—who I assume are the ones that you work with most during a crisis—particularly if it's some sort of national disaster or crisis of that nature? What's the trickledown effect?

LS: Essentially, the leaders have to establish that they're on it. Leaders can develop this skill through training and through experiences like problem solving, decision making, and conflict resolution.

Leaders can fine-tune these traits by paying close attention to such areas such as integrity, courage, and risk taking. They can take care of their direct reports so that they don't have to worry about accomplishing the mission.

For example, this can be fueled by reflecting and learning in an effort to bolster leadership competency and conflict—things that are really needed during a crisis.

Again, it's critical that they have a well-honed **communication strategy** and great personal communication skills. Quite often, as coaches, one of the first things we learn about is active listening. Listening to how the direct reports and the people within the organization are hearing and using the appropriate eye contact and responses can reassure people. Reiterating key points if they're not understood can also be crucial.

The leader needs to have a **clear vision** that can be communicated to direct reports so they understand it and so that they take some ownership of it and endorse it. That's a really powerful tool.

Then, the most important part—which is sorely lacking in leaders of today—is showing sincere interest and **genuine concern for others** and meeting their emotional needs. People will respond well to respect, dignity, appreciation, attention, and trust. This goes even further during a crisis because people have emotional needs that have to be met.

Once you meet your direct reports emotionally, they start feeling much better about themselves, they start understanding what the situation is, and they can filter that back through to their direct reports. It will flow right through the organization.

I: Are you finding that companies, governments, and so forth are acting more proactively and inviting you in before this happens as a proactive means to be able to deal with crisis? Or is it usually a reactive measure once a disaster has occurred?

LS: My experience is usually after the fact. Unfortunately, I think the majority of people go through life thinking, *It won't happen to me.* Although, with the amount of disasters we've seen in the last century, those attitudes are changing, but very slowly. The other thing that I tend to find is that in the last century, there has been a lot of emphasis on crisis management. People get that confused with what crisis leadership is really about.

Don't get me wrong, crisis management is very important, and every organization should have a crisis management plan. Crisis leadership, however, is more about those relationships that I talked about earlier. Having and showing sincere interest and a genuine concern for the people in your organization, establishing that you're a person of principles and that you have high standards, and having a clear vision and clear mission for your organization so that in times of crisis people can fall back on that is critical in these times. People already know the leaders. They've already established trust that the leader will do whatever it takes to guide the organization not just through the crisis, but also through the rebuilding process.

I: Do you do your consulting and coaching primarily from afar, or are you actually called to go on site? What's prevalent these days with this type of crisis consulting and coaching?

LS: I started my career working for the Australian government, and in that role, I found myself quite often going to the location. That, I must admit, is my preference. It's much easier to feel those emotional connections when I am face-to-face with the people. I have delivered assistance over the phone, although I don't feel that I can be as effective as when I can be there in person with the leader.

I started by telling you that crisis management is one of the biggest challenges a leader will face, and they have a lot of emotion going through them. Sometimes they just need someone to touch them on the shoulder or make that observation that the leader is also in emotional turmoil. Sometimes they just need you to do some work with them, one on one, to reassure them that they have all the strength they need inside them. All they need to do is dig a little deeper and put their self-limiting beliefs behind them.

It's never too late to start building those caring relationships and showing the people around you just how much you care for them. Have genuine concern for their emotional needs, because leaders don't always come from the top.

"Life is short and disaster can come from anywhere; it's borderless . . . there may be a day when we're called upon to lead the people around us. It's important for all of us to start honing some of those skills."

There are lots of instances where I've worked with organizations and there hasn't been anyone on the board or anyone at the C-level, the CEO, etc. involved. It hasn't been those people who had to lead the organization through the crisis. It has been someone in middle management who stepped forward and led their organization through the crisis.

For each and every one of us, there may be a day when we're called upon to lead the people around us—people we care about, people we work with at the office. It's important for all of us to start honing some of those skills. One of the most important skills is just having those caring relationships.

Life is short and disaster can come from anywhere; it's borderless. We never know when we're going to get caught up in a crisis. It could be a major motor vehicle accident or a natural disaster—you only need to read the paper and within a month you'll find that a natural disaster has occurred somewhere in the world.

Crisis can hit us at any time, and if you've already got those relationships and you've developed some skills in those three principles that I talked about—having good communication skills, being clear about who you are as a person and what you want for your own future, and being able to genuinely show concern and having that caring relationship—that will stand you in a good stead to be the crisis leader.

LEADERSHIP OPPORTUNITY:

We all face crisis. For a lot of us, losing a loved one through whatever means is a personal crisis that we face. My advice to those people is to reflect on that person's life. Reflect on what magic moments they gave you. What was their greatest gift and how you can take that gift and not only apply it to your life, but also apply it to all the people around you and the people that surround them to enrich their lives and to help promote their legacy?

Whether it's a leader leading an organization, a leader leading a nation, or a leader leading a family, I keep coming back to having clear communication, making sense of what has happened, and then really communicating that. You need to have a really clear understanding of what your goals are or what your mission is, what you want to achieve in life, and how you envision the future of your family or your organization or your country. Then you need to illustrate that through genuine emotional care for those around you.

LEADERSHIP SUCCESS:

One of the stories that I like to tell is about an earthquake and tsunami that occurred. I'd been working in the emergency medical facility all day, and I noticed a little girl standing outside. She was pacing up and down, and when I actually broke off about six hours later for a meal break, I went outside and just happened to stop and ask her if she was okay. She told me that her brother and her father were lying in the hospital, they needed some blood, and that she couldn't afford to pay for their blood.

I was horrified that at the end of the day, it all came down to fifteen dollars. I was able to help that little girl and help her brother and father survive; unfortunately, she lost her mother. For me, that story shows just how desperate things can get.

I guess I'm like a lot of people sometimes—my glass is half empty and I'm not focused on being grateful for all the things that I do have. When I get like that, quite often my partner will remind me of the little girl whose whole family and future rested on fifteen dollars. We think nothing of spending fifteen dollars in the majority of the countries; it would be a cup of coffee and a sandwich. Yet fifteen dollars was what it took to save two people's lives.

Sharon Melnick, Ph.D.
New York, New York, USA

Dr. Sharon Melnick is a business psychologist and coach dedicated to helping talented and successful people get out of their own way. She's informed by ten years of research at Harvard Medical School and trained in cutting edge stress-resilience techniques. She's a leading authority in helping business professionals move to the next level and feel secure about themselves in insecure times.

A dynamic trainer and executive coach for businesspeople in varying functional and sales roles, she has a strong track record of successful engagements at varied national organizations including Deloitte Consulting, Oracle Corporation, Pitney Bowes, Merrill Lynch, Korn/Ferry International, and many others. She has taught her effectiveness techniques at the School of Management at Boston College and at Fortune 500 companies and nonprofit organizations. Her training is from Yale University, UC Berkeley, and the Institute for Management Studies.

I: You have done a lot of work in helping people get out of their own way. Can you share, from your perspective, how that applies to leadership?

SM: Absolutely. In order to be a strong leader, there are certain capabilities you have to possess. You have to have a clear vision. You have to hold on to that vision. You have to be able to get people to the goal, which means you have to know how to get to that goal through the people with whom you work. You have to be able to engage others' hearts and minds, which means that you have to engage your own heart and mind.

The basis of strong leadership is to be secure in your own self. You have to be able to effectively lead yourself in order to effectively lead other people. That's often what I work on in terms of executive coaching—helping the client to be an effective leader of their own self so that they can use their natural capabilities to be an effective leader over other people.

I: We have so many leadership roles—some of which we aren't even aware. Can you share what you view are leadership challenges, regardless of whether our leadership roles are in organizations, in our business, or in our family?

"The basis of strong leadership is to be secure in your own self. You have to be able to effectively lead yourself in order to effectively lead other people."

SM: Sure. Let me do so by elaborating on the concept of how leaders get in their own way—how leaders get derailed.

I often find that leadership derailers stem from a confidence-related issue. Of course, in these turbulent times, any leader can be tempted to be distracted and overwhelmed, and they can make their focus very short-term and reactive. Situations can be overly complex, and it may be hard to make the right decisions. All leaders are facing those challenges these days. However, what I find to be a timeless challenge for leaders is the way leaders get in their own way, and this always seems to stem from a confidence-related issue.

To the extent that you have a doubt about your own self, it's going to set you up to act in a specific way. One way this shows up is instead of having a secure opinion and staying strong in that opinion and being able to communicate it to other people, you might tend to second-guess what your superiors want to hear. This may even drive you to make decisions for the wrong reasons—such as politically-based reasons that will affect how you're going to look—rather than basing your decisions on the right thing to do.

I find that people don't have a conviction. They don't really know what their convictions are, and therefore the people under them don't really know what they stand for either. They feel like they're being jerked around or that priorities are adjusted too often. In that regard, organizations don't get the best contribution from a leader; the leader's attention is often focused in the weeds.

When a leader is experiencing a confidence-related issue, it often causes them to stay within their comfort zone. It causes them to procrastinate and not really put themselves out there with their good

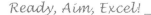

thinking. They're often very prepared and smart, but they won't speak up in meetings—they won't put themselves out there.

For example, I worked with a guy who was on the management team of a biotech start-up company. He was in charge of making the technology roadmap for the company. He was the CTO, he was the founder, and he knew more about the technology than anyone else. Because of his confidence-related issue, he never really spoke out with conviction about where he thought the company should go.

He would procrastinate on making that roadmap. He put a couple of things together and then he would go to the CEO and ask, "What do you think about this?" The company wasn't getting their best from him in terms of his leadership.

When he was able to build that confidence in himself and to trust his abilities—to feel that he was worth it—he was a much stronger voice on the team. He actually created that technology roadmap. He made choices about what they should be putting their money into and what they shouldn't, and his choices actually saved the company from a major loss of a client that would have led to company bankruptcy.

You might be prepared and you might be smart, but if you don't have confidence, you're not going to really put yourself out there. He held a senior role in the organization, but particularly for women in mid-levels of an organization, this is something I hear all the time.

In fact, I was talking with someone from one of the big food companies recently and that's exactly what she was saying to me. She's a mid-level employee in the Human Resources department. She said, "There I am in those meetings with the senior management, and I know that they need my information—that's why they have me in there. I'm the protector of the franchises. I'm the protector of the people. I have to make sure that senior management doesn't launch any new initiative that's going to affect our legal or our people policy. That's why they have me there. I think to myself, *Should I say it? Should I not say it? What if I say it? What if they think it's stupid?*"

That's a perfect example of the mind-churning that people go through. You can't be an effective leader if you're caught up in whether or not you have something of value to offer.

We were able to talk it through, and she was able to leave feeling purposeful and not allowing herself to be caught up in the moment worrying, *What are people going to think?* but instead to execute for the long-term. She was able to look at it from the perspective of being the protector of the people, to imagine when those senior leaders were going to be implementing those policies, and to really picture what it was going to be like—that made all the difference.

You can tell the quality of a leader by how far out they think. Someone who has a confidence-related issue is very "in the moment." They continually ask themselves questions such as, "What are people going to think when I send out this e-mail? What are people going to think if I speak up? Can I second-guess what my boss wants me to say?"

These are all immediate concerns—I call them sugar highs—when you're trying to do something to get an immediate response or to prevent an immediate criticism.

"A a true leader is executing and thinking for the long-term . . . There's an interesting connection between the degree of confidence you have as a leader and how far out you're able to have that vision and execute it."

A true leader is executing and thinking for the long-term. They're thinking way out in the future. They're asking, "Where are we going to go with the organization?" or "How do I need to lay out my team or my organization?"

There's an interesting connection between the degree of confidence you have as a leader and how far out you're able to have that vision and execute it.

I: That's an amazing perception. How do you help people start to gain confidence and think more strategically if they're in that place of real concern about what others are thinking of them?

SM: How do you lift yourself out of the weeds? In terms of the confidence issue, I think that there are a couple of exercises that leaders can do. One thing that's very simple but can make a quite powerful shift for people is to identify what their doubt is that leads them to have that gap in confidence—whether it's a big or small pocket of doubt.

I find that people tend to be pretty vague when I ask them what their doubt is about. They don't really know. They respond with something vague like, "I'm not as smart as my colleagues," or "I just don't have what it takes." That's not really a challenge that you can take on because you don't even know what it is.

The first thing that needs to be done is to dig down and get very specific. Really break out the components of exactly what it is that you have had a doubt about, because then we know what we're up against.

For some people, it might be their ability to think strategically, their ability to present in front of groups, or their ability to do certain financial transactions, etc. Identifying what it is, is a good first step.

Then there is an exercise you can do. Given that these are the areas you perceive as weaknesses and as prohibiting you from putting yourself out there in front as a leader, rather than staying vague and confused about this doubt that you have, you're going to tackle it head-on. You're not going to stay in that open loop thinking, *I should be smarter, but I'm not, and so therefore . . .* and spinning your wheels.

Here's what you can do to make a decision once and for all. I call this accept exercise Accept versus Accomplish.

Make a list of those things you have identified as very specific aspects of your doubt. Then, go through each one of those components and ask, "Is this something I can accept about myself?" What you are really asking is, "Can I really focus on my strengths? Can I embrace my strengths and appreciate them? Can I find a way to work around these kinds of things?"

Figure out what it is that you have a doubt about, and then make a decision—it's got to be one or the other: are you going to accept that component or accomplish it? Are you going to accept it as a part of you, or are you going to make a plan to accomplish it so that it is no longer an issue for you?

Usually, people list a couple of areas of doubt and they go through them, make their plans, and within weeks they're taking off like a rocket in their area of leadership.

LEADERSHIP OPPORTUNITY:

These days all of us are caught up, overwhelmed, and overloaded with information, and everyone's grabbing for our attention. In order to keep leaders thinking strategically about the big picture, it is important to set aside some time during the week—an hour is good if you can do that—to take yourself out of the everyday and the schedule and ask yourself those strategic questions: "Where am I going? Where is my business going? What's important to me right now? Is it the same or has it shifted? What can I be doing better? How can I feel better about myself?" All of that self-management and self-talk can be vital.

I find when clients do that, it really helps to keep them effective as a leader because they're always keeping that long-term vision in mind.

LEADERSHIP SUCCESS:

I worked with a woman who was at a big consulting firm. She was kind of a junior partner but she really wanted to be a senior leader. She aspired to be like those women in the senior-level positions within the organization. There she was, spending her time during the day answering e-mails with really thorough, technical responses. She was a bit of an order-taker. She was very good with people and she mentored her team, but she wasn't in the meetings with her C-level clients providing strategic thinking and really putting herself out there or taking her clients' thinking to the next level.

She had to feel that she was worth it and that she could bring that kind of value before she could step into the room. When she made that change in herself, she was finally able to be out in front saying to her clients, "Here's where your business is. Here's where I think it needs to go. Let me consult with you and help you think through what the next steps are for your business."

She did that, and she grew her clients' business. Within six months she was promoted to a regional leader of her area. Within nine months she was on the international decision-making committees for her huge international firm. She didn't trust her own value. When she changed that, then she was able to be out in front leading rather than behind asking how she was doing.

Kim Zilliox, MA, MBA, CPCC
San Jose, California, USA

Kim Zilliox is a leadership consultant and coach with nearly twenty years of experience in her field. She develops leaders in all industries and across all functions through one-on-one coaching, leadership workshops, and corporate webinars. She also speaks at conferences and to various organizations across the globe.

Using her prior experience in managerial roles both in high-tech and nonprofit sectors, she coaches her clients and program participants to increase their leadership skills, thereby contributing to organizational and career growth. As a published author, Kim has written about leadership strategies for women and often speaks to women's leadership organizations about leadership development and career growth.

I: Can you tell us a little bit about yourself and what you do?

KZ: Sure. I am a leadership facilitator: I facilitate the development of current and future leaders. I do that through one-on-one leadership coaching, company-sponsored workshops, webinars, and speaking at conferences, as well as through my books. The most recent book to which I contributed is called *Savvy Leadership Strategies for Women*. Fundamentally, I believe we all have a great leader inside of us that is waiting to be uncovered. I simply help people to bring that leader out.

I: That is beautiful. Women these days have so many leadership roles. What do you find to be your most common coaching topics?

KZ: There are about fifteen topics that are fundamental to my practice, and there are the four core fundamentals to all of my work:

- Developing high emotional intelligence
- Developing strong leadership presence

- Developing effective communication
- Building healthy confidence

Working with people on their brand, self-promotion, interpersonal skills, management skills, delegation, empowerment, etc.—all of these stem from those foundational skills.

Emotional intelligence is a core foundation for any great leader. By now, most people are pretty aware of the basics of this concept but have very little aptitude to move the needle in terms of their own "emotional quotient" or EQ.

In a nutshell, this concept is about the ability to be highly self-aware with regard to one's own emotions and emotional triggers, to manage their own behavior at all times, to have a keen awareness of what others are experiencing with regard to emotions, and to use all of this information to successfully facilitate interactions and build strong relationships through the use of effective communication.

Not all great leaders have strong proficiency in these areas, but we know that an overwhelming number of them do. Some of my clients are better at self-awareness and self-management, so I work with them on developing their skills in terms of other awareness; it is not a natural skill set for them. On the flip side, there are those clients who have an incredible ability to read people and situations, but their inability to self-regulate is impacting their career negatively, so that is the work that we focus on.

Emotional intelligence impacts us wherever we go, and it is amazing to see how my clients and workshop participants improve their lives by effecting behavior change in just this one area.

I also work with clients around leadership presence and building healthy confidence, which are strongly interrelated. In *Savvy Leadership Strategies for Women,* I wrote about building a strong inner core because it is fundamental to being a strong leader.

Truly amazing leaders have a strong, solid foundation that comes from authentic self-respect and confidence. When leaders don't have this solid foundation developed, it shows up in who they are and what they do.

We've all seen examples of this where people are overly arrogant to compensate for their lack of confidence, which does not work and can be very damaging to an organization and to one's career. On the other hand, a leader who doesn't feel fully grounded in who they are and in the decisions they're making is equally damaging to the organization. That person's career will stagnate at best.

We all struggle with self-confidence from time to time. I work with people to build a strong foundation and core in order to help them know who they are as a leader and to trust themselves to make the right decisions at any given point in time.

Leadership presence is critical for anyone wanting to move up to the next level inside of an organization. People forget that in order to be seen at the next level, they have to act as if they were already there. They typically have already proven themselves in terms of their technical or tactical abilities, but if this is the area for them to develop, they're still acting and presenting themselves within the measure of their current role. I work with clients to identify key competencies of leadership presence and together we work to develop the perception they are creating through their everyday behavior.

I: That is really important, powerful, and something we don't always think about. Your last book was focused on women. Can you tell us a little bit about your work within women's leadership?

KZ: Sure. I'm having a great time contributing to women in the workplace who are eager to contribute in leadership capacities. These women are absolutely amazing and are tremendously valuable to their organizations.

I have had the privilege of speaking to a number of women's organizations and networks and I love the energy and their veracious appetites for learning and applying the information that I present. Women have come a long way in the workplace over the last fifty years, but we still have quite a ways to go—which is tough to see—and I am happy to help.

I know I am an idealist, but I really would love to see what I call "50/50 by 2050." This means that 50% of senior leadership would be represented by women, and 50% represented by men statistically across all industries and functions domestically. Admittedly, it is quite a stretch goal, but what an amazing goal to shoot for, and hopefully eventually achieve! Women are still very under-represented at the executive levels, and it is not serving our companies, our communities, or our world.

I work with women to develop themselves for these roles from both the outside-in, as well as the inside-out. By this I mean that there are competencies that they need to make sure they develop such as physical leadership presence, strong communication skills, strategic thinking, being a visionary, etc. These are skills that everyone needs in order to be a strong leader and are a strong part of my consulting practice, with both men and women.

"Women are still very under-represented at the executive levels, and it is not serving our companies, our communities, or our world."

Then there are the inside-out areas such as self-confidence. I love working with both men and women on these areas, and as I have said, do more work with women about their self-confidence. These women do work around believing that they can do what they actually can do, and how to get out of their own way.

The great news is that it's an area that can be corrected and reprogrammed most of the time. It is actually easier than some of the behavioral changes that need to be made in terms of emotional intelligence and interpersonal challenges that more men potentially face than women. That is just to say that the good news is that we're able to do this work pretty quickly with women and then they catapult in terms of their productivity and impact in an organization.

Another aspect to consider is that, because the corporate environment has been so heavily male dominated in terms of leadership, women became programmed to think that's the only way it can be done. They think, *I am different, so I cannot be a great leader.* It looks ridiculous to actually read that on paper, but it is how we work as human beings; if we do not fit the mold, we think we are wrong. Once women and organizations start to embrace the tangible benefits that female leadership provides, these internal and external boundaries will be broken down more and more until we reach the tipping point—for which I cannot wait!

I: What are the challenges facing women today in this journey toward 50/50 in 2050?

KZ: I think the number one challenge facing women is getting out of their own way. Another challenge is believing in themselves and allowing themselves to move forward. It is still about overcoming prejudices, stereotypes, or the past mentality in terms of how women are seen, especially in executive roles. We have made strides, but it has not shifted yet.

"Once women and organizations start to embrace the tangible benefits that female leadership provides, these internal and external boundaries will be broken down more and more until we reach the tipping point."

Continuing to educate people—especially men in the organization—about how women work and communicate, and the benefits of having women represented across all levels is so important. It is also important to educate women on working with men, communication, and how they work. We are still two opposite sexes, and how we work together is probably always going to be a challenge, but the better both men and women can navigate that, the better the end result will be.

On a daily basis I see firsthand what works well and what does not work well in the areas of communication and leadership. I feel truly blessed to be able to do what I do and have the honor of contributing to people being successful and leading great lives.

LEADERSHIP OPPORTUNITY:

Create a future and then live into it. I suggest that people create a statement for themselves. They need to come up with something about their future—who they are as a leader, what their career looks like, who they will impact, or even a contribution that they may make to the world or to the planet.

It should be one sentence so it is easy to read and easy to take in in less than the time that it takes to brush your teeth in the morning. It should be written in the present tense and it should be in the first person. It should be extremely inspiring for you. If it is not inspiring or if it is something you "should" do, then recreate it. Make it inspiring so that you get excited when you read it and think about it. Read it every day to begin your day with purpose, and every evening to put your subconscious to work on it as you sleep. Say it until you mean it, and then keep saying it until it is true. It will be before you know it!

LEADERSHIP SUCCESS:

I had a client who was a senior manager at a large organization that we would all know. When she first came to me, her internal dialogue was incredibly limiting. She had numerous beliefs that were created by her culture and family while growing up that were stopping her.

They were conversations like, "I cannot speak up in that meeting," and "Who I am I to move to that next level?" and "Who am I to suggest that?" These are all limiting beliefs and thoughts that we can all have, and she was being stopped by them.

That became the focus of our work. She had to learn to let those go, to learn to speak up when appropriate, and to learn to do what she needed to do to get in the right place to contribute in the right frame of mind. She also needed to learn what she needed to learn in terms of the specifics of her role.

I am happy to say she is now a VP in her organization which means she received three promotions in a very short time since we started working together. She is unstoppable. She has always said that she would love to be the CEO of an organization. She is now coaching and mentoring female colleagues that have these same limiting beliefs. This is why I love what I do.

Rose Mattran, Ed.D.
Sarasota, Florida, USA

Dr. Rose Mattran began her career working in the field of public education. After earning a Doctorate in Education from Rutgers University, she served on the adjunct faculty of Rutgers University Graduate School of Education. She was the Director of the New Jersey School of the Arts under the direction of the New Jersey Department of Education and is a published author in the field of Creative Drama.

After a fifteen-year career in education, Rose opened an executive search firm with her husband. Over the last twenty-four years they have placed mid- to senior-level executives in companies across the country. Rose is a certified executive coach, a member of the International Coaching Federation, and has coached hundreds of corporate clients through career transitions.

I: I know you're coaching with the outgrowth of over twenty-four years in the executive search business and that you have placed hundreds of people in positions of either expanded leadership or entering into new leadership. I'm thrilled to have you share your wisdom on the subject.

Let me start by asking you to share how you've observed leadership requirements or demands changing in the U.S.

RM: One of the unique situations that our country is facing now is that we actually have four generations in the workforce at the same time. We have the Traditionalists, which are the people who are now in their senior years—age sixty-five and up—in the workforce. There are quite a number of those people. We also have the Baby Boomer generation, the Gen X, and then we have the Millenniums. Being able to relate to all of those generations at the same time is one of the very challenging issues leaders face. That in itself is unique to our current situation.

Then, of course, we can overlay the ability for people to communicate instantaneously around the world. In the prime of their career, it would have taken the Traditionalists maybe four or five days to get information. They also thought in concentric circles about their activities. It was local, then state, then regional, and then national. Millenniums today are thinking, *I can talk to someone in Singapore and connect with information over there at the same speed as I can with the person who's sitting in the cubicle next to me.*

These kinds of issues really have played significantly into the role of a leader being able to stay in touch with the constituency that he is leading. He must be able to understand them and work more effectively with them.

> *"Leaders today are not from the command and control school of leadership. They are much more collaborative in their leadership style."*

I: That's such an important perspective on the conditions today. I know that major companies look to you for placement of their future leaders. What attributes do you look for in identifying effective business leaders for these huge corporations?

RM: Aside from being well educated and well versed in vertical industry, today's leaders do not tend to come from the command and control school of leadership. They are much more collaborative in their leadership style.

Some of the attributes that contribute to that style might include:

- Being an extraordinarily good listener
- Being smart and creative
- Listening and formulating penetrating questions
- Openly sharing ideas with others
- Tending to listen to others rather than to speak
- Preferring not to be the smartest person in a room
- Synthesizing information well
- Not being afraid to make mistakes

Most of the leaders I talk to chuckle when they talk about making mistakes. There is one very prominent leader I work with who has a sign on his desk that says, "Always make new mistakes."

A willingness to consider all of the options and not be fearful in the current economic situation is key. The world is changing very quickly, and today's good leaders are saying, "Bring it on. I'm up for it." They're ready to fight the good fight.

I: What a wonderful change. How do you describe effective corporate leadership?

"The really effective leaders are taking the recent changes as an opportunity . . . There is no more linear thinking; they are thinking in a very holistic sense about their business."

RM: It is difficult to articulate one definition of corporate leadership in this particular moment. With the recession, we have some clients who have said, "Okay, we're not going to make any money, but we're not going to lose any money either. We're going to stay in the game, and we're going to drive a particular outcome."

Other people have absolutely cowered and believed everything that is coming across their desk in print or in media. Those people aren't very effective leaders.

The really effective leaders are taking the recent changes as an opportunity. It's definitely an opportunity to grab market share, to move in a different direction, and to look at people and have conversations like, "If money were no object, what would you want to do?" There is no more linear thinking; they are thinking in a very holistic sense about their business.

The creative leaders today are not, as I mentioned before, command and control, top-down kinds of leaders. They're surrounding themselves with creative people who are also very good leaders and listening to the managers that are below them who are gathering information in many different ways than they ever have before.

They treat employees in a very different way. Every person in their company feels that they have something to contribute, and as I said before, that "control down" concept is making its way out of the rolls of creative people—good leaders. There are some companies that are modeled in this elaborative style of leadership, and they're doing marvelously.

I: You're such a leader in your field and you are providing wonderful potential leaders to companies. What do you do for your own professional and personal leadership growth? Is there something you do on a regular basis?

RM: I am very involved in my community here in Sarasota. I like taking on challenges and leadership roles. When I see organizations that are struggling. I am frequently asked to step in, and I do.

The other things that I like doing, which are very helpful for me in our executive search business, is making it a point to continue to keep up with the trends in the industries in which we specialize. I like observing leadership styles and feel like I'm a constant student of leadership and business today.

I: What are some of the biggest challenges that you find with the candidates you interview for these positions to place in these companies today?

RM: There is a lot going on right now. The economy has certainly played a big role in who is willing to do what. There is uncertainty in the marketplace right now. But the challenges that candidates face right now are mostly linked to their ability to get their arms around change. Change will be a factor forever—not just right now. The world is changing faster and faster. The younger people in our marketplace right now understand that better than the older people.

Another challenge right now is that every company is faced with having to do more with less. Traditional roles, traditional job titles, and leadership roles are changing dramatically. For example, in the 1950s you probably had to work for a company for several years and make minor steps up the corporate ladder before you could get to become a leader in that organization. It used to be that leadership was something you earned by longevity and by doing a number of things right over a long period of time.

Today, critical roles in companies are given to people who have a particular skill that is needed quickly and on demand. That's what "Talent Acquisition" specialists in Human Resources are all about. Many of the candidates working now haven't really matured as leaders. They've got great horsepower, but they just haven't gotten their arms around their leadership style.

That's where I come in. That's where I'm coaching people. I can see that they're going to be great leaders, but the companies are needing them to step up faster than the natural maturation process would take them.

"It used to be that leadership was something you earned by longevity and by doing a number of things right. Today, leadership and critical roles in companies are given to people who have a particular skill that's needed quickly and on demand."

I coach on leadership and career transition. Some of these people are moving to different divisions within a company, some of them are moving straight up in their company, and some of them are moving out of their company.

I: We're definitely in a time of change, and it seems that the flexibilities you mentioned are really critical to anyone in a leadership role.

RM: Yes, indeed. Everyone has to be as open to all opportunities as they possibly can.

Photo on p. 268 by Andy Zirna

LEADERSHIP OPPORTUNITY:

For companies that really want to move ahead and capitalize on the talent they have, coaches can provide insight to a lot of their employees that they would not gain on their own. There's a lot of talent inside, but unfortunately they fall by the wayside because not-so-astute leaders aren't interested in looking down the ranks.

Coaching a transition within a company for the corporate side or coaching someone to move into an area where they've always had a passion to work is an enormously beneficial exercise to go through with people. It's sometimes difficult on the front end to convince everyone of that, but the people who come through the process are very pleased with what they have accomplished.

LEADERSHIP SUCCESS:

It's really important for people—especially young people who aspire to become leaders—to stay in touch with the company they're in at the time. In other words, grow where you're planted if you can. I've recently had two or three people come to me because they want to move up but they're apprehensive about it. Their coaching assignment was to see how they can get into leadership positions.

Interestingly enough, early on in the coaching process all of them spoke about going back to their current company and seeing what might be available there. Through those kinds of dialogues, every one of them wound up in a more challenging role that was a stepping stone. They didn't become leaders overnight, but they got on a leadership path or a management training path that they had not been considered for before.

I would say to anyone who is looking for something more than what they have in their current situation, don't just throw the baby out with the bathwater and think, *This isn't going to happen here.* Go back, and before you move on, make sure that where you are right then and there doesn't provide another opportunity. Be creative and flexible in your thinking about how that might get you further toward an ultimate goal. In the case of those folks, that actually worked very well for four people.

Scott Kerschbaumer
Pittsburgh, Pennsylvania, USA

Scott Kerschbaumer is a serial entrepreneur. Scott took his lead from his own father and grandfather and decided early on that he never wanted to work for anyone else.

Beginning with the iconic lemonade stand in grade school, Scott forged his own way through a number of really successful businesses from the ground up. With very little formal education, Scott had to go through an intuitive school of hard knocks to make him an expert in his field. Through the years Scott has become successful in a number of different business endeavors. He is a person of incredible action.

I: You have a tremendous energy about you that I really admire. What drives you as an entrepreneur?

SK: The number one thing that drives me is boredom. To be honest with you, I get bored fairly easily. It can be in terms of reading a book, playing a game, or building a business.

I am just a few years older than the generation that was either fortunate or not so fortunate to be immediately diagnosed and put on all kinds of medication for what ails me in terms of the tagline of ADD, ADHD, or name your own title. I'm a little bit older, so they didn't put that tag on me. They just kind of put me in a little box and said, "Oh, he's just . . . he's just . . . "

So with that in mind, I'm easily distracted. I can jump around from thing to thing and from project to project. Conversely, I can also be very focused on a task. I will stay up all night to make sure that something is finished if it needs to be finished. I forget to sleep—I just finish it and then move on to the next thing.

It's a weird kind of hybrid where I'm easily distracted and want to go and do the next thing but then I end up getting bored. At the same time, I'll spend forty-eight hours straight making sure that a project gets finished on time.

I am the king of the procrastinators. I procrastinate to no end. I use the phrase, "I have so much to do I'm going to the beach." I will say that in the school of hard knocks, I had a school of very soft knocks. I was fortunate enough to have a mom and dad who took great care of me. I was one of those coddled, silver spoon boys up until I was about sixteen or seventeen, and then my Dad lost everything.

If you're out there trying to reach for that brass ring if you've never had it before, keep on reaching for it, because it's great when you can get it. But if you've had it and lost it, it makes you really want to go back and grab it because you know what it is and what it feels like.

That was the only hard knock—to have to sit there and watch my dad, who was also his own man and an entrepreneur, lose everything. I am trying to do things a little bit differently. I'm trying to do all of the good things that he taught me and intersperse some breaks, if you will, and some different guide posts. A sign that he put up along the way—not necessarily because he knew he was doing it—was a sign saying, "This is where Dad went off on this road. You might want to take the other way." That's a great life lesson to have.

I'm very fortunate to have a family that gave me some great tools and a great early childhood. I thank God they're still around.

I: With your entrepreneurial spirit, how do you make a comeback? What do you do to face those challenging times from the standpoint of your own personal and professional leadership?

SK: The thing that I feel really separates entrepreneurs or those few people that really are successful from those people that just keep throwing darts against the wall is that no matter how many times you try something and fail, keep trying. What you may think is a failure may not be a failure at all. In essence, those are successes—the means upon which you can then build.

Those "failures" or things that didn't go as planned are nothing more than little keystones or building blocks that you can use to build something better upon. It is an education and in fact I think it's the best education because it's a real world education. This is where you can actually find out what works and what doesn't work outside the theoretical book-type environment. It's all well and good to sit and read about how something is going to work, but unless you really try it with the manufacturing process, the customers, and the regulatory process, you have no idea how it's going to end up. There are so many variables to consider that you can't simply read or study—you have to go out and try it.

A tough time is going to raise its head at some point, and if you have already had experience in dealing with a potentially rough spot, you're going to be infinitely more prepared to overcome and continue growing and being successful. That first time when you were either afraid or didn't know what to do and you were anxious and the stress seemed to overwhelmed you, that was all preparation. You were trying to tinker with it and you didn't have any confidence in yourself. Now you can say, "You know what? I experienced a situation like this thirty years ago (or ten years ago, or last year, or ten days ago), and I was able to do *this* to make it work."

> *"You have to continue doing the action. If you fail, fine. Move on. That failure can be very rewarding and may ultimately lead to a better success."*

Whether you do the same thing each time or not, having the ability to do it and the confidence that you can get through it makes all the difference.

If you consider successful people or companies such as Steve Jobs, Microsoft, Edison, or Sam Walton, everyone refers to them as "overnight successes." They're not overnight successes. Edison and the light bulb is a perfect example. He tried hundreds of different ideas before that light bulb worked. Someone said, "You failed." He said, "No, I just figured out a couple hundred ways that didn't work."

You have to continue doing the action. If you fail, fine. Move on. That failure can be very rewarding and may ultimately lead to a better success, as long as you approach it that way.

I: In an entrepreneurial environment, what do you think are the most important leadership skills that you call upon in order to create your success?

SK: It begins with being a leader. You are in that position if you've started your own company or if you are trying to set yourself up to be the visionary or the creative force behind a company or an industry. It is just that—you have to be a leader.

A leader leads by doing, by creating a plan. Creating a plan is my weakness in leadership. I can create a wonderful idea, but I struggle to put all the little pieces and details in place. But that's why you hire great people, so you can say, "Here's my vision. Go and put together all the little details that will make my vision happen."

There are three basic tenants to being a great leader:

- You have to have be unique.
- You have to have creative vision.
- You have to have a sense of humor.

That vision has to be something that is not so ethereal that people would sit there and say, "What are you talking about?" Your creative vision has to have something tangible that allows people to say, "Okay, I'm not quite sure about all that, but I get it, and I'm going to buy into that. I'll get on board to help you do that."

Once that vision is done, then you absolutely have to find those people who buy into your idea. The best possible people, in a managerial sense, are those who can dissect your vision and then interpret it for the people that are going to put it together and make it actually come to life—they are the translators, if you will. You have to find great translators.

I equate the term translator to the upper management people. They are your field generals. They're going to assemble the crew, give the crew the detailed instructions that are required, and then make that ultimate creative vision come to life.

As far as having a sense of humor, you first have to be able to laugh at yourself. You have to be willing to put yourself out there in a way that will allow others to laugh at you.

I specifically use the term *at you* instead of *with you*. Having the ability to allow other people to laugh at you gives you a wonderful way to move through life in a much more happy sense because a large number of people are going to sling large arrows at you, whether you're successful or not.

In fact, the more successful you are, the bigger the arrows and the more of them that are going to come your way. You had better have a thick skin. I think the best way to get a thick skin fast is to allow people to laugh at you. A sense of humor is very important.

I: Obviously you've been able to develop teams that have been able to step up and take your vision and help you make that a reality.

SK: I've modified my entrepreneurial way over the years. I've had teams that I've been putting together since I was nineteen or twenty, and for a certain period of time I didn't play well with others. I learned really fast that if I actually wanted to get something done, I'd have to learn how to play well with others. The best way to play well with others is to find the best people to play with you.

I'm give direction and lead them along the way. I refer to myself as their biggest cheerleader. You have to have great rewards. You have to have random rewards. I give a lot of leeway.

I really don't care how they get it done. When you find successful people, it's not just them. There are a lot of people behind them.

I: You say that it's really important to leave the world a better place for your children. What is the legacy you'd like to leave for your children?

SK: At the end of my days, if my son is sitting there saying that he wants to be as good a dad for his child—my grandson—as I was for him, that would be my greatest legacy. That would really be the best.

Forget anything else in terms of business, etc. If I could make my son want to be like me, then, there you go. That's the best thing.

LEADERSHIP OPPORTUNITY:

I would advise you to do two things. First, write down the absolute biggest fear you have. It can be anything—fear of sharks, fear of losing money, fear of being divorced, or fear of being alone. Whatever it is, write it down.

Second, after you have written that down and thought about it, write down a funny joke using that fear. It can be totally inappropriate, it can be totally out of left field, and it could make sense only to you. Whatever you write, it has to be humorous and make you laugh.

If you can laugh about the thing that you're most afraid of, you are going to be so much better suited to deal with anything that comes along. You'll find that the biggest problem in the world, if you can laugh at it, is not that big anymore.

This might be the biggest, quickest thing you could do to immediately change how you approach things.

LEADERSHIP SUCCESS:

My wife and I recently opened our second business location. We kept it very quiet; no one knew we were doing it. It's about three hours away from our current location, so it entails a lot of driving back and forth. It's in an area that's not known for high-end European spas. We're the first one in that area.

It's taken us two and a half years and pretty much every dime that we have ever saved. We don't have any partners. It is just my wife and I, and we don't have any family money. We only have what we raised from having one spa be such a growing business so far. We believe in organic growth and not getting loans and things like that.

So with that in mind, we've been working on this for two and a half years, and wouldn't you know it, we open in August of this year. Granted, we started this before the recession in 2008 when the bubble burst in the housing market, so everything was great when we put these plans together. Now it is 2011 and life doesn't seem that golden and rosy anymore. Everyone is talking about double-dip recession and so forth. I say to people all the time, "Just turn the television off. Things are cyclical."

I'm all about doing it. Just go and do it. You have to be risk-adverse and do it!

Diane Allen
Mt. Laurel, New Jersey, USA

Diane Allen, PCC, is a seasoned leadership coach and organizational development consultant. She coaches business professionals on building leadership confidences that include strategic thinking, communication skills, team building, and change-management. She has served on several boards for both profit and nonprofit organizations, and as a mediator for Ford Motor Company's Dispute Resolution Board. Diane developed and facilitates the Professional Coaching Certification Program for Burlington County College in Mount Laurel, New Jersey and Philadelphia Community College.

She holds a BS in Business Administration and MS in Organizational Development from St. Josephs University in Philadelphia, Pennsylvania. She also holds a Certification of Energy Leadership Index Master Practitioner from the Institute for Professional Excellence in Coaching and is certified in Booth Leadership Transition Survey, Myers-Briggs Type Indicator, Herrmann Brain Dominance Instrument, and DISC Success Insights Behavioral Instrument. Diane also serves as a leadership coach for the Ken Blanchard Companies.

I: You spend a lot of time focusing on the idea of leadership presence. What exactly does leadership presence mean?

DA: In short, I consider leadership presence to be the positive emotions that a person instills in others that makes them want to engage with you. Whether that engagement is face-to-face, in video, or in other forms of media, it doesn't matter as long as you are engaged. The key element is that others are drawn to you in some fashion because you exude confidence and credibility.

Some executives confuse having positional power with being an effective leader. They may even think having authority automatically converts to getting results and having a strong presence. They are missing how important it is to have strong emotional intelligence and authenticity. What I find is that those who are willing to devote the time to others and to understand others' concerns are the people who often have that presence. They enlist the support of others for a future vision and they help solve problems.

"When a leader exudes real presence, people become energetically engaged in common missions and they seek to do their best work."

I: How does presence relate to charisma?

DA: Some people confuse presence with charisma, but the two are not the same. Presence is developed over time, whereas charisma, by itself, is usually a matter of looks, charm, personality, and appeal. Charisma adds to presence, but you do not have to have movie-star looks to be a person of presence. In fact, having too much charisma could come off as being phony and even self-serving.

Just think about the very charismatic executives who have been involved in some of the worst scandals in corporate history. Those with strong leadership presence actually put the spotlight on others, and they are able to give others the time, energy, and effort to be heard. People are drawn to those types of leaders because they truly listen to others. That is presence.

I: How can leaders increase their presence?

DA: Many experts agree that the skills and the capabilities that translate into strong leadership presence can actually be taught. Some people have a natural talent for connecting with people, but we all have an interpersonal side that can be brought to the surface.

Leadership presence requires self-assurance and self-knowledge and—because leaders must communicate what matters to them in a way that makes it matter to other people—it is helpful to be able to show themselves and to let others know who they really are inside.

We have found that coaching and training can have a huge impact on the person who really wants to change. Once individuals start to think differently about themselves, they actually build more self-confidence and are more able to apply the techniques of developing presence. In short, when a leader exudes real presence, people become energetically engaged in common missions and they seek to do their best work.

One way that they can increase their presence is actually through a four-part model called SAGE.

The SAGE Model

Social Intelligence: Social intelligence is the capacity to comprehend what is happening around you and in the world, and then being able to respond in a personally and socially effective manner. So much has been written on the topic of social intelligence that at times it can seem overwhelming.

I think of social intelligence as wisdom, not necessarily just having "smarts." It involves being interpersonally competent. Being aware of how we use our social intelligence enables us to attract others into our lives, into our work, and into our avocations. I find that high social intelligence is beneficial for all of us, not just for those in official leadership roles.

"Knowing your strengths enables you to offer those strengths to others; knowing your limitations enables you to manage them."

There are three ways to further develop your social intelligence:

- Heighten your observations about what is going on around you.

- Set an intention to be present with others and observe how well you are able to connect with them. When you do that, you are able to gain more situational awareness.

- Do an honest self-evaluation. Knowing your strengths enables you to offer those strengths to others; knowing your limitations enables you to manage them. People with strong social intelligence have a well developed self-esteem, which means they do not have to convey it in words; people see it and feel it without the use of words.

Authenticity: Authenticity is the true respect that one has for engaging with others. Authenticity equates to being trustworthy; the driving force is a good will toward others. When we are authentic, we show others who we really are. That means we can have genuine conversations and show interest in others. We are also able to show some of our foibles, and we can do so with sincerity because we know people will relate to someone who is able to show that human side.

Gracefulness: I think of gracefulness in terms of someone who is a great communicator and who will listen, attend, observe, respond, and question in a way that is needed at the time. Someone who is graceful knows what is needed by the other person or parties involved in the conversation.

The graceful communicator's toolkit includes the following things:

- Building rapport easily. That means they are able to connect well with people in a natural way.

- Listening and responding with empathy. This is a key ingredient in all relationships. When a person has empathy, they are able to see and feel the world through the eyes of others. They are able to actively listen to another person and be genuinely involved in the conversation. It involves showing that they understand what the other person is saying. When someone with empathy is actively listening and present with another person, they can summarize the words the other person stated and how that person is feeling. Responding with empathy doesn't necessarily mean agreeing with the other person, but merely showing a sincere understanding. Exhibiting that type of empathy is very powerful.

- Keeping their own communication agenda free. They do not introduce personal biases and assumptions. That could be difficult for all of us, but it is not impossible. Ultimately, it will be critical to success.

- Showing a genuine, unconditional, and positive regard for others. A graceful communicator has the ability to be tough on issues, but not on the person. They are able to maintain or enhance self-esteem in others.

- Being congruent. What they say or do matches how they look and sound when they say or do it. There is an open and honest communication, and they draw very heavily on those kinds of characteristics.

Envisioning the Outcome: When we envision our outcomes, we can really identify with what impression we want to make with others. This includes things such as having others interests at heart, knowing how to solve a problem, and even painting a compelling vision for the future. We need to envision that within ourselves first. It also includes leaving a positive impression that builds long-term relationships. Instilling emotional memory in our interactions can prompt others to want more from us.

Having strong leadership presence really means having strong self-worth and self-confidence. If you think of the leaders you are attracted to, you would probably say one of the main things you see in them is an air of self-confidence. So many people question their confidence from time to time. It is hard to have a genuine presence when you are questioning your own confidence. You can try to fake it, but that takes away from true authenticity.

"It is hard to have a genuine presence when you are questioning your own confidence."

The best way to consistently build strong self-confidence is to reframe and rewrite your inner and outer conversations. Think about ways you can see yourself and have that inner dialogue. Anything negative needs to be reframed in a way that won't hold you back from having confidence in yourself. Another way to build self-confidence is to identify your negative beliefs and reframe them into positives.

Using all aspects of the SAGE model ensures that your leadership presence will become greater. You will attract those people into your life who are really interested in who you are as a person—as a leader. Leadership presence is something we're all drawn to naturally. It may look different for each person, but at the end of the day, there's plenty to go around.

LEADERSHIP OPPORTUNITY:

When we talk about presence, I believe having a positive outlook is also very important because people will see that within us. I call this exercise *My Most Prized Descriptor* because it helps us to focus on presence.

Identify three words that convey the meaning of what you most want others to think of when they hear about you. Those words could be anything, but here are some examples: confident, joyful, strong, sincere, an achiever, or even a visionary. They can be anything as long as they are your own words. Pick three and focus on them.

Find an opportunity every day to practice and express these descriptors. By doing this daily, you train your thought patterns to think in those terms. That will then relate to an expressed behavior so that you become those descriptors. Over time it will become very natural.

LEADERSHIP SUCCESS:

I coached a gentleman who had a very high-level financial management position in a large publishing organization, but he lacked the ability to make good decisions regarding people. He felt like he was being passed over formally for promotions and informally in the sense that he was not being heard. He felt as though he had things to contribute, so he turned to coaching.

Our work started out specifically in the area of assertiveness. He had a very introverted style, but over time our work transitioned to cover more than just assertive behavior and we started to work on leadership presence.

Through our coaching work, he learned the true definition of presence. He applied the SAGE Model to his daily thoughts and behaviors. These changes lead to a shift in his ability to relax, his ability to relate to others, and ultimately to his ability to build relationships. Once he learned how to increase his social intelligence and remain authentic to who he really was, he improved his communication skills dramatically.

He was eventually promoted to the next level, but more importantly, he found that he was able to express himself much more comfortably and much more gracefully.

Mary O'Loughlin
Dunsborough, WA, Australia

The term well-being is overused in today's world of overindulgences, but the dynamic with which Mary O'Loughlin, proprietor of Reach, approaches well-being makes you take a second look. She is a living example of the mental and physical fitness that can be achieved when we practice a healthy lifestyle.

Mary is a skilled practitioner, excellent facilitator, talented motivational speaker, and Certified Results Business and Executive Coach dealing with companies, elite athletes, performers, and individual clients. Mary's mission is to develop clients to a level which allows them to enjoy peak performance in all areas.

Mary is acknowledged both nationally and internationally as an inspiring, vibrant, highly motivational, and entertaining presenter and coach. She has the ability to tailor her presentations in coaching to match defined themes, and thus meet the specific needs, desires, and outcomes of all of the individuals and organizations she coaches.

I: You focus on the idea of belief in yourself and being able to create a wonderful day for yourself every day. Can you tell us why that's so important to you?

MO: Self-belief drives performance. One of the most important habits I recommend my clients develop is a disciplined habit of creating themselves every day. Most of us have a limited belief in ourselves to begin with. This limits our performance. Recognizing the best in you, the specialness in you, and acknowledging the gifts you have been given fuels your self-belief and the success you are seeking. To be successful in any area of life you must empower and inspire yourself daily. We have to take the challenge on at the beginning of the day. Spend ten to twenty minutes getting in touch with who you are and who you are developing yourself to be, and create a real feeling of excitement about being that person. You are now much better positioned to go out into the world and deliver the best that you have to give.

I: How do we learn how to develop the leader within us?

MO: Developing the leader within is first and foremost about appreciating who you are, acknowledging yourself, and recognizing your gifts and potential. From this position you can then recognize the qualities that you possess that will be of benefit to others. Developing the leader within is about standing in this attitude of confidence and gratitude for who you are and what you have been given and recognizing that your gifts are of immeasurable value to others. The final step is being courageous enough to follow your vision and offer your gift to the world.

> _"Developing the leader within is first and foremost about appreciating who you are, acknowledging yourself, and recognizing your gifts and potential."_

In the beginning, in order to develop the leader, you must give yourself time in the day to get in touch with who you are, what you're capable of, and where you're trying to go.

Discover your purpose by asking yourself the following questions:

- What do you believe is your purpose?
- What do you feel passionate about?
- What do you love doing?
- What type of work inspires you?
- What impact do have on the people around you?
- What acknowledgements do you get from others?

If you were to state your purpose in one succinct, specific statement, what would you say? Take this purpose statement into your "create" session daily and empower yourself to follow through.

I: I've heard you say that you believe in creating yourself every day and not living by default. What do you mean by that?

MO: You are the author of your own story, the director of your own production—or are you? Living by default means letting life happen to you. It is about being at the mercy of how the circumstances of your life pan out. It's about reacting to life and others because of who they have chosen or not chosen to be. Living life by default is living life in reaction not in action.

Creating yourself at the beginning of each day means taking the time to decide who you are and how you want your day to go. What is your purpose? Create such strong intention and clarity that your life then flows powerfully in a direction you have chosen.

This is the process I follow to create myself daily. I set my alarm for 4:30 a.m. and get up no matter what time I've gone to bed. I make a choice to honor this time. If I've had a late night and I'm tired, I have to correct it at the other end of the day. I've made a choice to prioritize this activity.

During my create session I relax and I pray. I have in front of me anything I've collected that inspires me and reminds me of who I am and where I am going—pictures, quotes, Bible verses, images of my goals, etc. I'll spend—as I recommend to my clients—at least twenty minutes immersing myself in my goals and my intentions. I review my purpose.

One book I use in my create session is *Think and Grow Rich* by Napoleon Hill. On page fifty-two there is a self-confidence formula that is very powerful. On page seventy-five there is valuable instruction to assist you to apply the principle of auto suggestion.

Your daily create session is a time to review goals, to affirm yourself for the successes you have achieved so far, and to invite the powers of your spiritual connections to assist you. You then step out powerfully into your day knowing who you are, where you are going and why, and allowing the whole day to flow toward you in alignment with your purpose and intention.

I: So you're actually creating a space to allow that flow to happen at the very beginning of the day.

MO: Yes. Set your intention at the beginning of the day. Decide how you would like your day and ultimately your life to go. See it, feel it, intend it, and watch your creation flow toward you.

In your role as a leader you will benefit greatly from having a balanced look at your goals every day. Balance is essential if you seek peak performance in your life.

I: You believe it's important to maintain balance. Can you elaborate on the importance of that idea?

MO: Balance is finding beauty, passion, and meaning in the different loves of your life and living those loves everyday at every opportunity. It is not a question of equal time, but rather making the best of the time you have and connecting fully with each experience.

"Balance is finding beauty, passion, and meaning in the different loves of your life and living those loves everyday at every opportunity."

As a leader, balance is important in two ways. First, balance is necessary for you to enjoy happiness and longevity, and second, it is essential that as leaders we "walk our talk" and that we are authentic and a true model of possibility.

I encourage you to set balanced goals for areas that might include your relationships, finances, family, leisure, career, mission, spirituality, and contribution.

In my career as a fitness professional I discovered the critical importance of balancing one more area—the one vehicle that makes all other success possible—your body. Peak performance is all about maximizing and maintaining your energy and positive focus. Daily exercise is essential to peak performance; it adds clarity, energy, and ease to your day. Eating life-giving foods adds vitality and longevity. In short, being in a fit and healthy body makes you a much more effective and powerful leader In every way.

I: What is your most important leadership practice?

MO: Creating yourself each day allows you to remind yourself of your potential, of what you can create, and to spend some time powerfully believing in yourself, your purpose, and your mission. When you walk out to face the day, there will be many challenges to face. You will benefit from having spent time empowering yourself to hold on to your vision, to hold on to your faith, and to keep taking those small actions, that are not always easy to take but that lead you to your desired outcome. You will achieve your goal; it's a guaranteed formula for success.

I: You are a busy mom with six children. How do you achieve your balance and still manage to run a successful company?

MO: I have five children between ages twenty-seven and sixteen and a surprise two year old. I maintain balance by creating my life on purpose. I have goals for all the important areas of my life, and I have trained myself over time to develop the mental focus and commitment I need to be as successful as I can be in all these areas. I pray daily in gratitude, and in my create session, I keep an eye on how I'm performing as a mother, a wife, a business owner, a friend, and a Christian. I acknowledge my success and examine any areas for improvement.

Now that we have our special two year old, I have needed to re-address the balance and spend more time parenting and nurturing my family. It is a fact of life that we will need to give more time and energy to our different loves at different times, and the skill of adjusting the balance is well worth developing. My early morning create session ensures I keep all these important areas in focus. It's wonderful to have developed enough balance to continue to run the company successfully and maintain a happy family life.

LEADERSHIP OPPORTUNITY:

Every day set aside time to create yourself. All of your success and powerful leadership will come out of your belief in yourself. In that time, empower and inspire yourself to recognize the best in you, the specialness in you, and the gifts you've been given, and acknowledge those things. Use this time to recognize who you are, what you've been given, and your purpose in life. Really strengthen yourself in those beliefs.

Remember that being fit and healthy is about making a choice moment by moment. Focus and commit to being who you need to be physically to achieve the results you are seeking. For me, it's a matter of diarizing my exercise session every day and just getting up and going—not giving myself a choice about it.

It's about habits. Moment by moment you're making a choice, and that choice affects your health, your fitness, your energy level, and ultimately your success. Create the balanced vision of how you want your life to be. Create it every day, do what is yours to do, and then enjoy the unfolding.

LEADERSHIP SUCCESS:

I remember a day, not so long ago, when I was a single mom with five small children earning a very small income as a fitness instructor. I decided to try coaching as a way of moving myself forward. My coach was able to see my potential and keep me focused on it. I started to create a picture of what was possible for me. Maybe I could create a gym and fitness club. It would have blue mirror-lined walls, there would be instructors with white uniforms and name badges, the clients would be happy and successful. With my coach's support and belief, within one year I was standing in the back of my own fitness club looking at the blue mirrored walls and watching the instructors working with many happy clients. I was looking at my own creation; it is a moment in time I will never forget. I became a coach to inspire people to see and create what is possible for them because I know how amazing that experience is. I have gone on to create more and more with each new creation putting me at a new vantage point from which to create anew.

I encourage you to hold on to your vision, to develop and lean into your faith, and to keep taking those small actions that make the big difference in reaching your goals.

Yogesh Sood
Gurgaon, India

Yogesh Sood has over thirty years of corporate experience and over fourteen years in the people-development aspect of corporate enterprise, including numerous organizational levels in varied industries. He has been a pioneer for this type of personal and corporate development in the Pacific Rim.

Yogesh is also a master trainer. He helps organizations to manage, change, and develop leadership based on competency models. He also helps them to manage the operational aspects of all of the learning and development that goes on within these corporations. He provides one-on-one coaching at leadership levels with top executives within an organization, and he also leads high-capacity project teams to change into greatness for the future of the organization. He has trained more than thirty thousand participants and he is the Founding President of the International Coach Federation in the India and South Asia chapter. He believes that coaching is a mutual win process between the coach and coachee.

I: You are one of the pioneers and leaders in the Pacific Rim with organizational development. What do you do to ensure your own personal and professional leadership growth?

YS: That's an interesting question because I personally believe that if you are sharing knowledge and helping others to develop, you constantly need to work on yourself. From time to time I go to leading management schools like Harvard Business School and Wharton to upgrade myself to a better education.

I am currently enrolled in a course called Owners, Presidents, Managers, which runs over the course of three years. In this course, you spend two years on the Harvard campus for a total of nearly seventy days. Twice during those three years, while on campus, you actually work on your leadership skills, your business skills, and your people skills. In addition to bringing informal learning to seminars and through working, I believe that one has to keep on learning from formal educational sources where the top minds come together. I continue to better myself by attending executive courses.

I am also an India partner for Dr. Ken Blanchard's company. I am their representative in India. I do a lot of internal learning on leadership and performance management through the learning center of Dr. Ken Blanchard. I have the privilege of working with him and his teams and being the only authorized and exclusive partner in this part of the world.

As far as my education, I earned my masters degree in business administration almost thirty-five years ago. Following that formal education, I continue working on my education through executive coaches, executive education courses, and also by learning on the job. I learn about leadership and I work on getting certifications from coaching. For example, I just completed my certification from the College of Executive Coaching working with Dr. Jeff, who is based out of Santa Barbara, California.

I: You work a lot with the development of people, the development of teams, and change management initiatives, which is sometimes very difficult for companies. How does leadership impact all of those arenas that you work with on a regular basis?

YS: Depending upon what level of leadership you are in, you have your area of influence in which you operate. If you're leading a team of twenty people, five hundred people, or you're leading a large organization with thousands of employees, people tend to forget the things that you say, but people notice what you do and demonstrate.

My personal view is that, as a leader, whatever you do is far more important than anything you say. A single action of leadership delivered at the right moment conveys much more than if you were to write a book in order to try to communicate and convince your audience about your philosophy.

For example, if the leader is trying to influence the importance of punctuality in a team and he or she is not punctual for meetings, then the leader will never have the ability to influence team members to be punctual and organized. People will not believe what

the leader is saying—they will observe what the leader is doing in this type of situation. They will follow their actions, not their words.

People believe that leadership traits are not displayed in certain situations. However, I personally feel that leadership is all around you. It is evident in your smallest actions. The higher you go, your micro-actions are also observed by those around you, and that is how others formulate opinions about you.

If you look at how leadership impacts the people and things around you, you are likely to pay closer attention to your actions. My view is that if you pay attention to how leaders behave—not only what they say, but how they behave, how they carry themselves, how they conduct themselves, and what kind of executive presence they display in interactions with people and how they handle situations—all of that influences and has an impact on the team. This is true whether you are a business leader or a leader in community and whether your leadership position is formal or informal. I have seen that this hold true in various walks of life. In essence, while your words may ask for respect, your actions earn respect.

"While your words may ask for respect, your actions earn respect."

I: You are in a position to be able to see a lot of change internationally, specifically in India and the Pacific Rim. How have you seen the leadership roles changing in your area?

YS: That's a very interesting trend which we have seen in the Indian market and this part of the world over the last fifteen years or so. For example, we saw that sometimes in the early 1990s, if you looked at learning and development as a function, most of the leaders would say, "It is a cost center; it is not required. Why do people need to be sent to training or why do they need to be educated on the job? This is kind of fun but a waste of time and a waste of money."

A big transition has happened in India and some Asian countries. Now learning and development have a function. Their department has become a core business driver where companies are looking at competency models. They're looking at competencies and how to integrate those competencies into leadership development with the business objectives. The same thing has been happening with executive coaching over the course of the last five or six years.

I participated in writing a book called *Diversity in Coaching*, which was written by Jonathan Passmore. He is based in the U.K., and my views from India were published in the book. What the book addresses is very interesting. I observed that a couple of years ago people were shy about being linked to a coach because they felt it indicated that there was something weak in them or they were being singled out by a company for some kind of poor performance. This mind-set is totally different now. It is undergoing a metamorphosis, and now people are looking at coaching as a positive development for them.

I have seen that at organizational levels, the very training that was previously looked at as a kind of dispensable function or something to be done only with leisure time and a plethora of money is now becoming an integral part as a business driver. Over the last few years, coaching has been seen as a fad or as a fashion; now it is becoming more and more a part of the DNA of organizations.

In the last ten to fifteen years we have seen great changes. Organizations have accepted the learning function, the development function, and also the ability to adapt and sustain change. At a personal level, people's acceptance of needing to continually grow and develop—which used to be only for a formal degree—has changed a lot. It's no longer only for engineers or people in a masters program.

If you look at the macro level, the economy has actually undergone massive change. Whether it's a government company, a private company, or other business sectors—telecommunications sector, insurance sector, retail sector—all of these have been transformed in India in the last ten to fifteen years. The companies are looking at growth, change, and learning and development as an integral and constant part of the organization's forward movement. Conversely, ten years ago, they were afraid of these changes and patterns which were not prevalent at the time.

The changes invested in this organization for individuals at all levels—personal levels, team levels, organizational levels, and even macro levels—because with the economy, every year something new is happening; there are new industries succeeding or expanding.

It used to be, "Oh my, another change, another way." Now people are learning to look at that change as necessity. Learning and adaptation are necessities; realignment is part of the game, and we need to brace ourselves to be part of that wave rather than trying to

> *"Learning and adaptation are necessities; realignment is part of the game, and we need to brace ourselves to be part of that wave rather than trying to fight it."*

fight it.

I: What is upper management looking at from the standpoint of individuals on their way up?

Top Three Factors Upper Management Considers

#1: How You Deal With Uncertainty and Change—This is going to be the order of the day whether you continue to come out of economic recession in a year or five years. Uncertainty and complexity of change are going to be a part of our life now. How do you deal with uncertainty and how do you deal with change?

#2: Your Ability to Build Teams and Carry People Along—All of us know the higher you go in any organization's hierarchy, the more you are dependent on people. As you move towards general management and C-level, you depend on all those below you in position. Your dependence on people becomes higher and higher. How do you build teams and are you able to carry people along?

#3: Business Acumen: This could be different for different functions, but you need to make sure that your business acumen and competencies are aligned to the organizational goal.

Your ability to adapt and change, your ability to carry people along with you, and business acumen and your understanding of the business are three key components that upper-level management will take into consideration when evaluating those on the rise within an organization.

LEADERSHIP OPPORTUNITY:

I prompt and encourage people to ask this question: "What am I doing today that is different than what I did last year in a similar kind of situation?"

They typically struggle to even tell me one thing. That's the start of a very interesting exercise.

Then I further challenge them by asking, "What are you doing in today's context which you think you should not be doing next year?" That gives you two directions: one thing you are doing today that you should not be doing a year down the road, and one thing you are not doing yet which you should be doing down the road.

This becomes a powerful exercise in terms of their own learning, in introspection, and linking directly to the business result and the behaviors they're displaying. I have found that to be meaningful in many situations.

LEADERSHIP SUCCESS:

I was in management school and it was Annual Day; I was the Master of Ceremonies. Suddenly the lights went off and we had no power. There were around three hundred students sitting in the hall and faculty members sitting on the stage, and as Master of Ceremonies, I was stumped. I didn't know what to do. I was feeling very nervous and uncomfortable and just when I was about to leave the stage, I asked a friend of mine, "What should I do? We're in a bad situation. I think we should leave the stage."

He said something very interesting that still lingers in my mind very heavily. He said, "Yogesh, you are responsible to handle this situation and you have to make sure that you take charge of these people who are sitting in the hall. You just can't go away because the lights are not there. Lights or no lights, that's an external factor. What you do is up to you."

I cannot tell you how many times that particular instance has haunted me. He brought me back, in a way. You are here standing on the stage and you're responsible for these people. You need to take action and take control of the situation.

Tina Rasmussen, Ph.D.
San Francisco, California, USA

Dr. Tina Rasmussen has worked for more than twenty-five years as a thought partner, trusted confidant, and creative strategic thinker who catalyzes individual and organizational change and growth for her clients. She was one of the first consultants to conduct empirical research on improving performance results while engaging people's hearts and minds to create healthy and vibrant organizations.

She has achieved measurable improvement in large, multi-year change initiatives and coached CEOs in a wide variety of industries from the Fortune 100 to nonprofits, including Kaiser Permanente, Levi Strauss, the YMCA, Odwalla Juice, and Nestle.

Tina is the author of three books: *Organizational Integrity, Diversity: The ASTD Trainer's Sourcebook,* and *Diversity Mosaic.* She is a contributor to Action Coaching and has guest lectured at Stanford Graduate School of Business and numerous well-known universities. She has presented at the Conference Board as well as other national events and is a Certified Professional Coach.

I: What are some of the greatest challenges you see in your field?

TR: From my clients' perspective, I would say the greatest challenges are the economy, having profitable performance, and the dramatic pace of change. From my perspective as a consultant and coach, I see three major challenges—that are also opportunities—for leaders today.

Three Challenges/Opportunities for Leaders Today

#1: Lifelong Development and Adapting to Change—No matter where they are—whether they're at a high point or a low point in their careers, whether they're facing challenges, or in a job that's very stable—it is important for leaders to keep growing throughout their careers. Yet, I see many leaders who—because of other pressures—find it hard to set aside the time to dedicate to their own growth and development. It's very easy to deprioritize this aspect of their leadership.

#2: Engaging Your Team—Regardless of how good a leader one is, all leaders need to make the most of their team. If your team isn't really with you—cohesive, energized, and motivated in the same direction—it is impossible to achieve sustainable performance beyond your own individual capacity, and things can easily start falling apart. Most leaders that I know want to create a high performing team, but they don't go about it in a purposeful way; it happens by chance or sporadically.

#3: Creating a High-Performing Culture—How do we create an organization in which the culture not only achieves the performance goals but also sustains lasting success in a rapidly changing world? As a leader, there's a real opportunity to create and leave a legacy— to build an organization that can last beyond the leader's tenure. It's a way to leave your mark on the world that can be very satisfying.

I: Can we delve into these one at a time? First, why would leaders not devote enough time to their own growth?

TR: Most leaders that I know agree that their own development is important, but it's not as urgent as so many other pressing business issues we face every day. Other things just come up and take precedence.

I see two scenarios among leaders that I work with. First, if one is successful, then the idea becomes, "I'm successful, so I'll keep doing what I've always done. That's what got me here."

The problem with this idea is that change happens all the time. The changes in the world that we're seeing are rapid and dramatic, such as the economy, technology, and globalization. In addition, for the leader who is moving up in their career or within their organization, that kind of movement is a change in itself.

Often leaders just keep doing what has worked for them in the past without recognizing that circumstances are changing around them. What they've done previously may not continue to work as well in the future, and they may not see it until something goes wrong.

In the second scenario, a leader may be in a challenging situation—maybe they've taken on a new role, their environment has changed, or they have a competitor who has come in who is making things difficult—and they're just putting out fires. They're not being strategic because they're in more of a reactive mode due to the challenging situation.

"The higher up you are as a leader, the more afraid people are to be honest with you."

The higher up you are as a leader, the more afraid people are to be honest with you. As a result, you don't know as much about what's happening. In addition, the old adage, "It's lonely at the top," can absolutely be true. There are fewer people whom leaders can confide in the farther up the ladder they move. Even within peer groups—even though your peers can be friends—there's sometimes competition, so there can be fewer people with whom to have unguarded conversations about things that matter.

This is where having a trusted thought partner who is there just for your success—someone who will tell you the truth, where venting is okay, and you don't have to be politically correct—is extremely valuable. I often work with senior executives, and that's part of the role I fulfill. Through the coaching relationship, the leader has a safe place to think through the difficult issues, where they can also be completely candid and receive honest feedback. A coach can also ask strategic questions that challenge the leaders' thinking and open up new possibilities.

Undertaking 360 degree feedback is also helpful for leaders. It's important to have a neutral third party to ask other people, "What are this person's strengths and what are their developmental opportunities?" Whatever is going on around you as a leader—it is happening anyway, whether you know about it or not. If you don't know about it, you're at a disadvantage. This is where having a coach as a trusted thought partner can help the leader see what's going on within a supportive context that's oriented towards growth and leadership mastery.

I: I would imagine that this is a critical component when the leader is trying to build a high-performing team. Is that right?

TR: That's right. With teams, you can extend the process that I've been talking about to the larger group. Most leaders want to build a team, but how do you actually go about doing that? Teams need a safe space where they can have authentic, meaningful conversations about what's working and how to address unproductive behaviors and obstacles that are holding the team back.

It is important to have an assessment of the team, including confidential interviews where team members can be fully candid with an impartial third party. The coach/consultant can then bring that information together for the leader as well as the team in a way that is productive for the team to take their work to the next level.

I use a triangle-shaped model in assessing a team's effectiveness (see page 302). In the lower left corner of the triangle is the "what." This is the team's goals, roles with each other, and responsibilities. What are we trying to achieve, individually and collectively?

In the lower right corner of the triangle is the "how." This includes our relationships with each other, how we make decisions, issues of diversity and inclusion, and how we run our meetings. The "how" greases the wheels in order to make the "what" happen.

At the top of the triangle, is the team's or organization's mission and vision, or the "why." What is the higher purpose for our being here? In the middle of the triangle is the heart of the people. Who are we, and are we fully engaged? It's only in putting all of these together that people can bring their full selves to work. As a leader, when your team is clear about the "what" the "how" and the "why," you engage people's hearts and they are willing to give their all.

This is how leaders create a high-performing team ensuring that they are "firing on all burners" with regard to these key areas. It is also helpful to dedicate time away from the office to get out of the day-to-day work, to have meaningful conversations, and to think strategically about these elements of effective team performance.

I: You also talked about organizational culture. Doesn't that just evolve organically?

TR: Culture does evolve on its own as an organization develops. There are also aspects of the organization's culture that can be influenced directly. Sometimes people ask, "What is it? We can't really measure it. How can we affect it?" Contrary to popular belief, we can actually measure culture through surveys and focus groups. Based on the results of those assessments, we can develop specific interventions that are designed to pull the strategic levers of the culture, such as how decisions are made and what gets rewarded. As a consultant, I've led many multi-year change initiatives throughout my career. I've found that many leaders find culture change work to be one of the most rewarding highlights of their career, to leave a legacy that outlives their own tenure.

LEADERSHIP OPPORTUNITY:

Creating a High Performing Team =

Clear direction (what) + effective norms (how) + engaged heart (who, why)

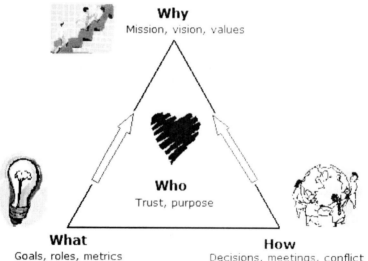

Why
Mission, vision, values

Who
Trust, purpose

What
Goals, roles, metrics

How
Decisions, meetings, conflict

LEADERSHIP SUCCESS:

I recently worked with a client who had just entered a new organization as a divisional President. Prior to that, he was the COO of a similar organization. He had a leadership team of fifteen people reporting to him directly, and an organization of several thousand staff.

Over the three years that we worked together, he went from "good to great." While he entered with solid leadership skills and technical knowledge, we discovered several development areas that were starting to derail him. He was already aware of some of these, and some were new insights we gained through 360 degree feedback and having candid three-way conversations with his new boss and team.

One of the most helpful tools we used was one that I use for my own development. We created a pocket-sized matrix with his three goals on it, targeting the new behaviors he had committed to doing every day. For example, "When meeting with my team and the larger staff, I use direct customer stories to engage people in meeting our service goals (rather than just metrics)." He put this in a visible place (I use the inside of my medicine cabinet near my tooth brush) and rated himself at the end of each day on a scale of one to ten on how well he did. Over time, these new behaviors became habits, and the change in his leadership improved the overall performance of his division.

This client became the highest performing President in the organization on annual goals for his division, with the corporate CEO acknowledging him and his team publicly as a model for others.

Bernice Boyden
Pittsburgh, Pennsylvania, USA

Executive/Leadership Coach and Consultant Bernice Boyden is fiercely committed to showing women in leadership how to unleash their influence, enhance their leadership presence, be politically savvy and be the "go-to" leader in the workplace.

As CEO of The Masterful Leader, an executive coaching and leadership development firm, Bernice partners with women in leadership who want to maximize their success by having a strong leadership presence (without compromising who they are) that builds connections across all levels of the organization. Guiding women to achieve the ultimate success as a leader with time-tested, proven, and easy-to-learn tips— without losing their sanity—are her passion and commitment.

Bernice offers her no-nonsense, truth-telling, personal transparency and open communication style with all of her clients. Using her "best-friend" charisma, clients often feel like they've known Bernice all of their lives. She is often described as the "The Leader's Confidante" as she blends keen intuitive instincts and human resource knowledge with strong leadership skills and savvy.

For almost two decades, while working as a Human Resources professional in several large Fortune 100 companies to include AT&T, Verizon Wireless, and FedEx Express, Bernice has coached many entry- to senior-level leaders. By implementing one-of-a-kind techniques that unleash strengths, maximize influence, and increase respect, her clients are able to produce immediate results in their lives. Bernice is certified as both a professional coach and senior human resources professional, which brings a unique perspective to her clients, and she is the author of two books,

Inspirations to Leadership: Words of Wisdom for the Leader in You and **Seven Secrets for the Successful Professional Woman.**

I: Why do you feel leadership presence and the branding of a leader is so important to successful leadership?

BB: Basically, your brand is what you bring to the table. Other people's perception of you is all you have. Their perception is their reality and that's what you carry as a leader.

When I work with people on their brand, their persona, it's really not about creating a new person; it's just about looking at what's already there and at some creative ways that we can work to strengthen those positive attitudes. In that way, the perception, the brand, comes across stronger.

> *"The most important things to remember while leading and influencing others are to be fair, to be consistent, and to have a clear and distinctive brand."*

As a leader, the key thing you need to be able to do is to influence others. People get to see who you are, and the most important things to remember while leading and influencing others are to be fair, to be consistent, and to have a clear and distinctive brand. When you're conscious about how you come across to people, consistency comes through. As a leader, you must have consistency while you're leading others.

I: In addition to consistency, I'm sure you probably work with some of these leaders to determine what is unique about the way they lead as well, correct?

BB: Yes, absolutely. We work on boosting their strengths! We don't focus on what's missing, but at what they already have with their strengths, and then work to increase and maximize those. Then we can come back to look at ways they can fill the gaps through their strengths.

Five Components to Leadership Presence

#1: Be Clear—Know exactly what it is you're going for and what you want/need others to focus on. You have to have vision and clarity.

#2: Communicate—Be able to communicate in a way that comes across to others clearly.

#3: Have Confidence—Don't confuse confidence with cockiness or arrogance. When people are sure enough of themselves to exude a level of confidence, others tend to look and listen. They will want to know what it is you're talking about.

#4: Be Credible—This is key. You have to have credibility.

#5: Create Connections—Be able to connect with others across all levels.

If you look at some of the strengths you already have and tie these five in, your leadership presence will grow tenfold!

I: Would you say that those are the main ingredients to being a good leader?

BB: I think those are very key ingredients. What's funny about being a good leader is you could probably read a thousand different books and find that there are a thousand different views on what being a good leader means. As far as my work is concerned, in close to twenty years of working in various companies and working with leaders on all levels along with the research that I've done, I have found that those are the foundational keys that make someone a good leader or what I call a "masterful leader."

I: What do successful leaders look like in this day and age? Do they really exist, considering all the challenges we face today?

BB: It's very hard in this day and age to be a good, successful leader. I don't know that there's any one perfect leader because everyone brings something different to the table. The difference is that the really good leaders are driven; they always want to improve and to keep growing. They are also very aware of what's going on around them and aren't afraid to jump in at any level and create change for the good.

As we discussed earlier, there are so many different models of perfect leadership, but undoubtedly, to be a successful leader you need to have vision and influence. You need to be able to coach and mentor people, to delegate, and to connect—connection is crucial.

That's what a successful leader looks like. I'm not sure that there's ever been a perfect leader, but if you're able to take your strengths and hone them into those five areas, you're bound to have success. I think there's definitely a successful leader in all of us. Perfection isn't always the goal.

I: We all have leadership roles—sometimes we're not even aware of what they are. We are all leaders. What do you see as some of the major challenges facing the leaders you work with nowadays?

BB: One of the main challenges I see—and it's probably been consistent outside of just what we're facing globally—is their ability to deal with the people issues. I've always said that a good worker doesn't always make a good leader. A lot of people are very successful workers and they know their work well, but when it comes to leading, they struggle with conflict. I tell people all the time when they're looking to move into a leadership position or move up in their roles that leadership is 80% people and 20% business. You can learn the about the business, but if you can't learn how to deal with people, that's going to be a problem. I see that as an issue that continues to be a challenge for some of today's current leaders.

Leadership is like a chess game; you have to learn about and understand who you're playing with. Each person on your team is an individual. You need to handle them like they're the only person around. You have to learn what makes them tick and you have to meet them on that level.

Actually being able to do that can be a challenge, especially when you're responsible for driving a message that doesn't always connect with everyone. You have to be able to connect that message to each person on the level that they need it in order to fully understand it. If you can do that—there are a lot of people who have that charisma—it will afford you a way to influence others like you'd never thought possible.

I: You are able to connect with so many leaders in so many different arenas and you've been so successful in doing so. How do you ensure your own personal and professional leadership growth?

BB: I never stop learning. You never reach the end. There's always more to learn. I do that through self-study. I'm always interested in the books that the leadership greats offer. You want to read those books and gain the various perspectives on leadership.

I also attend various trainings. Go back to school—I've done that—

whether you want to take one class or earn another degree in college.

Most importantly, you need to have a great coach. Having a coach that's able to pull out some of the things in you that you don't see in yourself or that you tend to take for granted is something you can't put a price tag on.

I continue to grow through coaching and through continuous learning. One of the other things I do is study some of the successful (and not so successful) leaders around me. Take notes of what worked and what didn't, and then look at where you fall in that arena. In that way you're able to look at how you want to move forward. Take some of those positive traits and see if they work for you. Take some of the ones that don't work for you and improve upon those.

I think self-growth is a cyclical idea. You need to look from your inner layers to the leaders around you. Get some outside training and then look from a thirty thousand foot view at what some of the gurus of leadership are saying is important.

Getting all of these different perspectives gives you your own ability to lead and grow to a tremendous level of depth.

LEADERSHIP OPPORTUNITY:

One of the most important things you can do is to spend quality time getting to know the people on your team. A lot of times leaders are separated from their people. You may be there communicating the message, but you're not always connecting with the people. Get to know your team and get to know your team's team. Take some time and get to know the people outside of the direct work that you're focused on at the time. Get to know how they operate, what they like, and what they don't like.

If you take these steps to develop relationships, it will be beneficial the next time you need to deliver a message to your team—especially since a lot of negative messages come from the top down. People will remember that you got to know them and they will take into account that you are actually a person too, not just Mr./Ms. So-and-So, the VP of Marketing. They will give you that extra drive—their discretionary effort. They'll give you that extra oomph if they know you as a person and feel that you really care about them.

It's well within everyone's abilities to take that time—schedule it in if you must—to really get to know your people and who works for you. You need to know who's down there driving the message that you're giving. That's the best thing you can do for yourself. It's rewarding for you as a person, it's rewarding for you as a leader, and it's rewarding for your employees.

LEADERSHIP SUCCESS:

Once I coached a senior-level executive who hadn't really done well at getting to know her employees. She had been promoted because she was very driven and very good with her work. However, she was missing out on the people part as she was moving up the ladder. She actually took my advice and worked on that.

We did employee satisfaction surveys at this company where we worked, and I had her put that into play. She couldn't understand why her employee satisfaction survey was very poor while she was still able to produce results. On the surface she was successful, but with relationships—with people—she wasn't.

She took that tip and made time in her schedule to meet with all of her people, and I'll tell you what, she soared on her next satisfaction survey. She also soared in her results. She had always been successful in her team's results, but they really skyrocketed after she stopped to take the time to get to know the people on her team.

When people know you, they're willing to do more for you. They understand, they know you, they trust you, they like you, and they're willing to give you that extra mile.

She was able to come out of her shell and not just look at them as numbers but as people. It helped her immensely, and she said never will she go back to being strictly results-focused. She'll focus on the people first because if you focus on them, they'll give you the numbers. They'll get you the results you need.

That was very rewarding for her, and it was rewarding for me to see her blossom and expand. It goes back to branding and the perception you bring across to people. It's so important when you're building relationships and connections in your career.

Gina Hiatt, Ph.D.
Reston, Virginia, USA

Gina Hiatt, Ph.D. is a clinical psychologist. She received her undergraduate degree in psychology from the University of Pennsylvania, graduating Summa Cum Laude in 1973, and she was one of only twelve people inducted into Phi Beta Kappa in her junior year at Pennsylvania. She received her Ph.D. from McGill University and did her postdoctoral year at UCLA.

Gina is also the president of Finish Agent, Inc., a company that provides both innovative client-accountability software and a psychologically-based system that ensures client retention and success. It is a full-service software that provides such features as a daily progress grid where participants answer customized questions and get daily responses from other small group members, coaching comments, a forum, progress graphs, chat rooms, and content pages for class information. It is thrilling for coaches to see their clients form bonds with each other, support each other, and succeed.

Gina first created this software system in her other business, Academic Ladder, Inc., to help her academic clients (graduate students and professors) who were struggling with procrastination on long-term writing projects. She had phenomenal success—her system became a membership site (the Academic Writing Club) with over four hundred members, which provides recurring income for her, and raving fans who stay for years. Last year she made over $350,000 in mostly passive income from the Club.

Now, with Finish Agent, she is licensing this same system so that coaches can reproduce her success and have thrilled clients and recurring, predictable, leveraged, and passive income.

I: You have such an interesting background. What changes did you go through that set the stage for your career, and what do you feel are the important aspects of leadership that have enabled you to be successful in all of those different venues?

GH: I had a private practice for many years as a clinical psychologist. I became burned out, and switched to coaching graduate students and professors. Once I developed a practice, I realized that my clients needed more and different service, and ideally at a lower rate than individual coaching. So I developed a membership site which consisted of software that I conceived and created using Web developers. It's a daily accountability membership site that enables people to be in small groups and get the support they need while being held accountable by others. The format encourages social interaction. Each group has its own coach who writes in twice a week. There's also a forum, a chat room, and other ways to interact. There is space for content as well.

That venture has been very successful; I have well over four hundred clients who pay $70 every four weeks. What's made it wonderful is the fact that I hire coaches to run it, enabling me to have free time. Last year I made over $350,000 in mostly passive income. I also made additional money that wasn't passive income.

Because of the success of this business model, I wanted to make it available to other coaches. That's why I started my second business, Finish Agent, Inc. I license the software system to coaches, teachers, or anyone who nudges people to change—in other words, change agents. That's where the name *Finish Agent* came from. Our system allows change agents to help their clients actually take action instead of to just listen to their classes, say, "That was great," feel inspired, but not follow through with the life-changing actions that they just learned.

That's what I'm doing, and I'm in the end of the beta part of the launch. I have all kinds of coaches trying it out during this beta period with great success. I went from being an academic—doing research in neuropsychology—to being a clinician with a private practice for twenty five years, to becoming a coach, and then to becoming a business owner running the Academic Writing Club. Now I'm the owner of a software business—software as a service. It all just kind of happened.

Being a therapist doesn't predispose you to being a good businessperson. It's poor training for it, actually. In the therapist

mind-set, things are private, confidential, and one-on-one, and you don't really discuss money or business. What I am doing now is so radically different on every level. It's been a real shift for me.

I: What are some of the stumbling blocks you ran into as you stepped into this role?

GH: I had trouble in the beginning just going public and marketing myself, talking about myself, and talking about what I had to offer. It felt like it was illegal. I'm used to licensing boards that watch that you're professional and that you do things the way psychologists should do things. You get used to this quiet confidentiality, so it was very hard for me to make that leap into going public, beating my chest and saying, "Here I am, I'm great, and here's the Academic Writing Club and it's wonderful." I did it with the help of coaching along the way, but it wasn't an easy transition.

From what I've seen, a lot of therapists who move into coaching, business, or marketing struggle with this issue. It's difficult. I don't have business role models. My father was a physics professor. My mother was an artist. They were great role models, but not for business. I really had to learn from the bottom up.

Also, for me, the mind shift was the big thing—stepping into the idea that I was a businesswoman. I used to walk around and say to myself, "I am a businesswoman. I am a businesswoman. I am President of my company." It wasn't easy, and it's a continuing struggle as I become more successful.

Recently I was told by Max Simon—one of my mentors, along with Andrea Lee, Lisa Sasevich, Lisa Cherney, and Melissa Evans—that I needed to hire a CEO. I went through this whole jumbled up feeling in my mind and I finally decided that I want to be my own CEO and learn how to do that. I might eventually hire someone, but until then I want to learn. It's quite a learning process. Now I've hired a new coach who specializes in helping CEOs and other leaders in larger companies so that I can learn more about running a software business as opposed to a therapy or coaching business.

I: What kind of leadership skills or qualities within yourself are you finding you have to call up to meet these challenges?

GH: I need to make decisions. I just read an article that someone sent me from *The New York Times* titled "Do You Suffer from Decision Fatigue?" It's true; making decisions can be exhausting.

I have been developing this software that I'm working on with the Web developers who are high-level programmers, and I have to decide practically every button—every way that we're going to do the automatic billing, etc. It reminds me of when we had a house built and I had to decide every doorknob and hinge. If you spend a lot of time agonizing over every decision, you don't get anywhere. I found that over time I've gotten better and better at making decisions and not being so cowed by what others think.

An initial stumbling block in developing the Academic Writing Club was that I got pushback from people. Some said, "This isn't the future of what you want to do. You just want to run telephone coaching groups. This lower priced way of offering services just won't work."

I got a lot of pushback from my family as well in terms of the amount of money it cost to develop something like this initially. They were afraid that I wouldn't get the money back. I really feel that these situations developed some strength in me to be able to insist and say, "This is the right way, and I'm not going to listen to these naysayers. I'm going to forge ahead."

You have to be ready to stand your ground and say, "This is the way I intend to do it." You can listen to what other people have to say, but you have to make your own decisions. I've gotten better and better at the decision-making process.

I: Do you find that your intuitive nature kicks in to help you decide if you're making the appropriate decisions?

GH: Absolutely. I think I'm very intuitive. I feel like a lot of the decisions really are people decisions. Even if you're wondering about a button and its usability, what it will look like, and how will people react, everything boils down to people. I feel like my background as a psychologist helps me understand people better and be attuned to what they would want.

I trust my intuition when it comes to certain things, and when it comes to other areas where I know I have weaknesses like details, billing, etc., I have no trouble delegating.

I: This is different from your work in psychology or coaching because you're guiding people to their vision. How did you make that leap? Was that a different process than coaching or therapy?

GH: Yes. It's different because I'm not asking them about their childhood or helping them understand deep significant problems about themselves. If they've got them, I don't want to know about them. I've learned so much about people and interacting with them. A lot of my patients were businesspeople or people who worked for the CIA. I learned a lot about what people go through in business, and I gained a lot of insight from that.

Now I think that I do pretty well with what I guess you would call managing. I have to own up to the fact that the people I manage are people with whom I already have a good rapport. Even my subcontractors all say they really like working with me and they want to increase their hours. I think I maintain a good environment; so far, so good. I trust them, I trust that they're good at their job, and I'm trying not to micromanage. I just check in when it is necessary. It's a combination of trusting and verifying. I'm pretty good at dealing with people.

In therapy, in a way you are using persuasion because the person usually comes into a therapy session upset about something in their life. You need to persuade them that by looking at this or that or by doing this technique, you're going to help them and that you're doing it for a good purpose. I find that business is like that too. There's a lot of persuading involved. I think a lot of marketing is educating and persuading people to understand your point of view.

I was shocked to find out that my software is so different from what's out there. It's wonderful, and it's difficult. There's a lot of explaining and persuading that needs to be done to help people understand the advantages, even though they hear my story and they know it works. They may disagree when it comes to some of the premises of it. The ability to educate and persuade is important.

I: You've been able to draw a connection with your skills from your previous line of work and bring that to the forefront in order to remain consistent all the way through your experiences.

GH: Psychology is everywhere, and I think it's really been a great help to me because business is about people. It's about your clients, your customers, and the people with whom you work. Having those people skills helps when you're negotiating, when you're marketing, when you're managing, and when you're being a thought leader.

LEADERSHIP OPPORTUNITY:

This is an exercise that Melissa Evans had me do, and it helped me feel more powerful and capable. Write down your own biography as a business person, "bragging" as much as you can about everything that you've accomplished, including numbers, and don't ignore things that you might think are small. It could be anything from, "I led the PTA to grow from twenty-eight to forty members," or "I started my business without any financial backing and was able to bring it up to thirty thousand dollars a year."

It doesn't have to be huge, but the exercise of writing it down and bragging is helpful. Women might find this more helpful than men, but I think that is a step in the direction of believing in yourself and starting to see yourself as really successful. I think everyone has it in them to be completely successful. It's those voices inside that hold you back.

LEADERSHIP SUCCESS:

One of my favorite success stories is in the Academic Writing Club, which is the same system as Finish Agent. There was a graduate student who joined the Club. What we emphasize is small, daily actions that move them steadily towards their goal of working on the most important thing in their life (in this case, a Ph.D. dissertation). The action involved could be very small, such as fifteen minutes of writing in the case of this graduate student.

She wrote to us that she knew that it was time for her to do her fifteen minutes, but, "I think I was cold because my hands were shaking so hard I couldn't type. I kept putting sweaters on, but it was still so hard to type, and the shaking didn't stop until I typed for fifteen minutes."

We all said to her, "You weren't cold; you were terrified." That's how blocked she was when it came to writing. That's why she hadn't written anything in months.

During the time she was in the Club, I watched her go from being a terrified graduate who was really in danger of dropping out of graduate school to finishing her dissertation, getting a tenure-track position at a major Canadian university, and becoming a professor. It just shows the power of small group support, along with the daily accountability. Step by step you can pull yourself out of that hole and really succeed. As a coach, it just warms your heart to see someone like this make tremendous progress, one step at a time.

David B. Savage
Calgary, Alberta, Canada

David Savage is the cofounder of Global Negotiation Insight Institute, the Company to Company Dispute Resolution Council, and Synergy Alberta.

He works with organizations and professionals to explore, engage, and energize their negotiation and leadership awareness capacity and success. He convenes negotiation, leadership, and public engagement circles to realize collective and collaborative wisdom and also provides business consulting.

David engages, challenges, connects, creates, speaks, writes, and so much more.

I: Because you're so prominently known in this field, I want to start out by asking if you could share what you do personally and professionally to continue your own leadership growth.

DS: I think it all starts personally. Leaders in today's challenging roles must first be grounded. I have really pursued curiosity and mindfulness so that I develop the leadership strength of openness to what's possible. This allows me to not only be gentle with myself but also with others. Curiosity allows me to be sensitive to what needs to be heard, seen, done, or created. It also allows those possibilities from the people that I lead and I negotiate with to be noticed. From that strong, centered, balanced, grounded, and present approach, I don't have to be reactive. I can witness others and create that trust—create that possibility.

I: You're an explorer and a developer and you're always seeking new paths. How does that curiosity draw you into this tremendously creative environment?

DS: Curiosity really allows possibilities to arise that I may not have seen otherwise. If I go into a leadership or a negotiation event with a position, a goal, or a specific deadline, it can really disallow the opportunity for much more than that.

Through my career of thirty-five years in business and in conflict management, one thing I have learned: I don't know it all, and others do have answers that can create "Aha" moments. I just need to be strong enough to not be strong and to be open enough to allow others to actually see me and see themselves as most important.

I: So really, seeking out that connection and the understanding of others is what brings all of that to fruition?

DS: Yes. The "busyness" of our business, the distraction of communication styles, and modern technology really minimize the opportunity to allow what needs to come naturally. So often in management we tend toward acting under stress and deadlines, focusing a lot of our energy on logic, economics, science, technology, accounting, law—all of those left brain types of things. At the end of the day, those are so incomplete. They're important, but they're so incomplete.

We can create our breakthroughs when we allow others in and allow other wisdoms to flourish. There is a great opportunity in this world to come together to deal with the challenges and not be in such a hurry; we must go slow before we can go fast.

I: I've heard you refer to learning as something you continually seek through every challenge and with celebration. Can you share a little bit about that?

DS: In leadership in particular, it's all about building rapport and understanding. There's no real point in having one-sided communications. There is power in all the people that we surround ourselves with, so let them in and allow disputes, conflicts, and diverse opinions—let in those people that you don't easily get along with all the time. Their perspectives are very valuable resources to management and leaders. They're so valuable because people wouldn't fight against us or be positional toward our cause unless there was a basic underlying value or interest that we hadn't yet seen. Once we spend time honoring and respecting their diverse opinions and their different perceptions, we can get a better understanding and perhaps shift our own perception so that we can all move forward.

I: In your area of specialization, you're really helping leaders understand how to hone their negotiation skills and communicate on this level. As far as leadership is concerned, what impacts that area of specialization the most today?

DS: Leaders are looking for additional tools, strategies, and approaches. I'd like to share a comment that one of my major clients said. This client is a very successful international oil and gas company. When they brought me in, I initially said no. I wasn't interested in coaching their organization, their negotiations, or their management because they're a top-down, "this is the way it will be," successful and positional company.

When I asked them why they were interested in bringing me in, they said, "Because we have such major challenges in front of us that we know now that we need to empower and engage our five thousand employees. We need to learn how to treat them instead of simply expecting them simply to be messengers." I think that says a lot.

I: It does say a lot, and it's a very progressive stance for them to take. Are you seeing that this type of stance is becoming more prevalent?

DS: Both are needed. At times, a company, a leader, or a President must simply be directive—hard and fast— and hold people accountable. As companies grow, they realize that if they want to attract, retain, and build the best people and the best organization, this is one of the best ways.

The best people don't want to work anywhere other than a place where they can learn, be valued, and make a real contribution to their organization.

I: That has probably always been true and it's just now coming to the forefront. This idea is now becoming almost a necessity for organizations to realize and act on in a way that creates a positive environment.

DS: Yes. In a boardroom, in decision-making, strategic processes, or in any situation like that, it is so valuable to have contrary opinions. Leaders need to appoint people to actually research and argue the contrary in order to really hone the decision so that you've shaved it down to its most powerful impact before the proposal or decision goes out the door. It is not effective to simply to be surrounded by people who agree with each other. It is effective to have a diverse circle of opinions and then have the executive—the leader of the team—make an informed decision as to where they want to go.

I: You've mentioned that we're all leaders and that perhaps we don't always realize what leadership roles we play. Some of us don't even think of ourselves as leaders. Could you elaborate on that?

"It is not effective to simply to be surrounded by people who agree with each other. It is effective to have a diverse circle of opinions."

DS: We are all leaders in every organization. Every organization increasingly needs people to act in a leadership role at all levels. I guess the piece of leadership that resonates most with the work that I do is that you can only lead when you know what's most important to you, where your boundaries are, and where your values are, and then you need to be prepared to speak them and live them in your organization. That's transformative leadership—where power, respect, and transformation come from.

To be the leader, you must see yourself and stand for what's most important to you before you can expect others to acknowledge your vision. Today's definition of leadership is very different from what we've traditionally felt. Leadership used to be the people with the authority got to tell others what to do. There are many people with authority who are not leaders because they haven't yet made the connection and found out what's most important.

When some of my clients in the oil and gas industry have trouble with communities, with the public, with environmentalists, etc., it's often because people within the organization feel that when they go to work, they can't be environmentalists, they can't be the public, but we're all of those things. We are all of those things, and that's how we need to act in organizations and as leaders.

I: Since you specialize in helping leaders with their negotiation mastery, how does that strengthen them in their leadership role?

DS: First and foremost, they figure out where their center lies. They allow their intuition, artistry, creativity, and all of the aspects of who they can be to simply be. From that point, they allow themselves to look for the same in others. They coach people that they work with to look for the same in themselves and to speak their truth, speak what's most important, and to hold each other truly accountable from that place of grounded values, interests, and respect.

Once you get to that "realness" point with people in your organization, with those in your community, with the stakeholders of your company, etc., then everything will run much more smoothly. The bumpiness, the conflict, the friction is gone. That leader may not agree with those stakeholders or those others, but there's respect first, so the communication is clear, and the game plan, the resistance, and the hostility is diminished.

I: So bringing in authenticity and awareness of self and true presence of those skill sets really helps with the process of making that clear within the organization?

DS: Yes. The next thing that that we must share is that oftentimes the women and men at the top of organizations already know that to be true. It's often the people in the middle who think they don't have permission to be themselves and to be great within their organizations. It's that middle chunk from organizations that are so important to show up, to lead, and stand for what's most important.

I: You talk about the challenges of this amazing, beautiful, toxic, and challenging world of the twenty-first century. Can you elaborate on that?

DS: We have gotten to where we are through so much brilliance, so much productivity, so much connection, and so much respect. I think that is what's called for now in the challenges we face with our environment, with our organizations, and with communities.

The biggest challenge isn't innovation or resources, it's giving people the opportunity and the expectation to actually show up and giving ourselves permission to be fully in our world—not just the left brain, all of ourselves. That's the challenge. If people choose to be little, avoid conflict, or to just get through their day, it is so sad and such a waste of resources. When people choose to stand up for what's most important, they'll find that it's not easy. They'll find that it will not be comfortable for people in their organization. However, when they go home each night, they'll be able to say, "I was really there. I was really there for what's most important."

LEADERSHIP OPPORTUNITY:

Once you think you understand, once you think you've got a deal, once you think the person working for you knows exactly what needs to be done and why, ask three more questions and then notice what comes up. Read and react from there.

It's fluid because you think you know, but once you ask those three more questions, you'll realize that the conversation is never complete and learning is always possible.

LEADERSHIP SUCCESS:

About twelve years ago, we were running a small Canadian natural gas exploration company. We were drilling in an area that was very controversial. There was a lot of anger in the community. The lead company in the area was of the old school mind-set, the "here's what I need to do so get out of my way" approach.

We spent about six months getting to know the people and finding out what their interests and fears were. We were trying to build their respect so that we could illustrate that we had an interest in their interests.

It was difficult. I was called a used car salesman, a lawyer, and all of those horrible things people can be called. But we found that by seeking first to understand and respect the landowner's interests, then they understood that we weren't actually pushy, positional, and hardnosed, rather that we wanted to find a way to make it work for everyone, we were able to work together. Through their resistance, we found that we didn't actually have to build the production facilities that we would normally build. We came up with fresh solutions that saved our shareholders many millions of dollars and got our production going very quickly.

Our share price tripled within three months of that breakthrough with the community, with the landowners, with the public, and our wells were on production within months of them being drilled. Here we are twelve years later and the wells of the competing oil and gas company with the old style of thought—the one that said, "Get out of the way!"—are still not on production.

Go slow so you can go fast!

Cathy Greenberg, Ph.D.
Tucson, Arizona, USA

Dr. Cathy Greenberg is a number one national best-selling author, a top ranking executive coach, a global guru on leadership and positive psychology, and ABC TV's First Lady of Happiness. Cathy helps executives and their companies maximize success using her unique Happiness=Profit business formula.

Having done so successfully for more than two decades, Cathy wins rave reviews from clients and leadership experts including Warren Bennis, Marshall Goldsmith, and Noel Tichy. Cathy is the cofounder of XCEL Institute with Dr. Relly Nadler.

I: Cathy and Relly, you have brought your expertise together for the leadership development and organizational population out there. Tell us more about this.

CG: Most leaders tend to underestimate just how much they influence others, and as a result, they and their teams can underperform. But doing just a few things differently will make an impact. We believe that when you are focused on developing yourself and others in your organization as leaders, you will systematically improve. We know that when we provide you with information about what happy companies know about performance, emotional intelligence, brain and neuroscience, gender differences, or generational differences, that we help you make a difference. We are going to be combining our strengths in these areas with the XCEL Institute.

RN: We know that leaders have 50%-70% influence over the climate of their team. They are the ones we call the "emotional thermostat." We all know that if the emotional thermostat of a team—whether it's you or someone else—is clear and calm in the midst of a storm, then the team looks at the leader and says, "I guess everything is going

Relly Nadler
Santa Barbara, California, USA

Dr. Relly Nadler was educated as a clinical psychologist and is a world-class executive coach, corporate trainer, and author. He is the President and CEO of True North Leadership, Inc., an executive and organizational development firm, as well as the cofounder of the XCEL Institute, which stands for eXcellence in Coaching for Executive Leadership.

Dr. Nadler brings his expertise in emotional intelligence to his keynotes, consulting, coaching, and training. He has designed and delivered many multi-day executive boot camps for high achievers and for Fortune 500 companies.

to be okay." If the leader is frazzled, stressed out, and tense, the team gets the message that maybe it's not okay. They end up picking up that anxiety because emotions are contagious. We really want to zero in on leaders because they have so much influence.

One of the things that we are focusing on is how to get someone on your team who may be solid "B" player—let's say 85% or so—to be in the top 10%. That really is the tipping point, because when someone gets into the top 10%, a lot of the literature shows that they produce twice as much revenue for the organization as managers in the eleventh and the eighty-ninth percentiles.

We tend to spend a lot time with our "C" players when we really need to focus on how to get the "B" players—and maybe that's you— to do just a few things differently in order to be an "A" player. We call these micro-initiatives and ask, "How can you do a few things differently to make a difference?"

Some of the things we will highlight in the XCEL Institute are training and coaching. Some of the research about these goes way back, but if you have training alone, there is about a 22% bump in performance.

We've all had training. I dealt with someone last week who said, "I really like what you are doing with the coaching by adding coaching to training." Most of the time you go to a training session and it's two days or so and it's over. If you can add coaching to the training—which we are going to do in XCEL—research shows that instead of a 22% increase in performance, you can get as high as an 88% increase. With coaching you can tailor the message; you can really drop into specific tools and techniques that the person can use.

Then we talk about these micro-initiatives that can create a macro-impact. We know that if you can bring a coaching network inside your company—some of the things we do with XCEL—studies have shown that Cathy's sweet spot—happiness—is tied to profit by more than 93%.

I: Can you share a few words about your mission, about value, and how you are bringing your expertise together?

CG: XCEL stands for eXcellence in Coaching for Executive Leadership. Our mission and our goals are pretty clear; emotional engagement is where leadership meets performance. For those of you that know me, I love formulas, so the easy way to remember it is E2P. "E2" means "emotional engagement," and the "P" is for "performance." We would like to provide cutting edge tools and practices to become the "CEO of you," as my friend Susan Butler says. That means being a better leader and a leader who coaches.

Relly and I often walk into organizations where they have had profiling assessments, some team leadership development, or some of the foremost models and leadership thinking, whether they are from Warren Bennis, Marshall Goldsmith, or Steve Drotter. They are essentially looking for solutions sets to take them to a new level of performance. Now that they understand their profile, they understand what the team needs in order to be successful. Now that they have a strategy or an idea of the direction that they need to go, they need to actually organize, align, energize, and engage. That's where we are coming from, as well.

RN: One of the things I'm so excited about is how we bring these skills to our leaders. In the organizational development world, when you have training, you learn all these good things, but then it becomes very challenging to put them into place. Many of the leaders are also working, and they have reports and strategic meetings that they are going to and many things they are doing as well. They don't always make the time for leadership. We all know about the idea of work/life balance, and often I think what we are talking about is work/leadership balance. How do you balance the work and the leadership?

What happens regarding leadership is that it becomes easy for that to get ignored or to do it later because it may not be as immediate of a concern as the pressing problem. So what we are going to do with XCEL and our work is to teach you how you get more balance so that you are doing the work, but you are also doing these micro-initiatives that are critical for the work/leadership balance. The good news is that while work is going to take most of your day, these leadership things, if done daily, aren't going to take a whole day. They will take five minutes here or fifteen minutes there.

Leadership is all about the relationship. Cathy and I are focusing on what the relationship is between you and your direct reports. Are they getting the time? About 66% of workers, when surveyed, say they do not get enough time with their leader. Their leader is doing work, but they are not balancing their work/leadership.

I: Why is this leadership program needed?

RN: There are a lot of programs out there, but our focus is going to be a little bit different. Cathy and I have seen that there are three different kinds of what we would call "brain drains" in the workplace. We will address these through XCEL and I'll go through this.

Three Key Brain Drains

#1: Fewer Brains—There is going to be a leadership drought. Forty percent of organizations today will be experiencing a significant gap in the number of skilled leaders. One of the reasons for that gap is the seventy-eight million baby boomers who are going to be retiring while only forty-six million new Generation X leaders are coming into the workplace. That right there is a huge amount of fewer brains coming into the workplace.

#2: Emotional Intelligence—The Baby Boomers have been known to have higher Emotional Intelligence. The reason is technology; interfacing with the computer or phone verses a person lowers the amount of time spent face to face with people. So hour for hour, the more time you have with your phone or screen versus face time, the less time you have dealing with conflict, less time looking at how I am communicating and my communicating depth, and less time reading someone's responses. *Do they like what I said? Do they not like what I said? How do I alter that?* So that less face time and ability to readjust your communication adds to this emotional intelligence drain in each generation that is up and coming.

One of the aspects of emotional engagement and emotional intelligence is that all of these skills can be learned. I had a meeting yesterday with someone who had a twenty year old and a twenty-two year old. She was saying that one was in the front seat and one was in the back seat and they were texting each other in the same car.

CG: That's not atypical. In fact, for those of you who work in an office setting, often you'll look in the cubicles as you walk by them and you'll see young people who are sitting there texting the person in the cube across from them. You wonder why they don't just turn to each other and have a conversation. Well, the reality is that cubicles reduce privacy, and as a result, they can't speak openly. So they use texting as an operating model for honesty and trust. Relly, what you saw was a first-hand example of how young people interact. Whether you use the analogy of being in a car or in a cubicle, the reality is the same. We have created an open environment for communication and people think that texting is a more trustful way of getting information to the other person. Interesting, isn't it?

RN: Yes, it's very interesting on numerous levels. That's why I think the emotional intelligence drain, which is the second of three, is really important, especially for the leaders that we will be dealing with because they are going to be working with Generation X, Generation Y, and the Millennials who have grown up on this kind of communication. One of the other obvious things when it comes to texting is that you can't hear what is going on in context. If you are in a world where you can give feedback and someone raised their voice, then you'd know how to react. That isn't the reality with texting. We don't know. All we hear is clicking.

From the standpoint of social learning theory, we also miss learning how someone deals with conflict. We used to be able to overhear or watch a conversation. Now we are in this silent world so we miss another critical variable around learning, which is mirroring and being able to learn from watching others model behaviors.

So the first drain is fewer brains, the second one is the emotional intelligence drain, and the third one is more about this environmental issue, and I'll let Cathy cover that.

CG: Absolutely.

#3: Environment—The third drain is the environmental drain. It's fascinating to me that we are going to have a leadership drought very soon, if we don't have one already. In 2011, a major portion of our Baby Boomers will be retiring. We know through the work I have focused on for the past five or six years that environments are changing. An environment where an individual works to create negativity or toxic energy will impact their life satisfaction, their work satisfaction, and their overall happiness on the job.

"We give leaders tools to counter-attack "brain drain," to be more effective in their decision making and in their ability to genuinely and authentically develop others, and to live a well-being focused lifestyle."

A lot of people would laugh at the idea that people have to be happy on the job, but for those that have been following the last season of *The Boss*, we can see that a person's role, their level, their gifts, and their strengths speak directly to their sense of purpose. If they are satisfied and delivering on their sense of purpose, then they feel a connection to the work and the people or the mission of the company. That is when their performance improves by well over 90%.

My dear friend Jessica Pryce-Jones has a brand new book out called *Happiness at Work*, and in addition to my work on *What Happy Companies Know* and *What Happy Working Mothers Know*, we have a whole host of data and statistics on what it means when your environment is draining you. So the drain relative to this environmental condition is really important.

Most leaders and organizations are, in fact, experiencing a brain drain, and they are operating in what Relly and I would call a "dummied-down" manner. We need to teach leaders the tools to understand themselves and to influence others by understanding themselves as a result. We give leaders tools to counter-attack "brain drain," to be more effective in their decision making and in their ability to genuinely and authentically develop others, and to live a well-being focused lifestyle.

Most executives and employees are operating with ten to fifteen fewer IQ points daily. That's a big data point. We can't afford to lose ten to fifteen IQ points in our operating environments—in the places where we work every day. The visible factor affecting this organizational brain drain is the daily chaos that results from complexity or an urgent situation; things have to be done during a certain time constraint. Someone might be asking you to do something you haven't done before or to do it in a new market or with a new team member; these changes can create stress.

RN: We have been talking about the three brain drains: fewer brains, the emotional intelligence, and the environment, and how those affect someone's IQ. The IQ decreases because there is so much stress that the amygdala is more activated. When the amygdala is activated, there is less blood and oxygen going into the prefrontal cortex, thus we have less executive functioning. Therefore, that affects IQ.

For some people it could be drastic, for others it may be just a few IQ points, but when stress and chaos affect your IQ with less brain power, you can become more defensive, blame others, micro-manage, check out, or avoid a critical decision affecting the organization and/or individual's future.

When stress comes in without the inoculation of emotional intelligence and if you can't really manage that stress, then IQ goes down. So we are saying things are dumbed down in a lot of organizations because as the stress comes in, the EQ goes down, and the IQ quickly follows.

When a lot of smart people are together in a room, very rarely is the IQ maximized by everyone. If anything, the IQ of the entire team goes down if there isn't a skilled leader who knows how to handle conflicts—how to hear from people. I would say it decreases to the tune of two to three points per person unless the leaders—which are the folks that we would be training—really know how to maintain that capacity and to ask good questions. In most of these meetings you have people with high IQs who are just advocating their own position. Therefore, you get debates and people who are either in conflict or avoiding the conflict. Those are some of the key points about the brain drain.

I: Who would benefit from XCEL?

CG: Well, this is a real hot spot for me. One of my favorite subjects is to have an abundance mentality, which means let's think about everyone. Existing leaders who have been through established profiling processes and have given themselves up to development and to strengths and weaknesses discussions have been exhausted. They have simply been told what they need to improve and where they need to do more, and frankly, no one ever gives them a pat on the back.

> *"Things that haven't won for you before will probably never be winning formulas in the future. Stop exhausting yourself by trying to do things that are not your core talents and gifts."*

Instead of focusing on what you need to do better, let's focus on what you do really well. Let's incorporate that into the XCEL Institute's process and maximize who you are—not develop components of you that have never been a winning formula for you. Things that haven't won for you before will probably never be winning formulas in the future. Stop exhausting yourself by trying to do things that are not your core talents and gifts. We want to make sure that existing leaders who are trying to get through current challenges do not lose talent. Such challenges might include how to make better judgments or thinking about the leadership pipeline and how they fill it.

What can we help teach all of you out there about yourself to make you even better? We call that personal mastery. For existing leaders, we have an entire week of tools and techniques to help make you the best performer you'd like to be as well as to help you increase your emotional engagement to exact performance from yourself and others around you.

For emerging leaders, we know that you are on a fast track. Many of you have some industry knowledge, many of you have some experiences that are going to be appropriate for being a leader in the near future, and many of you are in the process evolving. You are looking for ways to maximize your potential to get to that leadership role as fast as you can. This isn't about the time or the race; it's about the journey. And again, personal mastery is an important character trait to develop. The younger you develop this, the more masterful you will become.

XCEL Institute is for both existing and emerging leaders who wish to truly create engagement around them. The model that I love to use is happiness=joy, joy=full engagement. When you are in a joyful state—when you are in the moment of joy—you are engaged fully in whatever you are doing. Engagement should be truly focused on emotions. As we say, where leadership meets performance and exceeds performance standards, you become the best and the brightest. We might say you become the most that you could possibly become. What we are saying is that when you are the best possible leader you can be, you are going to be your best. That's up to you, your standards, your organization, and your role. So we feel that this program is for all leaders who really want to be their best.

RN: I would agree, and I think it goes back to something we always say that I think is so true. Every time I speak, I say, "Every leader that I have dealt with has underestimated their influence over others." There are a couple of key reasons for this, but I think most people agree.

People are just doing their job. They are doing the work side of their job and they don't realize that the employees and the people they are trying to develop want the leadership side of their job. So there are almost two different checklists. They are doing the work side but they are not doing the leadership development side. People don't realize they are under the spotlight 24/7. That is one of the reasons that leaders underestimate their influence. We want to give them the proper tools. You may already be a solid "B" performer and we are here to help you find the few things that are going to get you into that top 10%.

I: What are some of the benefits of the program?

CG: What I think would be helpful is if we were to explain a little bit about what training does for people. Most training only exposes people to new information. We want to help all of our leaders personalize this and practice these skills once they leave us. So as you said, they are going to get a 22% bump in their knowledge base by being with us. Additionally, they are going to go back to their resident environment where they are going to develop and continue to be working with us through telecourses and Web seminars on a regular basis. This will help to continue their growth through coaching as well as to teach them how to approach each other. We will engage them in education, learning, and skill building, and then we are going to get them back in their organizations, still working with their team members that they have been through the program with, helping to coach each other and learning from each other.

I: Could you talk about the elements of your program?

RN: I'd say 90% of all training is exposure to interesting information and interesting research. You leave saying, "Oh, that was interesting."

Maybe 10% really get a chance to move to the second level after they have that exposure. The second level is actually practicing something. That's about where it ends.

The third level is proficiency and the fourth level is mastery. Most training that happens in a couple of days gets to the exposure phase and maybe even to a little bit of practice. Then people get caught up in their world and they never get to proficiency.

Proficiency, I would say, is when you are about 60% of the way to the finished product. Mastery is getting to about 80%. We know that it takes a lot practice to move through proficiency to mastery.

We are going to have technology on these teleconference calls so that it's almost like being in a live classroom. You are not only listening to someone speak, but you'll have a chance to do a breakout session and be in your own room. You will have a chance to practice one of the tools with someone in the moment, live on the call. So it's like having a group where we do a breakout session and then we come back. That will be one element of practice. Another element of practice is that you'll have some homework. We'll have some partner exercises to try and move you on that continuum at least to proficiency.

We can't guarantee mastery. We know from Malcolm Gladwell's newest book, *Outliers*, that success takes about ten thousand hours, which is about five years or more of concentrated effort. He gives some great examples that all of us who are at the Baby Boomer age will remember, like the Beatles and how they suddenly became an overnight hit while they were so young. They didn't just get together and become incredible musicians at nineteen years old; they put a lot of hours into practice. They had a couple of gigs in Hamburg where they played for eight hours a day for about three months, day in and day out. They put together all the music and had this engagement three different times in Hamburg prior to their explosion in the U.S. They put in close to ten thousand hours of being experts before we ever knew about them. That's what it takes for us. You can hear about feedback, how to give feedback, delegating, coaching, and how to do self-mastery and think that you are all of a sudden going to grab it, just like that.

CG: Some of the learning aspects that we will emphasize in our program are how to delegate, how to get feedback, how to coach, and how to manage stress for yourself and others. In today's chaotic environment we know that being adaptive is a critical skill. Learning how to build relationships and how to manage yourself and your boss is invaluable.

Relly and I stress that the best people practices that companies actually do provide show a 64% total return to shareholders over a five year period. That's more than three times the 21% return for the companies with the weakest practices. This is based on a survey of 750 companies worldwide. Again, we like to be data-driven. What that means is that nourishing relationships mentally benefits our health and our people. Your emotions are managing others, so it's really important to understand how to manage your boss and how to manage your energy.

We are focused on how you want to manage your time—not how to manage time in general, but how you as an individual want to manage your time. Everyone is different. We have people who are calendar/clock—those people who always watch how much time you are taking in a meeting. Then we have people who are rhythmic and paced. How you manage your time and team around you is critical.

How to manage diversity is really important, as well. If you know the distinct style and point of view, it can add value to your market share and to your individual strengths. Knowing other people is critical to our success now and in the future, especially given the changing world around us.

LEADERSHIP OPPORTUNITY:

Relly Nadler's Emotional Intelligence Tips for Newly Promoted Leaders

- Be clear about your top five responsibilities.
- Be clear with your team about what you want to see happen.
- Learn about the team's strengths and each individual's strengths—so often that's discovered simply by talking to them.
- Let your team know the best ways to work with you.
- Be aware if you are adding too much value. New leaders may try to add too much value and then take away the team commitment to carry it out.
- Have one-on-one meetings with your people where you can talk about some of the things just mentioned.
- Be aware of what your triggers are. This is where the 360 degree feedback comes into play. Talk with your team, friends, spouses, and loved ones so that those situations don't end up turning into derailers.

LEADERSHIP SUCCESS:

Dr. Cathy Greenberg's Triumph Over Tragedy

I was a managing partner in a very well-known firm called Accenture and part of the Computer Sciences Corporation—two of the largest consulting firms in the world. I was traveling on a daily basis to far and wonderful parts of the world, serving our client base and doing executive and strategic coaching, and I wound up with two potentially terminal illnesses. Basically, I hit the wall of life after going through a divorce, losing my parents, and experiencing the loss of a child while I was pregnant. I realized I had to get it together; even though I was considered successful by society's indications of success in terms of title, income, and lifestyle, I was not happy.

I took time down here on earth to get it together. I learned a lot about the science of happiness and positive psychology. Being a behavioral scientist, I was able to apply what I knew to myself and then turned it into a model that I now use to help others as well.

Happiness is not something you seek. It is found in the things you *do,* such as offering and receiving forgiveness, growing friendships, and pursuing wisdom and knowledge. When you deliver on your sense of purpose in a way that enables others to achieve their goals, then happiness follows. Happiness is something we *do*, and in the process of doing it for others, we gain it ourselves.

The following books were referenced by our experts within their interviews:

Nineteen Eighty-Four by Geroge Orwell
AïM© for Life Mastery by Raymond Perras
Community: The Structure of Belonging by Peter Block
Directions: A Guide for Life by Linda Cobb
Diversity in Coaching by Jonathan Passmore
Diversity Mosaic by Tina Rasmussen
Diversity: The ASTD Trainer's Sourcebook by Tina Rasmussen
Don't Bring It to Work by Sylvia Lafair
Execution: The Discipline of Getting Things Done by Larry Bossidy, Ram Charan, Charles Burck
Good to Great by Jim Collins
Gutsy: How Women Leaders Make Change by Sylvia Lafair
Happiness at Work by Jessica Pryce-Jones
His Sufficiency for My Authenticity by Candice Smithyman
How to Multiply Your Baby's Intelligence by Glenn Doman, Janet Doman
Inspirations to Leadership by Bernice Boyden
Know Can Do! by Ken Blanchard, Paul J. Meyer, Dick Ruhe
Lead With Your Strengths Wherever You Are by Peter Kaldor, John McLean
Leadership From the Inside Out by Kevin Cashman
Megatrends: Ten New Directions Transforming Our Lives by John Naisbitt
MOJO by Marshall Goldsmith
Organizational Integrity by Tina Rasmussen
Outliers: The Story of Success by Malcolm Gladwell
Savvy Leadership Strategies for Women Coauthored by Kim Zilliox
Seven Secrets for the Successful Woman by Bernice Boyden
Stop Spinning Plates by Susan Guiher and Mary McHenry
The 21 Irrefutable Laws of Leadership by John C. Maxwell
THE BOOK "I'm Doing the Best I Can!" by Lisa Hein
The Discipline of Solitude by Candice Smithyman
The Five Dysfunctions of a Team by Patrick Lencioni
The Leader of the Future by Frances Hesselbein, Marshall Goldsmith, Richard Beckhard
The Leadership Challenge by James M. Kouzes, Barry Z. Posner
The One Minute Entrepreneur by Ken Blanchard, Don Hutson, Ethan Willis
The One Minute Manager by Kenneth H. Blanchard, Spencer Johnson
The Success Principles by Jack Canfield, Janet Switzer
The Uterine Health Companion by Eve Agee
Think and Grow Rich by Napoleon Hill
Triple Your Time Today by Kathryn McKinnon
What Got You Here Won't Get You There by Marshall Goldsmith, Mark Reiter
What Happy Companies Know by Dan Baker, Cathy Greenberg, Collins Hemingway
What Happy Working Mothers Know by Cathy Greenberg, Barrett Avigdor

Eve Agee	www.eveagee.com
Diane Allen	www.dianeallencoaching.com
Ken Blanchard	www.kenblanchard.com
Bernice Boyden	www.themasterfulleader.com
Gilles Brouillette	www.TransformationalLearning.ca
Sherry Buffington	www.sherrybuffington.com
Stacey Chadwell	www.blogtalkradio.com/coachchadwell
Linda Cobb	www.lindacobb.com
Tony DiRico	www.profithunters.biz
Ann Farrell	www.quantumendeavors.com
Alison Forbes,	www.elevatedleaders.com
Theresa Garwood	www.lifecoachchicago.org
Zeina Ghossoub	www.zeinaghossoub.com
Marshall Goldsmith	www.marshallgoldsmithlibrary.com
Cathy Greenberg	www.xcelinstitute.com
Susan Guiher	www.sueguiher.com
Lisa Hein	www.LisaRHein.com
Gina Hiatt	www.FinishAgent.com
M.J. Jiaras	www.integratedcoaching.org
Juracy Johnson,	www.juracyjohnson.com
Scott Kerschbaumer,	www.esspa.com
Joan C. King	www.cellular-wisdom.com
Sylvia Lafair	www.ceoptions.com
Ruth Littler	www.ruthlittler.com
Bert Martinez	www.bertmartinez.com
Rose Mattran	www.mattrangroup.com

Sharon McGloin	www.experientialalternatives.com
Kathryn McKinnon	www.kathryn-mckinnon.com
Sharon Melnick	www.sharonmelnick.com
Anastasia Montejano	www.visionaryleadersinternational.com
Relly Nadler	www.xcelinstitute.com
Katinka Nicou	www.integrateod.com
Clara Noble	www.success-academy.org
Joyce Odidison	www.interpersonalwellness.com
Mary O'Loughlin	www.reachfitness.com.au
Jodi Orshan	www.coachjodiorshan.com
Laura Pedro	www.leadandflourish.com
Raymond Perras	www.repars.ca
Tina Rasmussen	www.TinaRasmussen.com
Teresa Ray	www.nwacoach.com
DuaneReed	www.Micro-Leadership.com
David Savage	www.savagemanage.com
Michael Simpson	www.ebacs.net
Candice Smithyman	www.dreammentors.org
Yogesh Sood	www.doortraining.co.in
Lee Strauss	www.leestrauss.com.au
Ann Van Eron	www.potentials.com
Agnès van Rhijn	www.theconsciouslifeacademy.com
JoAnne Ward	www.growforwardyouthsuccess.com
Karen Wright	www.parachuteexecutivecoaching.com
Kim Zilliox	www.kzleadership.com
Terry Zweifel	http://tinyurl.com/TerryZweifel

1 Integral Element to Career Success
For 50% off *Savvy Leadership Strategies for Women,* go to the link below and look for the drop down option of "RAE." Additionally, e-mail Kim Zilliox directly at kim@kzleadership.com for a FREE recording of "The #1 Integral Element to Career Success."
www.kzleadership.com

2 Complimentary Weight-Loss Coaching Sessions
Two complimentary weight-loss coaching sessions to inspire your vision and clarify your winning strategy. E-mail Mary O'Loughlin at mary@fitness.com.au.
www.reachfitness.com.au

3 Secrets to Impactful Leadership
For great leadership tips and strategies, receive a complimentary report and join the e-zine family by visiting the link below.
www.themasterfulleader.com/freereport.pdf

5 Passive Income Secrets for Coaches
Change the way you think about coaching—these out-of-the-box ideas will introduce you to ways to leverage your income while providing even higher value to your clients. Stand out from the crowd, expand your reach, and become the coach in your niche that everyone turns to.
www.FinishAgent.com

7 Keys to Reinvent Your Life
These audios from Anastasia Montejano are designed help you achieve the breakthrough you are longing for.
www.VisionaryLeadersBreakThrough.com/7keystoreinvent.html

10 Skills for Great Parenting
Go to the link, click on Message, and say, "meet with me" to receive a Rapid Coaching Session for FREE! That's one question and twenty minutes alone with Jodi Orshan.
www.theparentingplan.com

30-Hour Basic Biblical Life Coaching Course
Receive a certificate in biblical life coaching. Join now as a FREE Social Media Member and access our online university.
www.dreammentors.biz

30-Minute Coaching Session
Free 30-Minute coaching session with Sharon McGloin. Contact Sharon at the e-mail address listed below or call 816-309-8543.
www.experientialalternatives.com

30-Minute Consultation and Assessment
This offer from JoAnne Ward is based on the needs of youth, ages 16–22 years. Walk away with hope, support, and easy tips for how to increase grades by 10% within a semester or less!
www.joanne@growforwardyourhsucess.com

Abundance Audit Assessment
How would you assess yourself in key areas for applying an appreciation for abundance in your professional and personal life? Find out now with this offer from Dr. Cathy Greenberg.
www.h2cleadership.com/resources/tools.shtml

Are You Talented But Getting in Your Own Way?
Receive the free webinar *Confidence at the Core: 3 Steps to Own the Room, Earn What You Are Worth, and Ensure Your Hard Work Leads to Success*. Get Ready to land your biggest client ever, have the confidence to be effective and respected in your position, and have ease and power in your personal relationships.
www.sharonmelnick.com

Assessment of Needs and Complimentary Coaching Session
It is possible to integrate peak performance in your daily life by applying a simple recipe that will help you learn to master your thought process and guide your emotional intelligence for optimal results. If you are longing to be a better leader and peak performer, and are aiming to maximize results while reducing stress, aim for life mastery with Raymond Perras, certified professional coach. Request a free assessment and coaching session. To take advantage of this offer, visit the link below.
www.repars.ca

Complimentary Consultation
To take advantage of this free offer from Agnès van Rhijn, visit the link below:
www.theconsciouslifeacademy.com

Complimentary Strategic Thinking Assessment
Gain insight into your strategic thinking skills. To take our complimentary strategic thinking assess, please visit the link below.
www.dianeallencoaching.com/assessment.php

Consultation From Kelsa Coaching
To take advantage of this offer, visit the link below.
www.lifecoachchicago.org/

CORE Gets Right to the Heart of What Really Matters
With CORE, analysis of natural and conditioned traits, development levels of essential competencies, emotional intelligence, coping patterns, and which behaviors create stress and which motivate and energize are all presented in one unified system. Access your CORE profile.
www.coremap.com/index.php/core-profile.html

Formal 90-Minute Web-Based Training
To take advantage of this offer from Duane Reed on the topic of Company Culture and Leadership Development, send an e-mail to the address below.
duane@ceofocusdenver.com

Free 30-Minute Coaching Session
E-mail Coach Zeina at the e-mail address listed below or call her at 011961-3-998313/011961-4-413280
zeinag@viesaine.org

Free 30–Minute Consultation and Free Negotiation Success Checklist Download
David B. Savage offers these to support your transformation and success! Go to the link below for the download and then e-mail David to schedule the consultation.
www.savagemanage.com

Free Breakthrough Change Leadership Resources
To take advantage of this offer from Dr. Alison Forbes, visit the link below.
www.elevatedleaders.com

Free Chapter of *Triple Your Time Today: 10 Proven Time Management Strategies to Help You Create & Save More Time!*
Discover Kathryn McKinnon's secrets in her new best-selling book on Amazon. Pick up a FREE chapter of her book and a copy of her *Time-Saving* e-zine here:
http://www.kathryn-mckinnon.com

Insights Magazine: Life—Love—Bliss—Health—Wealth—Inspiration
Receive a free issue of this incredible resource in which top visionaries share their wisdom, success secrets, and the defining moments that have shaped their lives in exclusive interviews.
www.getei.com/BillCGift.html

Leadership Assessment
These assessments from Dr. Relly Nadler are designed to give you insights while the accompanying Action Plan helps you design a path forward.
www.truenorthleadership.com/assessments-opt-in

Leadership Skills Assessment
To take advantage of this free offer from Linda Cobb, visit the link below.
www.coachcobb.com/lsa

Leadership Tips
To take advantage of this offer from Ann Van Eron, visit the Web site below.
www.Potentials.com

Learn to Lead and Flourish
Laura Pedro offers free gifts to help you get started!
www.leadandflourish.com/ready-aim-excel-gifts/

Measure Your IWQ (Interpersonal Wellness Quotient)
Find out where you are right at this moment and set a goal for where you want to be.
www.interpersonalwellness.com/test_instruction

MP3 Download: Create Your Best Life
To take advantage of this guided meditation from Dr. Eve Agee, visit the link below.
http://eveagee.audioacrobat.com/download
createyourbestlifemeditation.mp3

***Profiles of Success* Radio**
This offer from Stacey Chadwell includes interviews with top leaders, where performance meets excellence.
www.blogtalkradio.com/coachchadwell

***PUBLISHED!* Magazine**
Receive a free issue of this publication in which authors and publishing professionals share their treasured resources, success secrets, and the defining moments that have shaped their lives in eighty pages of interviews, articles, and exclusive writing tips and techniques each quarter.
www.getei.com/p2011/JGHPGift.html

Ready, Aim, App!
The world is moving to a mobile platform. Smart Phones, Tablets, The Cloud, etc. Put your message where the 21st Century lives, works, and plays. Award-winning marketer Scott Kerschbaumer will deliver your customized App in less than one week. Your choice: waive all set up fees or save 40% per month. Take advantage of this limited-time offer today and visit
www.appthis.biz

Take 5 to Thrive Workbook
Including The Thriving Values Exercise and The Personal Thriving Sphere along with a strategy session to implement them. To take advantage of this offer from Sue Guiher visit the link below.
www.sueguiher.com/excel

The Big Time Management Lie E-Book
To take advantage of this offer from Clara Noble, visit the link below.
www.success-academy.org/readyaimexcel

The Coach Exchange—Free Membership
Receive a free membership to The Coach Exchange, where coaches from all over the world and opportunity meet. To take advantage of this offer from Viki Winterton, visit the link below.
www.thecoachexchange.com

The Marshall Goldsmith Library
To take advantage of this offer from Marshall Goldsmith, visit the link below.
www.marshallgoldsmithlibrary.com/html/marshall/resources.html

The Mattran Group—Contingency and Retained Search Services
These services are offered for your domestic and international positions.
www.mattrangroup.com

The Top Three Things Super Successful Executive Coaches Do
Karen Wright offers a free report! Visit the link below.
www.coachbiz101.com

TMG Sales ConsultantsContingency and Retained Search Services
These services are offered for your domestic and international positions.
http://www.mattrangroup.com/refresh/templates/tmg_sales.php?id=22

Write Away, Write Now! Complimentary Class and Free Membership
Receive a 6-week complimentary journaling class and a free membership to the global community where writers find literary mentors and all the resources they need for their personal journey.
www.WriteAwayWriteNow.com

Your Corporate Success
Complimentary strategy session with Ann Farrell, corporate success coach, plus two months complimentary membership in her group executive coaching program, Your Corporate Success.
www.yourcorporatesuccess.com